Tourism in Destination Communities

Tourism in Destination Communities

Edited by

S. Singh
Department of Recreation and Leisure Studies
Brock University
Canada
and
Centre for Tourism Research and Development
Lucknow
India

D.J. Timothy
Department of Recreation Management and Tourism
Arizona State University
USA

and

R.K. Dowling
School of Marketing, Tourism and Leisure
Edith Cowan University
Joondalup
Australia

CABI *Publishing*

CABI *Publishing* is a division of CAB *International*

CABI Publishing
CAB International
Wallingford
Oxon OX10 8DE
UK

Tel: +44 (0)1491 832111
Fax: +44 (0)1491 833508
E-mail: cabi@cabi.org
Web site: www.cabi-publishing.org

CABI Publishing
44 Brattle Street
4th Floor
Cambridge, MA 02138
USA

Tel: +1 617 395 4056
Fax: +1 617 354 6875
E-mail: cabi-nao@cabi.org

A catalogue record for this book is available from the British Library, London, UK.

Library of Congress Cataloging-in-Publication Data
Tourism in destination communities / edited by S. Singh, D.J. Timothy, and R.K. Dowling.
     p.   cm.
Includes bibliographical references (p.).
  ISBN 0-85199-611-6
  1. Tourism. 2. Tourism--Social aspects. I. Singh, Shalini. II.
Timothy, Dallen J. III. Dowling, Ross Kingston.
  G155.A1 T59212 2002
  338.4'791--dc21

                                               2002005998

ISBN 0 85199 611 6

Typeset in NewBaskerville by AMA DataSet Ltd, UK
Printed and bound in the UK by Biddles Ltd, Guildford and King's Lynn

Contents

Contributors

G.J. Ashworth, *Faculty of Spatial Sciences, International School of Spatial Policy Studies, University of Groningen, PO Box 800, 9700 AV Groningen, The Netherlands*

S.W. Boyd, *Department of Tourism, Otago University, PO Box 56, Dunedin, New Zealand*

R.K. Dowling, *School of Marketing, Tourism and Leisure, Edith Cowan University, Joondalup, WA 6027, Australia*

M. Fagence, *Department of Geographical Sciences and Planning, University of Queensland, Brisbane, Queensland 4072, Australia*

D.A. Fennell, *Department of Recreation and Leisure Studies, Brock University, St Catharines, Ontario L2S 3A1, Canada*

C.M. Hall, *Department of Tourism, Otago University, PO Box 56, Dunedin, New Zealand*

D. Ioannides, *Department of Geography, Geology and Planning, Southwest Missouri State University, 901 South National Avenue, Springfield, MO 65804, USA*

A.M. Johnston, *International Support Centre for Sustainable Tourism, PO Box 1212 Lillooet, BC V0K 1V0, Canada*

G. Moscardo, *Tourism Program, James Cook University, Townsville, Queensland 48111, Australia*

P. Pearce, *Tourism Program, James Cook University, Townsville, Queensland 48111, Australia*

K. Przeclawski, *University of Warsaw, Wilcza 55/63-37, 00-679 Warsaw, Poland*

R. Scheyvens, *Geography Programme, Massey University, PO Box 11222, Palmerston North, New Zealand*

S. Singh, *Department of Recreation and Leisure Studies, Brock University, St Catharines, Ontario L25 3A1, Canada; and Centre for Tourism Research and Development, A-965/6 Indira Nagar, Lucknow, India*

D.J. Telfer, *Department of Recreation and Leisure Studies, Brock University, St Catharines, Ontario L2S 3A1, Canada*

D.J. Timothy, *Department of Recreation Management and Tourism, Arizona State University, PO Box 874905, Tempe, AZ 85287, USA*

C. Tosun, *School of Tourism and Hotel Management, Mustafa Kemal University, Numune Mah., 31200 Iskenderun, Hatay, Turkey*

Preface

This book owes its inception to the international journal *Tourism Recreation Research*, which had proposed a special issue on the theme of host communities in 1996. For various reasons, this special issue never came to fruition, so the idea to create a book on the subject was introduced, which we were pleased to spearhead with some important guidance from Dr Tej Vir Singh. At the time, sufficient evidence existed within the tourism literature to indicate that there are unique and unmistakable dynamics at play in places where tourists spend their time and money, as well as the unavoidable and important involvement of destination community members in the growth and management of tourism. Also, new destinations are constantly being 'discovered' in regions that heretofore have been largely ignored (e.g. places on the world periphery) by traditional tourists as people have started seeking out destinations that are as yet unspoiled by the ravages of mass tourism. At the same time, traditional, well-developed destinations have experienced rapid tourism-induced change and have begun looking for alternative ways of mitigating the negative side of tourism and enhancing its positive outcomes. Thus, we felt that further efforts were needed to consolidate the extant knowledge and substantiate existing findings into a book form that would provide guidance to students, educators and tourism community managers regarding how best to enhance, control and critically examine tourism in the places where its effects are most notable.

The primary objective of this multi-authored book is to create an understanding about the role of tourism in solving and creating problems simultaneously in locations where tourist experiences are created. A great deal of brainstorming was done between the editors and other reviewers regarding the most critical and apparent subjects at the level of destination community and which should be included in this volume. The themes identified herein are the results of this collaborative effort. The book provides a review of many of the primary issues, concepts, themes and theories related to tourism from the perspective of the destination community.

The making of this work brought together people from a wide range of backgrounds. Academics, activists, field workers, consultants, colleagues, friends and family members came together for the cause, and we are grateful for their cooperation and support.

Shalini Singh
Lucknow, India

Dallen J. Timothy
Tempe, Arizona, USA

and

Ross K. Dowling
Perth, Australia

Acknowledgements

The editors wish to express their gratitude to the contributors, who kept to the initial schedule and produced high-quality reviews of current thinking in the research on destination communities. We would like to offer a special thank you to the reviewers of the initial book proposal and the anonymous reviewers who meticulously read and helped improve each individual chapter throughout the editing process.

To Dr Tej Vir Singh we owe a special debt of gratitude for his initial encouragement, and his support throughout the entire project. Rebecca Stubbs at CAB *International* was amazing! Her patience, professional attitude and gentle encouragement were appreciated very much. Thank you, Rebecca, for supporting our endeavours from the beginning.

We would like to extend our appreciation to our families and colleagues who have supported us throughout this project. Shalini would like to thank her mother for her support in times of near absence from family events, her sisters and brother (Seema, Ratna and Mohit) for their patience with her exhausting discussions. Shalini also wishes to acknowledge a debt of gratitude to the staff at the Centre for Tourism Research and Development, especially Masood Naqvi and Prachi Rastogi for their continuous support in retrieving unsaved data and bearing an extra share of administrative workload to allow her to have longer hours of uninterrupted silence. Dallen wishes to acknowledge the support of his colleagues at Arizona State University and his wife Carol and four children (Kendall, Olivia, Aaron and Spencer) for giving dad some much-needed quiet time while finishing off this book. Dallen also wishes to acknowledge his sisters (Denise Reninger, Teresa Bundy and Tammy Panek and brother Bruce Pettus) for their kindness and interest in his work. Ross wishes to thank his wife Wendy for her unfailing love and support throughout the duration of the project. Thanks also go to his two sons and their partners (Simon McLennan and Lynette McGrath and Mark and Kelly Dowling) for their interest and support. Ross also wishes to extend a special thank you to his daughter Jayne, her husband Trevor Belstead and his granddaughters Shenee and Paige for hosting him and Wendy in London on their visits to CAB *International* in 2001 and 2002.

COMMUNITY TOURISM PERSPECTIVES   I

Tourism and Destination Communities

SHALINI SINGH,[1] DALLEN J. TIMOTHY[2] and
ROSS K. DOWLING[3]

[1]Department of Recreation and Leisure Studies, Brock University,
Canada, and Centre for Tourism Research and Development,
Lucknow, India; [2]Department of Recreation Management and
Tourism, Arizona State University, Tempe, USA; [3]School of Marketing,
Tourism and Leisure, Edith Cowan University, Joondalup, Australia

Introduction

Tourism has proved to be one of the most ingeniously crafted, deliberately propagated and expedient opportunities for social exchange. Its philosophy enshrines some of the most ennobling aspirations of peace, enlightenment, self-actualization, social exchange, mutual understanding and learning. In principle, it is a remarkable largesse bequeathed upon humanity by humankind. At the same time, it has been a culprit of negative change, wherein destination environments have deteriorated, cultures changed and economies faltered.

Ever since tourism was proclaimed to be a universal and fundamental right of all citizens of the world in the Universal Declaration of Human Rights of December 1948, the tourist floodgates have opened dramatically. Immediately following the declaration, new records in tourist arrivals, receipts and expenditures were reached, with each year increasing upon the previous. In less than half a century tourism grew into a phenomenon that overwhelmed economies, societies and environments and firmly established itself as the veritable service industry of the last century. The fine art of travel was inevitably displaced by Fordian patterns of tourism, popularly termed mass tourism (Wang, 2000: 223).

Mass tourists are a generation of travellers characterized by a cultivated lifestyle, disposed to habituated travel to experience the 'expected'. Thus, their behaviour reflects a peculiar combination of doing much of what they do at home, as well as what cannot be done at home. Hence, while they express their desire to experience the unfamiliar, they also demand the familiar, simultaneously. This behaviour is natural. Krippendorf (1987) argues in favour of the much-maligned tourist who has been unintelligently 'insulted' for this legitimate 'right' to leisure. The industry cashes in on this right. Entrepreneurs leave no stone unturned in producing dream holidays, and governments follow suit for various reasons (Richter, 1989). As such, value-based tourism was brought under the dictates of capital economic logistics. To quote Waters (1978: 13), 'there is reason to believe that . . . the worldwide interweaving of trade, tourism and financial relations is beginning to inhibit the national exercise of self serving economic and political policies'. Tourism's cowboy economics (Korten, 1990) profaned the very soul with which it was born by creating social repercussions.

As tourism grew, tourists could be found in practically every accessible corner of the world. In some cases, their ubiquitous presence gradually drained the lifeblood of societies. Even governments that were aware of the parasitic nature of tourism could do little to protect themselves against the ills of tourism culture, which had an inherent tendency to pit people against people (e.g. tourists against locals, humanists against technocrats, rich against poor, and practitioners against intelligentsia). Tourism essentially alienated tourism.

Despite the prevailing trends, and considering the noble side of tourism, it is unlikely that tourism itself is bad, it is simply badly planned and managed. Although it is clear that tourism is not the root of global crises, its practitioners and researchers have been called upon, time and again, for collective action to revive its lost charm and vitality. The Brundtland Commission (WCED, 1990) believed strongly in the power of humanity to reorient existing patterns towards sustainable development. Section III of Agenda 21, an impressive documentary outcome of the 1992 Rio Conference, reasserts the role of public participation in the realization of the ideologies upon which sustainable development is based. Although neither of the two documents made any direct mention of tourism, their efficacy in putting people in the spotlight is unquestionable. Never before has there been such an awareness of the diversity, difference and variety among places and people as in recent times. This perception has evolved over decades of social interaction and was openly acknowledged only after the two documents were made public.

Tourism social scientists have been quick to respond to this clarion call. While the sociology of tourism particularly addresses societal and cultural aspects (Wang, 2000: 221), contributions by anthropologists and psychologists are also worth noting. It is difficult to overlook influential publications by MacCannell (1976), de Kadt (1979), Krippendorf, (1987), Smith (1989), Stokowski (1994), Dann (1996), Nash (1996), Pearce *et al.* (1996) and Wang (2000), among many others. An interdisciplinary mix is more relevant to the study of host–guest interaction.

Existing practices in mass tourism raise myriad issues of consumption, exploitation and globalization. In the context of these concerns, tourism originally did not seem to discriminate between the lesser-developed world and the developed world, the North and the South, or the East and the West. Socioeconomic problems derived from mass tourism afflicted Africa as they did Hawaii, Indonesia, Ecuador and Thailand (Smith and Eadington, 1992; Butler and Hinch, 1996; McLaren, 1998). The last two decades have witnessed a sudden upsurge in remedial forms of tourism. Worldwide there was an inquisitive search for some alternative form(s) of tourism – forms that would slow or arrest the deterioration process, seek to maintain and retain resources, place people in the centre, and reposition tourism as a humanizing force. Basically the objective was to devise or design a type of tourism that would be an antithesis to mass tourism. A form that would work as a double-edged sword, piercing through the hardened layers of capitalism and permitting the penetration of 'good' tourism into communities.

Scholarly attempts to pinion tourism from its corporate and administrative heights and secure it to local strongholds were emerging issues in the tourism literature from the late 1970s. All suggestions were accompanied by a directive for sustainability, wherein benefits permeate into the grass roots in a manner that would connect the socio-sphere to the biosphere in a symbiotic system. Emanating from the compelling need for alternative practices to prevailing forms of mainstream tourism, recommended formats included ecotourism, other forms of nature-based tourism, farm/rural tourism, cultural tourism, senior tourism, youth tourism and heritage tourism.

Of the many alternatives to 'bad' tourism, ecotourism emerged to be the most 'dramatically captivating' (Boo, 1993: 15). The term was initially coined exclusively for travel to natural realms, and those practicing it were ecotourists, who were said to possess a dedicated love of nature (Western, 1993: 7). Nature-dominated ecotourism was essentially a 'green' panorama in which residents were denied access, particularly in protected areas, since they did not fit in with the 'colour scheme'. However, visitors were permitted in increasing numbers until it was realized that local and indigenous people were indeed in the 'scheme' of ecotourism (Wells and Brandon, 1992). It took some time for protagonists of ecotourism to acknowledge the concept as an amalgam of interests arising out of environmental, economic and social concerns. Nature could not be saved at the expense of local people, and economics was identified as a viable binding force between the two. Conservation, preservation and development later became implied facets of ecotourism, which now began to be pursued for the well-being of local communities (Ceballos-Lascurain, 1996).

Thus, while ecotourism, like alternative tourism in general, acquired a new status, the strong undercurrent of community-based tourism became an underlining principle in the realm of alternative tourism. A proactive revival of community-based tourism was spurred on by de Kadt's (1979) treatise advocating strongly in favour of 'life chances and welfare' of the marginalized and the less privileged in society.

Tourism Issues in Destination Communities

Over the years, community tourism has evolved from the simple practice of visiting other people and places, through the overt utilization of community tourism resources, eventually culminating in seeking out resident responsive tourism experiences. This pattern conforms to Jafari's (1989) consolidated platforms of tourism, namely: advocacy, cautionary, adaptancy and knowledge-based platforms. Studies in community tourism have followed a similar pattern. Early writings seemed to emphasize the economic good that tourism was capable of generating. This perspective is part of the advocacy platform. With the rise in tourism activities worldwide there was a gradual realization that tourism may not be all that good and that it extorted a price from the common pool of the public. On the cautionary platform, Young's (1973) book *Tourism: Blessing or Blight*, was perhaps the first to reflect the complexities accruing at the local level from increasing international tourism. In the wake of modern tourism, more and more researchers began to concentrate on the sociocultural and socioeconomic impacts of tourism (see Bosselman, 1979; Rosenow and Pulsipher, 1979; Smith, 1989). It is an interesting fact that prior to the publication of the Brundtland Report, scholars like Murphy (1985) and Krippendorf (1987) had already begun advocating pro-community tourism, thus heralding the adaptancy platform. Since then there has been a deluge of literature on the varied character and constructs in community-based tourism. Currently, most research on this alternative approach has focused on the study of community perceptions (Pearce *et al.*, 1996), structural networks (Stokowski, 1994), cultural conflicts (Robinson and Boniface, 1999), development options (Dahles and Bras, 1999; Dieke, 2000), nodal growth (Bosselman *et al.*, 1999), social exchange (Ap, 1992), partnerships (Bramwell and Lane, 2000) and a global grass-roots movement for change (McLaren, 1998). These publications provide the knowledge-based foundation for a holistic treatment of issues emerging from community-based tourism.

Community-based tourism continues to remain an amorphous concept in realistic terms and hence tends to elude attempts at a solid definition. Attempts to define community tourism began almost two decades ago. With the mission well in place, its objectives and *modus operandi* remained un-addressed. While researchers grappled to define the concept precisely, practitioners were engaged in selling it. Some operators have achieved some measure of success in terms of positive outcomes from tourism in destination areas. Academics, on the other hand, have afforded the basic requirements for, or principles of, community tourism. If community tourism is defined in terms of participation, power and profits (Stonich, 2000), as has so far been argued, it is certainly a perplexing proposition.

The notion of community conjures up a mental picture of a defined set of people living together, symbiotically bound to each other and their habitat, thereby rendering themselves a distinct collective personality. Murdock (1955) suggested that any social group, existing in a territory and meeting all its problems of survival and continuity, should be considered a community. By itself, this definition may be considered adequate in the context of traditional settlements. However, as the world shrinks into a 'global village', obscurities in the concept of social continuity are increasing as never before.

In the tourism literature, communities have usually been researched and described in the form of case examples (e.g. Singh, 1989; Smith, 1989; Butler and Hinch, 1996; Price, 1996; Lew, 1999), rather than being defined. Jackson and Morpeth (1999: 5) agree that even in documents such as Local Agenda 21 'the term "community" is accepted and utilised, but is not defined or used consistently. What constitutes a community and what gives a community its lifeblood is . . . something still to be clarified'. At best, some researchers (e.g. Murphy, 1985; Swarbrooke, 1999) offer their views of community. There are, however, instances where tourism scholars have brought in background knowledge from conventional disciplines to define communities. The following sections examine the meaning of community from some geographical and social anthropological perspectives.

Meaning of Community

Geographical perspective

The importance of location has long been endorsed by spatial scientists (e.g. Nobbs *et al.*, 1983; Savage and Warde, 1993; Hodgson, 1995) and the idea of geographical space, with all its physical endowments, is an indisputable element in the meaning of community. This is because one of the basic requisites of community living is that its members relate to their physical environment in several ways, which are vividly reflected in their lifestyles and economic activities. Examples of the binding of humans and their environment exist throughout the world. For instance, Singh (1989: 89) reports on 'the uncanny ways of the people of Malana [a Hermit Village, North of Kulu Valley, in the Indian state of Himachal Pradesh] and of their closed socio-ecological systems'. The Goan community on the west coast of India is another example. Goans are essentially 'coastal people, occupying a marine niche. [They] have harvested their principle [*sic*] source of nourishment from the seas' (Alvares 1993: 2). For them the coast is their wherewithal and way of life. A Native American community, the Zuni Indians, is another good example. Mallari and Enote (1996: 27–28) argue that it is virtually impossible to separate the land/environment from Zuni society, culture and religion, and in fact this human–earth relationship underlines the meaning of the word *Zuni*. In the western plains of Australia's Cape York Peninsula, the Aboriginal community and the white cattle farmers are another example. Strang (1996) reports the close and continuous interaction between communal land ownership and local ecology and resources. While these examples are taken primarily from traditional societies, attachment to place is also an integral part of community in developed societies as well (see Cohen, 1985; Macdonald, 1993; Monti, 1999). In short, place and people are often viewed as being indivisible, thereby making the relationship holistic, lasting and intimate. Realizing this fact, the Northern Tourism Conference on Community and Resources, held in Canada in 1991, declared a community to be 'an area with close links between people and their habitat' (Haider and Johnston, 1992: 583).

By virtue of the finer sensibilities and sensitivities evolving out of the above discussion, a metaphysical binding becomes consequential. Thus, a belief system evolves centred on human spiritual conception from within the land and its people. As early as 1966, Wright, a noted geographer, identified this unique outcome of human–environment relationships and subsequently coined the term *geopiety*. Turner (1973: 69) reverberated the mystical aspect that defines *communitas*, his definition relying heavily upon 'sacred values' and 'high emotions' as a patrimonial endowment of a core group. Essentially a religious concept, geopiety subsumes the themes of ecology and territoriality through the byway of attitudes, beliefs and values (Tuan, 1976: 11). In this line of thought, a cultural group resonates through the physical environment in which its members live. Hatcher (1996: 182) calls it the 'human eco-system' that wraps a sense of ownership and belonging into it. The vitality of this relationship is the feelings of warmth and belonging that transcend specific religions and cultural contexts (Tuan, 1976: 29). It is the 'rooted-ness' of values arising from such soulful attachments to place that create communities.

By way of caution, Little (1994) clarifies that 'community' is usually a misused term that can invoke a false sense of tradition, homogeneity and consensus. Communities are not as definable as Ascher (1995) and Western *et al.* (1994) make them out to be. Rather, easily defined communities are said to be fragments of scholastic imagery of an idealized paradise, devoid of realities of everyday life (Stonich, 2000). This concept, which was coined 'imagined community' (see Anderson, 1991), is put to good use by the tourism industry to sell quaint destinations irrespective of the locale.

Socio-anthropological perspective

From the constant intra- and interactions within and between people and habitats, two hybrid dimensions of community living arise: culture and society. Society, community and system are all accepted elements of the overall community structure (Mogey, 1975; Savage and Warde, 1993; Stokowski, 1994). Urry (2000) deviates from the factual realistic terms and replaces them with 'ideology' to bring out the intrinsic meaning of community relationships. He considers a community to be a cluster of like-minded people and, where the unlike-believer is isolated as a non-commune. Terms like 'affiliation' (Warren and Lyon, 1988), 'mutuality' and 'emotional bonds' (Bender, 1978) are generally used in this context.

In the preceding discussion, the reality of humankind's changing nature has remained quite neglected. People change, landscapes transform and communities evolve with the passage of time. The spirit of communes, too, undergoes metamorphosis, following erosion in intrinsic values and subsequent breakdowns of community structures. Possibly, this was the reason Schmalenbach (1977) preferred to introduce the concept of 'bund' wherein people can freely choose to join or leave a group or community.

For the continued survival of social groups, it is imperative for members of a community to uphold their root values at the same time as they are being threatened by extraneous factors, which have potential to devalue their cohesiveness. Values translate into visible actions in everyday life of community members. Such value-based expressions are the lifeblood of community living. Similarly, Pearce *et al.* (1996) examine in depth Social Representations Theory, which blends the overt (tangible) and the covert (intangible) assets of a community. Overt expressions of this binding force are generally the cultural attributes of a community, made vivid through language, dress, cuisine, festivities, settlement types and lifestyle. The more subtle or covert aspects are the underlying beliefs, ethics and attitudes that shape overt behaviour and action.

In summary, tourism academics have generally referred to communities as locals, residents, natives, indigenous people and hosts, with much importance placed on the latter term. A *host* community, or destination community, is practically all of what has been described so far. Within the particular context of tourism, Swarbrooke (1999) highlights how complex the term is, stating that it involves geography, ethnicity, demography, governance, stakeholders and the power structure that exists within the community. Bosselman *et al.* (1999), adopt a non-controversial meaning of the term *host* community. They include it to mean all such persons and public and private bodies who are potentially affected, both positively and negatively, by the impacts of tourism development within the boundaries of the destination area.

A related issue, which has bearing on the overall discussion, is whether or not the host–guest analogy is somewhat of a misnomer. Does a community regard itself as a host, and can this hold true for all sections of a community? Equally, do all visitors consider themselves guests with the expectation that the community at the destination is there to cater for all their needs and desires? For some this analogy will hold true, but others would never conceive this type of relationship to exist. Hall and Butler (1995) addressed this issue when they argued that the host–guest analogy, while a useful one to examine the links between tourists and the places they visit, exists to justify what is actually taking place between both, namely that of an economic transaction. Many residents within the host community do not necessarily see their function as that of a host, primarily because they do not benefit directly from the economic transactions that take place.

Given the range of responses community members can express towards tourism, not surprisingly much diversity exists in terms of types of destination communities. For instance, while there are those communities where tourism is the primary mainstay, there are cases where tourism plays a minor role. The relationship function between tourism and the community itself can therefore range from those that are in outright support for tourism to those opposed to tourism as a development option. In addition, communities exist within different real world contexts (e.g. developing versus developed) where differences might also be obvious regarding the level of tourism development. Furthermore, communities are living entities and subject to change over time. As a result, the relationship between destinations and tourism may also change for better or worse. Hence, it becomes somewhat difficult to classify communities neatly under specific typologies with respect to tourism–community relationships.

These varied debates on the meaning and nature of community notwithstanding, destination communities in the context of this book are the locations, together with their natural and human elements, where tourist experiences take place and where the tourism product is produced.

This Volume

It is clear that tourism and its role in destination communities is a multi-dimensional phenomenon that encompasses economic, social, cultural, ecological and political forces. Most studies of tourism destinations focus on market demand or the supply side of tourism, at the expense of understanding community dynamics from the perspectives of both physical location and the socioeconomic life of destination residents. This book aims to address this dearth by examining together many of the issues and critical concepts that pertain to the relationship between destination communities and tourism. These issues include economics, society and culture, heritage identity, politics and power, indigenous rights, ethical stakeholder interactions, development theory, planning, environment/ ecology, management and marketing. Each of these matters forms the nucleus of an individual chapter. This volume is not a collection of case studies. Instead, each chapter is grounded solidly in, and focuses on, theoretical/conceptual knowledge, with additional support provided by the use of empirical examples.

This book is divided into three parts. The first comprises Chapters 1 (this chapter) and 2, which set the tone of the volume by establishing definitions and outlining the parameters of tourism in destinations. Chapter 1 introduces community-based tourism and tourism in destination communities. Furthermore, it provides a description of the book's contents chapter by chapter. Chapter 2 (Boyd and Singh) discusses issues of scale, tourism community types and the supply side of tourism. It also critically examines the relationships between different types/structures of destinations and tourism and presents a typology of these relationships.

Part II expands upon the previous part. These six chapters take a closer look at the principles and processes involved in the development of tourism in destination communities. In doing so, the authors impart reasoning to why the outcomes of tourism in destinations occur as they do. In Chapter 3, Ioannides summarizes how host communities adopt tourism as a means of diversifying their economic base, particularly in situations where they may be heavily dependent on a narrow range of activities. He presents logical thought on the indiscriminate use of tourism's multipliers, thus affording a degree of reality of tourism at the regional and local levels. For sustainable tourism development to occur, the economics of tourism cannot be accorded a greater or lesser status than the sociocultural and environmental dimensions of tourism.

Dealing with the twin aspects of society and culture, Fagence (Chapter 4) reverberates similar opinions. Commencing with the notion that tourism has both positive and negative impacts on destination communities, he observes that scholars have a general tendency to concentrate only on tourism's negative side at the expense of seeing the positive. He acknowledges that there are difficulties in understanding the visitor–resident interactions and that observation and measurement of impacts poses a massive challenge. Exploring the case example of the Amish and other Anabaptist groups, Fagence demonstrates how some cultural groups are commonly seen as attractions in their own right and how they protect themselves from the influences of tourism.

The cultural past is very much a part of a community's identity and an important resource for tourism. In Chapter 5, Ashworth explores assumptions about community and place identity, tourism and destination communities, and the goals of local policy. Against this context he develops a model to explain the relationships between local and tourism senses of place. With the help of three examples from Newfoundland (Canada), New Mexico (USA) and Kraków-Kazimierz (Poland), Ashworth introduces two concepts in relation to the presentation and interpretation of community heritage. The 'Disneyland Effect', demonstrating the effectiveness of deliberate planning action, is presented in tandem with the concept of 'Replication of Venice', which implies that if place identities can be created then it follows that places are reproducible and tourism places are more easily replicated than most.

Hall's discussion of destination community politics (Chapter 6) raises questions about the power dimensions of tourism and place, and the strength of certain interests within a community to dominate over others. The chapter adopts a three-dimensional approach to analyse power in the decision-making process. According to Hall, the uneven development of the qualities of place, as well as the representation of place, together reflect the existing ideologies and power relations in destination communities.

Closely related to the issue of power, is concern for indigenous peoples, who have traditionally been shut out of development decision-making by colonialists and ruling classes. Johnston provides insight into indigenous rights within the framework of human rights in Chapter 7. The central principle of indigenous rights, she argues, is self-determination with respect to the entitlement of a community to decide whether or not it wants a tourism economy, which parts of its culture will be shared and which will remain private, and what protocols will govern access to, and use of, cultural property. Indigenous knowledge about development has spiritual dimensions, which need to help create 'Sacred Balance'. Johnston strongly advocates the principle of prior informed consent, while suggesting steps to bridge the policy–indigenous community divide.

Fennell and Przeclawski in Chapter 8 discuss ethics among and between tourism stakeholders. According to these authors, tourism is a form of human behaviour and the act of travel should be viewed as a window into the soul of the individual and of society. Their chapter examines tourism's impacts from an ethical perspective and considers the many actors involved in tourism, including tourists, residents, brokers, and the broader social and ecological environments in which they interact. Through the development of a conceptual framework they demonstrate how ethics can assist in a broader understanding of the impacts of tourism.

The third and final part pertains to the *how* of sustainable community tourism. The chapters in this part are critically poised to afford some solutions to the myriad issues mentioned in earlier chapters and some additional ones ensuing from the business of tourism in destination communities.

Exploring the linkages between tourism and development theory in Chapter 9, Telfer highlights the changing if overlapping nature of the two. Telfer begins by examining tourism development in the context of four main development paradigms, specifically: modernization, dependency, economic neoliberalism and alternative development. Destination development is explored in terms of empowerment, participation, partnership, community capacity and community change. Through the application of a three-part 'framework theory', an effort is made to understand community development on a continuum from the micro level to the global level.

Chapter 10 is about planning for community tourism. There is a substantial literature on strategies for tourism planning. Most studies of tourism planning emphasize vertical and horizontal integration in planning practices. Timothy and Tosun affirm that principles, such as equity, efficiency, integration, balance, harmony, and ecological and cultural integrity are more effectively brought about when community members are allowed and encouraged to participate in tourism planning and development, when collaboration and cooperation are allowed to occur, and when tourism is developed in an incremental fashion. Besides explaining scales of planning, the prime focus of this chapter is the various planning approaches in destination communities. On the basis of participatory, incremental and collaborative planning principles, the authors present a normative model that combines the three styles into one under the abbreviation 'PIC'. This implies that a combination of strategies is a more sure technique in the planning process than a singular method or approach. However, several obstacles exist in implementing the PIC planning model in both developed and developing societies.

Dowling (Chapter 11) discusses why community consultation/participation is vital from an environmental perspective. Assuming that community members understand the benefits derived from tourism, such as the preservation of historic sites, Dowling emphasizes the importance of incorporating the perceptions of destination residents in evaluating the effects of tourism development for planning purposes. Sustaining the environment is the principal idea behind a healthy tourism economy and an equally healthy environment that can be achieved through the social mechanisms of interconnectedness, intrinsic values, conservation, intergenerational equity and individual responsibility.

Scheyvens, in Chapter 12, pursues the question of who should manage tourism in host communities. This raises the issue of participation and empowerment, which lie at the heart of the development process, and thus the diverse facets of empowerment (i.e. economic, social, psychological and political) are explored. These multiple views of empowerment require the involvement of multiple agencies. Scheyvens identifies governments, the private sector and non-governmental organizations (NGOs) as critical stakeholders in facilitating the involvement of destination communities in managing the industry.

Chapter 13, on the marketing processes in destinations, emphasizes the tensions and contested values at work in human social groups. The authors, Moscardo and Pearce, discuss Social Representations Theory, with the purpose of emphasizing community–tourism relationships in a holistic way. It is clear that such an approach alone can encourage community participation in destination marketing. Social Representations Theory is useful in establishing appropriate links between the marketing of communities for tourism and sustainable tourism issues.

While various issues have been dealt with separately in each chapter, and while contributors to this anthology have presented their concerns with fresh perspectives wherever possible, the notion of sustainability is notably present in all chapters. This was not a part of their initial assignment. Instead, concepts and principles of sustainability have appeared as a natural part of all aspects of tourism in destination communities. This is not surprising given that the sustainability debate in tourism has heretofore focused on the long-term viability and health of physical, economic and sociocultural environments in destination communities.

References

Alvares, C. (1993) *Fish, Curry and Rice: a Citizen's Report on the Goan Environment.* Ecoforum Publication, Goa.

Anderson, B. (1991) *Imagined Communities.* Verso, New York.

Ap, J. (1992) Residents' perceptions of tourism impacts. *Annals of Tourism Research* 19, 665–690.

Ascher, W. (1995) *Communities and Sustainable Forestry in Developing Countries.* ICS Press, San Francisco.

Bender, T. (1978) *Community and Social Change in America.* Johns Hopkins University Press, Baltimore, Maryland.

Boo, E. (1993) Ecotourism planning for protected areas. In: Lindberg, K. and Hawkins, D.E. (eds) *Ecotourism: a Guide for Planners and Managers.* Ecotourism Society, North Bennington, Vermont, pp. 15–31.

Bosselman, F.P. (1979) *In the Wake of the Tourist: Managing Special Places in Eight Countries.* The Conservation Foundation, Washington, DC.

Bosselman, F.P., Peterson, C.A. and MacCarthy, C. (1999) *Managing Tourism Growth: Issues and Applications.* Island Press, Washington, DC.

Bramwell, B. and Lane, B. (eds) (2000) *Tourism Collaboration and Partnerships: Politics, Practice and Sustainability.* Channel View, Clevedon, UK.

Butler, R.W. and Hinch, T. (eds) (1996) *Tourism and Indigenous Peoples.* International Thomson Business Press, London.

Ceballos-Lascurain, H. (1996) *Tourism, Ecotourism and Protected Areas: the State of Nature-Based Tourism Around the World and Guidelines for its Development.* International Union for the Conservation of Nature, Gland, Switzerland.

Cohen, A.P. (1985) *The Symbolic Construction of Community.* Ellis Horwood, Chichester, UK.

Dahles, H. and Bras, K. (1999) *Tourism and Small Entrepreneurs: Development, National Policy, and Entrepreneurial Culture: Indonesian Cases.* Cognizant, New York.

Dann, G.M.S. (1996) *The Language of Tourism: a Sociologistic Perspective.* CAB International, Wallingford.

de Kadt, E. (1979) *Tourism: Passport to Development?* Oxford University Press, New York.

Dieke, P.U.C. (ed.) (2000) *The Political Economy of Tourism Development in Africa.* Cognizant, New York.

Haider, W. and Johnston, M. (1992) Tourism and community development. *Annals of Tourism Research* 19, 580–583.

Hall, C.M. and Butler, R.W. (1995) In search of common ground: reflections on sustainability, complexity and process in the tourism system. *Journal of Sustainable Tourism* 3(2), 99–105.

Hatcher, R.L. (1996) Local indicators of sustainability: measuring the human ecosystem. In: Nath, B., Hens, L. and Devuyst, D. (eds) *Textbook on Sustainable Development.* VUB University Press, Brussels, pp. 181–203.

Hodgson, S. (1995) Local Agenda 21 and social dilemma. Paper presented at the 1995 International Sustainable Development Research Conference, 27–28 March, Manchester, UK.

Jackson, G. and Morpeth, N. (1999) Local Agenda 21 and community participation in tourism policy and planning: future and fallacy. *Current Issues in Tourism* 2(1), 1–38.

Jafari, J. (1989) An English language literature review. In: Bystrzanowski, J. (ed.) *Tourism as a Factor of Change: a Sociocultural Study.* Centre for Research and Documentation in Social Sciences, Vienna, pp. 17–60.

Korten, D.C. (1990) *Getting to the 21st Century: Voluntary Action and the Global Agenda.* West Hartford, Connecticut, Kumarian Press.

Krippendorf, J. (1987) *The Holiday Makers: Understanding the Impact of Leisure and Travel.* Butterworth Heinemann, Oxford.

Lew, A.A. (1999) Managing tourism-induced acculturation through environmental design on Pueblo Indian villages in the U.S. In: Singh, T.V. and Singh, S. (eds) *Tourism Development in Critical Environments.* Cognizant, New York, pp. 120–136.

Little, P.D. (1994) The link between local participation and improved conservation: a review of issues and experiences. In: Western, D., Wright, R.M. and Strum, S.C. (eds) *Natural Connections: Perspectives in Community-based Conservation.* Island Press, Washington, DC, pp. 347–372.

MacCannell, D. (1976) *The Tourist: a New Theory of the Leisure Class.* Macmillan, London.

Macdonald, S. (1993) *Inside European Identities: Ethnography in Western Europe.* Berg, Providence.

Mallari, A.A. and Enote, J.E. (1996) Maintaining control: culture and tourism in the Pueblo of Zuni. In: Price, M.F. (ed.) *People and Tourism in Fragile Environments.* John Wiley & Sons, Chichester, pp. 19–31.

McLaren, D. (1998) *Rethinking Tourism and Ecotravel: the Paving of Paradise and What You Can Do to Stop It.* Kumarian Press, West Hartford, Connecticut.

Mogey, J. (1975) Society, man, and environment. In: Jones, E. (ed.) *Readings in Social Geography.* Oxford University Press, Oxford, pp. 168–176.

Monti, D.J. (1999) *The American City: a Social and Cultural History*. Blackwell, Oxford.

Murdock, G.P. (1955) Statistical relations among community characteristics. In: Lazersfeld, P.F. and Rosenberg, M. (eds) *The Language of Social Research*. Glencoe, Chicago, pp. 305–311.

Murphy, P.E. (1985) *Tourism: a Community Approach*. Methuen, New York.

Nash, D. (1996) *Anthropology of Tourism*. Pergamon, Oxford.

Nobbs, J., Hine, B. and Flemming, M. (1983) *Sociology*. Macmillan, London.

Pearce, P., Moscardo, G. and Ross, G. (1996) *Tourism Community Relationships*. Pergamon, Oxford.

Price, M.F. (ed.) (1996) *People and Tourism in Fragile Environments*. John Wiley & Sons, Chichester.

Richter, L.K. (1989) *The Politics of Tourism in Asia*. University of Hawaii Press, Honolulu.

Robinson, M. and Boniface, P. (1999) *Tourism and Cultural Conflicts*. CAB International, Wallingford.

Rosenow, J.E. and Pulsipher, G.L. (1979) *Tourism: the Good, the Bad and the Ugly*. Century Three Press, Omaha.

Savage, M. and Warde, A. (1993) *Urban Sociology, Capitalism and Modernity*. Macmillan, London.

Schmalenbach, H.S. (1977) *Herman Schmalenbach: On Society and Experience*. University of Chicago Press, Chicago.

Singh, T.V. (1989) *The Kulu Valley: Impact of Tourism Development in the Mountain Areas*. Himalayan Books, New Delhi.

Smith, V. (ed.) (1989) *Hosts and Guests: the Anthropology of Tourism*, 2nd edn. University of Pennsylvania Press, Philadelphia.

Smith, V. and Eadington, W.R. (eds) (1992) *Tourism Alternatives: Potentials and Problems in the Development of Tourism*. University of Pennsylvania Press, Philadelphia.

Stokowski, P.A. (1994) *Leisure in Society: a Network Structural Perspective*. Mansell, London.

Stonich, S.C. (2000) *The Other Side of Paradise: Tourism, Conservation and Development in the Bay Islands*. Cognizant, New York.

Strang, V. (1996) Sustaining tourism in far north Queensland. In: Price, M.F. (ed.) *People and Tourism in Fragile Environments*. John Wiley & Sons, Chichester, pp. 51–67.

Swarbrooke, J. (1999) *Sustainable Tourism Management*. CAB International, Wallingford.

Tuan, Y. (1976) Geopiety: a theme in man's attachment to nature and to place. In: Lowenthal, D. and Bowden, M.J. (eds) *Geographies of the Mind: Essays in Historical Geosophy*. Oxford University Press, New York, pp. 11–39.

Turner, V. (1973) The center out there: pilgrim's goal. *History of Religion* 12(3), 191–230.

Urry, J. (2000) *Consuming Places*. Routledge, London.

Wang, N. (2000) *Tourism and Modernity: a Sociological Analysis*. Pergamon, Oxford.

Warren, R.L. and Lyon, L. (eds) (1988) *New Perspectives on the American Community*. Dorsey Press, Chicago.

Waters, S. (1978) *Travel '77/'78: the Big Picture*. Child and Waters, New York.

WCED (World Commission on Environment and Development) (1990) *Our Common Future*. Oxford University Press, Oxford.

Wells, M. and Brandon, K. (1992) *People and Parks: Linking Protected Area Management with Local Communities*. World Bank, Washington, DC.

Western, D. (1993) Defining ecotourism. In: Lindberg, K. and Hawkins, D.E. (eds) *Ecotourism: a Guide for Planners and Managers*. Ecotourism Society, North Bennington, Vermont, pp. 7–11.

Western, D., Wright, R.M. and Strum, S.C. (eds) (1994) *Natural Connections: Perspectives in Community-based Conservation*. Island Press, Washington, DC.

Wright, J.K. (1966) *Human Nature in Geography*. Harvard University Press, Cambridge, Massachusetts.

Young, G. (1973) *Tourism: Blessing or Blight?* Penguin Books, London.

Destination Communities: Structures, Resources and Types

2

STEPHEN W. BOYD[1] and SHALINI SINGH[2]

[1]*Department of Tourism, Otago University, Dunedin, New Zealand;* [2]*Department of Recreation and Leisure Studies, Brock University, Canada, and Centre for Tourism Research and Development, Lucknow, India*

Introduction

Lately researchers have strongly recommended community-based tourism for a sustainable tourism industry. Studies of tourism development repeatedly emphasize the importance of people's participation through power sharing, social cohesion and knowledge enhancement (Prentice, 1993; Drumm, 1998; Timothy, 1999; Tosun, 2000; Mitchell and Reid, 2001). Mechanisms for accomplishing this have been proposed with the intention of facilitating judicious use of common endowments for the benefit and perpetuation of community values and for the promotion of community health and well-being. However, putting these mechanisms in place is a daunting task. At the very outset, even the concept of community poses a major challenge as described in Chapter 1.

In response to this challenge, this chapter discusses issues concerning tourism communities. The first part of the chapter examines the diverse structural nature of destination communities, which can be classified through a set of morphological traits. These characteristics are discussed in the second section of the chapter, with the purpose of gauging the range and forms of communities. With this background, the latter part of the chapter makes an effort to place destination communities into a broad-based typology of tourism–destination relationships.

Types and Characteristics of Destination Communities

Types, scale and functions

Destination communities exist in different forms and at different scales. One of the most obvious forms is that associated with seaside resort towns, where tourism has grown around a resort community, or where a community has developed around enclave-type resort development. Other resort-type communities centre on tourism that caters for a particular activity-based experience. Ski resorts, for example, represent one element of host communities that exists primarily within rural areas. At the opposite end of the scale, host communities may be large urban centres where the proportion of the population involved in tourism can be great or small depending on the role tourism plays within that specific urban context. In the middle of the spectrum exist destination communities within a rural context, ranging from non-specialized villages where tourism plays a minor role to those that are best described as craft and tourist shopping villages, where tourism can often be their *raison d'être* (Getz, 1993). Another type of destination community associated with tourism is indigenous groups, which may be urban or rural. In all cases, these have had a long history of development, but it is only recently that tourism has come to play an important role in the life of these communities.

Because destination communities differ over time and space, their functions also vary. To meet demand, they need to ensure that supply elements, such as transportation, attractions, services, information and promotion, are provided. Jansen-Verbeke (1986) viewed such aspects as comprising the primary (attractions), secondary (services) and additional elements (infrastructure) that make up the tourism product of places. The extent to which these functions are provided by communities will depend on the type of community itself. Space limitations do not permit a detailed breakdown of specific functions within different types of communities. Instead, what is offered here are a few comments on how the focus will shift between different types of communities. For instance, in resort communities, emphasis is usually directed at attractions (often theme park related and not geographically related to the actual place itself) and services (particularly accommodation available at different levels of quality), with less attention given to infrastructure and promotional needs. In contrast, urban destinations, while also providing attractions, services and accommodation, are often seen as markets as opposed to users, and therefore stronger emphasis is given to catering for functions that address infrastructure and promotional needs of tourism outside the community itself. In other communities (e.g. craft villages and indigenous settlements) where there is often a single or specialized tourism product, their function is to ensure that the demand is met, albeit often with a limited base.

Community structure

The role of tourism can have a direct bearing on how the destination community is structured. Communities are rarely homogeneous in their composition. Sproule and Suhandi (1998: 216), for example, saw from their research in Indonesia that while:

> communities can have many things in common, they are complex entities and should not be thought of as one homogenous group. Communities are comprised of specific groups, such as tenants and landowners, the wealthy and the poor, and old and new residents. Different interest groups within the community are likely to be affected variably by the changes associated with tourism . . . [and] . . . depending on the issue, a community may be united or divided in thought and action.

It is possible therefore to suggest that community structure can range across a number of polar extremes – complex to simple, heterogeneous to homogeneous. While there is danger in oversimplifying how terms are categorized, it is suggested here that communities will often exhibit those characteristics found at the same extremity of each spectrum. For instance, complexity is more likely to be present in those communities viewed as having a high degree of heterogeneity (Ryan and Montgomery, 1994; Mason and Cheyne, 2000). This is often because tourism is viewed as being only one product of a number that the community is involved with, and hence will only involve a sub-element of the host community (Joppe, 1996; Lawson *et al.*, 1998). In contrast, communities that predominantly cater for tourism are more likely to be homogeneous, as the majority of the host community is seen to be involved in the same activity. As a result a simpler community structure develops.

It is, however, important to note that other factors are involved in shaping community structure. Primary among these are endogenous factors, such as local population mix, length of residency, extent of local ownership, level of local involvement in tourism, and the existing decision-making power structure and processes in place (Mitchell and Reid, 2001). Given space limitations, only a few comments will be offered regarding who is involved in providing services to tourists within the community. In most destinations, these comprise two major groups: the public and the private sectors, although in some places, non-profit or volunteer-sector services also exist. The first group includes the policy makers, planners, government agencies, regional and local authorities operating in a predefined system (Torkildsen, 1983). The second group, the private sector, comprises entrepreneurs, corporations and the resident populations (Burns, 1999). Finally there is the volunteer/non-profit sector, which in the context of tourism might include museums, non-governmental organizations (NGOs) and community groups. While all three groups described above are very different from each other, they are often mutually interdependent.

Exogenous factors are also important in shaping community structure. These may include factors such as the extent to which in-migration into the community is linked to the provision of tourism as well as the extent to which businesses are owned from outside of the community. In light of the foregoing comments, it is important to stress that communities operate individually and may not display all of the characteristics noted above. However, if taken at a broad general level, it is not unreasonable to assume that complexity and heterogeneity would best typify urban destinations and to a certain extent coastal resort communities, particularly those that have had a long history and have had to diversify beyond tourism to exist. In contrast, a more homogeneous structure would be expected within indigenous communities, rural areas, craft and shopping villages, as well as those linked to resorts that cater for a single activity (e.g. skiing).

Community partnerships

The importance, utility and nature of tourism partnerships have recently emerged in the literature (e.g. Bramwell and Lane, 2000). Timothy (1998) identified several types of tourism partnerships that need to exist for communities to develop more sustainable forms of tourism. The most critical in this discussion include cooperation between public sector agencies, different levels of government, and public and private (including volunteer) sectors. One area within Timothy's public and private sector cooperation that has not received much attention in the literature is NGOs. It is critical in host communities to understand the extent to which partnerships can be forged between the community and the various levels of government responsible for tourism. Tourism NGOs differ from relief-based NGOs in that the former cater more for community development, with strong emphasis on environmental protection particularly of a community's resources and assets (e.g. the Ecotourism Society), while the latter are focused on aid development, particularly relieving the suffering of the poor around the world. Tourism NGOs exist at all levels, but more often are community based, and as such may acquire the label of CBOs (community-based organizations). Because variation exists both in their nature and in how effective they are, it is difficult to make generalizations, but some strengths may be noted. These organizations are characterized by strong grass-roots links, the ability to innovate and adapt, emphasize the need for participation, a long-term commitment, and an emphasis on sustainability. As such, they provide a base on which host communities can adopt, develop and deliver their tourism products. Despite limitations such as limited financial and managerial expertise, being isolated and only making small-scale interventions, NGOs can often serve as the bridge that promotes cooperation within communities, establishing the initial links with the local and regional government tourism sector to form partnerships (Burns, 1999).

Partnership is a term that has become inextricably linked to sustainability as it is tied to the broader concept of involvement. There is an emerging literature on tourism partnerships which focuses on a number of related aspects, namely their type (formal or informal), the approach that can be adopted (grass-roots or agency driven) and the degree of cooperation expected (great to limited and issue-based) (Boyd and Timothy, 2001). Destination communities need to form partnerships if they intend to maintain their product base and attractiveness (Selin, 1999). Their type may often depend on broader development issues involving the community and the role that CBOs can play to galvanize support to form partnerships across the community and with external agencies. One means of ensuring the integrity of community resources is through cooperative development that encourages local participation effectively.

It is not easy to assign types of partnership to different communities, as it is important to stress again that no one community is like another and that if generalizations are to be made, they should be made with caution. In complex urban-based destinations, partnerships are more likely to be directed at particular subsets of the tourism product, for instance how to promote the existing product base over protecting it. In contrast, tourism partnerships associated with communities like resorts, rural areas, craft villages and indigenous peoples, are more likely to focus on protection of the tourism base, as opposed to just promoting the tourist product, for the simple reason that these communities are more reliant on the quality of their resource base, which is often individualized.

Host reactions and extent of change

By virtue of their dynamism, communities change over time in how they perceive tourists as well as how they react to increased demand for more tourism. While some early models of resident perception of tourists (e.g. Doxey's Irridex) were quick to suggest that feelings were unidirectional, moving from tourist arrivals as a positive experience to seeing the 'guests' in a negative light, others recognized the fluidity of destination residents' experiences, noting the exchanges that could be had from interaction with visitors and that within a community there can exist a range of views from acceptance to avoidance and that these positions could also change over time (e.g. Getz, 1994). Factors that account for this range of reaction include the physical distance between where residents live and work compared to tourist spaces, the ratio between hosts and guests, as well as the extent of support for tourism that exists within the host community as a whole. In looking at different types of communities, only broad generalizations can be made with respect to residents' perceptions of tourists and the extent to which this changes. As observed earlier, large urban centres can more readily absorb large numbers of visitors and so the impact is not as recognizable. While tourism is an important economic activity for many urban areas, the fact that distance separates residential space from tourist space mitigates the degree of negative feeling that may be generated. Issues at the fore that will have a bearing on residents' feelings are that urban places with obvious tourist attractions face growing problems of congestion, accessibility and higher prices, and a decline in the quality of the local product (see Fagence, Chapter 4 this volume). In contrast, resort-based and rural communities vary between those with little resident reaction, often where tourism development is enclitic in nature, and those where residents are outnumbered by tourists and, as a consequence, are made to feel of secondary value in their own communities. Because many resort communities have a long history of tourism they have well established feelings towards visitors, ranging from active involvement to avoidance. The opposite scenario is emerging for destination communities associated with craft villages, rural areas and indigenous peoples, where they once avoided tourism in the past, they are now actively encouraging it as a vital tool for economic development (Getz, 1993; Timothy and White, 1999).

Community tourism resources

Given the previous description of what constitutes a community and the range of people within it, a community may be regarded as a repository of tourist resources by way of its biocentrality and ethnocentrality (Murphy, 1983). In 1985, Murphy argued that 'the natural resources of a community (both physical and human) are often the *raison d'être* for the industry', and hence justifies the notion of community as a resource for tourism. In the words of Cohen (1985: 118), communities are symbolic constructions that make them 'a resource and repository of meaning, and a referent to their identity'. Thus, a community offers its nature, culture, society and even its economy as commodities (Fry, 1977) for tourism and to tourists. These assets are packaged, commoditized and then merchandized by brokers as 'local colour' to potential buyers. The 'everyday life' of residents would include an unlimited range of assets, from the basic resource of water to the sacred site located in the remote vicinity of the area, to the seasonal festivities marking occasions of community cohesion and solidarity.

Space does not permit a detailed discussion of what tourism resources exist within communities. However, a useful way to address this is to take the key supply elements of tourism that were identified by Jansen-Verbeke

(1986) for urban areas and see how each relates to other types of community. Within an urban context, she argued that attractions are the primary elements, comprising activity places (e.g. cultural, sport and amusement facilities) and their leisure setting (physical characteristics and sociocultural features). For most resort communities emphasis is placed on providing entertainment (e.g. casinos, night clubs, bars, bingo halls, amusement parks, cinemas) and quality sporting facilities, particularly water-based, with less attention to cultural facilities (e.g. museums, galleries, theatres) though these are, to a certain extent, also provided. As for the leisure setting, physical characteristics of places are place-specific where the mix of features found is often dependent on the location of the resort, and its history. Older resort communities have had this because they contain several attractions, including nature, cultural and built heritage, as well as distinct sociocultural features (e.g. folklore, customs, traditions, dress). This array of features is not often found in planned resort areas where there is less of a community presence, but where emphasis is placed on facilities provision. The nature and extent of attractions will vary for communities found in rural areas. The emphasis here shifts to leisure-based attractions where the rural landscape can be the attraction or act as the context in which various leisure pursuits and sporting facilities are offered to tourists. As for sociocultural features, rural areas and their communities offer a wealth of interest to visitors, with their folklore, local customs, language, architecture, ambience and general friendliness. It is often these attractions that account for the growth of tourism in rural areas. The same comments apply for indigenous communities, but where the attraction of a unique natural heritage can often have the same appeal to visitors as the sociocultural features these types of communities offer.

Secondary elements of supply focus on the services these communities offer such as accommodation, shopping and markets. The extent to which these services exist within different destination communities is often a factor of how they are marketed. Virtually all offer accommodation, but this will vary depending on demand and ability to meet it, with less of a choice being available to tourists as one moves from urban and resort areas, as many rural communities have set themselves up as exclusively market and shopping places. An example of this is St Jacobs, Ontario, Canada, where nearly the entire village is given over to tourists, who buy crafts and produce, particularly items related to the Mennonite culture of the region (Dahms, 1991; Getz, 1993; Mitchell *et al.*, 1998).

Tertiary elements of supply are those relating to infrastructure (e.g. transportation, information offices, parking). Again, the extent to which these can be provided by destination communities will vary across the spectrum from urban to rural places. As with the secondary elements, the complexity and diversity of the infrastructure will diminish as one moves from an urban to rural environment, although it is likely that some of these will be easier to provide in rural areas where visitor numbers remain small.

One useful way to examine the supply side of destination communities is to identify whether communities of different types and scales can be classified according to the relationship they are perceived to have with tourism. The extent to which that relationship remains a favourable one is often dependent on how well the host community is structured to cope with, and respond to, the nature of tourism development taking place locally. Clearly, there are challenges with using this approach. The above discussion has highlighted a number of aspects associated with host communities. Based on this it is possible to develop a typology of destination communities and tourism.

A Typology of Tourism–Host Community Relationships

Typologies have been widely used within tourism literature as a useful way to establish broad classifications. In the context of impacts, Burr (1991, cited in Pearce *et al.*, 1996: 28) has put forward four theoretical approaches germane to community structures and systems. These include: human ecology (habitat), social system (structural processes), interaction (social exchanges) and critical opposition (power groups). He argues that a pluralism of these theoretical approaches would be necessary to ensure the inclusion of the diverse range of destination communities. So far, these have ranged from macro aspects such as tourist development (Pearce, 1989), types of tourism (Burton, 1995) and types of tourists (Smith, 1977) to more specialized micro aspects like partnerships (Selin, 1999; Boyd and Timothy, 2001). The approach taken here to establish a typology is based on assessing the relationship that exists between tourism and the destination community. The following four possible relationship scenarios may develop: win–win, win–lose, lose–win or lose–lose (Cater and Lowman, 1994; Nepal, 2000).

Win–win

The win–win scenario is one where both the community and tourism benefit. The obvious example of this is what is termed community-based tourism, where the community is in support of tourism, participates and benefits from it and where tourism ensures the maintenance of the resource base of the community itself. Some of the best examples of community-based tourism are linked to indigenous peoples. The Communal Areas Management Programme for Indigenous Resources (CAMPFIRE) projects in Zimbabwe, the Annapurna Conservation Area Project (ACAP) in Nepal, and Aboriginal tourism at Uluru (Ayers Rock) in

Australia are some that have received significant attention from tourism scholars.

> ### Win–win: indigenous communities – Uluru National Park, Australia
>
> Uluru (Ayers Rock) is internationally recognized as one of Australia's leading tourist attractions. Tourists are overwhelmingly motivated by the desire to see the spectacular inselberg, but unfortunately they rank learning about Aboriginal culture in the area as low (Hall, 2000). Aboriginal communities take a different view and have decided to become involved in tourism, defining their relationship with tourism as having control and exercising choice (Mercer, 1994). They have representation on the management board that administers the park and have control over how tourism is presented, ensuring that the cultural and religious significance that Aboriginal people attach to the park is accorded the highest degree of protection and respect (Wells, 1996). As for choice, the Aboriginal communities can decide if they want to be involved in tourism or not. Much of this involvement has recently become symbolized by the interpretive and educational services they offer visitors at the Uluru – Kata Tjuta Cultural Centre located in the park. Their position is summed up in the words of a senior Anangu traditional owner:
>
> > we want tourists to learn about our place, to listen to us Anangu, not just to look at the sunset and climb the puli (Uluru) . . . In the Cultural Centre we will teach the minga (tourists) better. We will teach them about the Tjukurpa (law creation period) teach them inma (dancing), show them how we make punu (woodcarving). We will teach them about joint management. We are always saying, 'Pukulpa pitjama Ananguku ngurakutu – Welcome to Aboriginal land'.
>
> In this case a win–win relationship is being established. Local communities in the park benefit economically, as all businesses in the Cultural Centre are Aboriginal-owned. They also benefit from a sociocultural perspective as the park's interpretive and educational programmes place greater emphasis on Anangu explanation of the surrounding landscape. One could also argue that as a result tourism has benefited. Uluru remains a top tourist attraction, despite the fact that Anangu ask tourists not to photograph them or climb on the rock. Instead they offer tourist walks around its base (the Mala and the Mutitjulu) to highlight their living traditions better.

Win–lose

Win–lose scenarios may exist where the community benefits but mass tourism does not necessarily. This can arise by restricting numbers of tourists to ensure that host–guest ratios are appropriate to cope with numbers. The community benefits as emphasis is often on encouraging quality tourism, stressing meaningful interaction between residents and tourists, encouraging higher spending, minimal leakage and less negative impact. Bermuda is a good example of a destination that has promoted quality tourism by restricting numbers of tourists to the benefit of local communities.

Win–lose: island tourism with narrow niche markets – Bermuda

In having a tradition in tourism that dates back to the late 1800s, Bermuda has enjoyed the status of being one of the world's premier island tourism destinations, where tourism represents half of the islands' economy (Conlin, 1996). Bermuda's contemporary tourism has been characterized by initial rapid growth followed by a conservative tourism policy that promoted quality tourism (high spenders, low numbers) via narrowly defined niche markets, placing a moratorium on new development, promoting an upgrading policy on hotels and restricting cruise ship arrivals. As a result, there was less of an imbalance between hosts and guests and because emphasis was on high-spending tourists, the island community continued to benefit. However, with a downturn in arrivals since 1990, Bermuda has started to recognize how inextricably linked its economic well-being is to a robust tourism industry. A Commission on Competitiveness created in 1992 encouraged residents to become involved in future tourism planning, stressing they were an important part of the tourist experience. The win situation for this community may be short lived as one of the key findings of the commission was that one of the island's essential tourism services (the large hotels) was losing business, which in turn was translated into a loss of jobs, income and domestic business (Conlin, 1996). In a sense, tourism has lost out owing to restrictive policies and a narrow niche market philosophy that focused on smallness, exclusivity and affluence.

Lose–win

Lose–win is the third scenario. According to this scenario, the community loses while tourism gains. Many tourist–gambling communities fall into this category as gaming often destroys the fabric of communities both in physical (areas are pulled down to make way for more casinos) and social terms (increased deviant behaviour, addiction and organized crime). In contrast, tourism gains as all-inclusive packages of gambling, entertainment, shopping and accommodation are offered to potential visitors.

Lose–win: gambling tourism – Atlantic City

Atlantic City, New Jersey is often quoted as a premier example of a travel destination that went through one life cycle (from a fashionable to a rather seedy seaside resort) and then got a completely new lease of life as an exciting gambling destination (Morrison, 1989). While there is no disputing that gambling has rejuvenated many tourist destinations, and the trend is for more gambling centres to develop (Eadington, 1999), the impact of gambling on the resident population in Atlantic City, for example, is nearly beyond belief. The community has clearly been the loser, with the loss of agricultural land and urban decay best describing the area surrounding the casinos, with more and more residential areas declining, being bought up and torn down by the casinos to accommodate increasing parking needs. Crime figures are high, prostitution is all too evident and problem gambling has affected many in the community. Local businesses cannot compete against the all-inclusive package that the casinos offer. There have been some winners within the community, but the majority of them are employed by the gaming industry. The accommodation and hospitality sector has clearly been the winner over the local population. Since city leaders welcomed the casino corporations into Atlantic City, people from all walks of life have come not to walk along the famous boardwalk, but rather to spend money in the casinos. There is little evidence to suggest this will change in the near future.

Lose–lose

Lose–lose is the last scenario. In this case, both the community and tourism lose out. One obvious example of this would be uncontrolled mass coastal resort-based tourism where emphasis is short-term economic gain at the expense of long-term community and environmental loss. Many of the resorts along the Mediterranean coast fit this scenario, where traditional fishing villages have been replaced with masses of visitors who have a superficial relationship with their hosts, and are low spenders with significant negative impacts. This situation has improved somewhat recently as recognition has grown that there needs to be a good relationship between residents and tourists.

Lose–lose: uncontrolled coastal tourism development – Benidorm, Spain

Spain enjoyed dramatic and uninterrupted growth in visitor numbers from the early 1950s to the late 1980s (Burton, 1995). As a result, quiet fishing villages along the Mediterranean coast were transformed over a short time into tourist destinations for the short-haul European market interested in a sun–sea–sand (3-S) experience. Over time, much of the coastline became synonymous with the worst excesses of mass tourism: unsightly resorts, polluted beaches, degradation of natural areas and the ubiquitous lager lout. As a result, markets declined over competition from elsewhere and the changing tastes of a more demanding clientele (Klemm, 1992). Tourist numbers declined throughout the 1980s, only for this trend to be reversed in the late 1990s. While many of the resorts are displaying signs of recovery, Benidorm being a good case in point, the host population has lost out in the sense that their culture and traditions have been changed as a result of tourism and the relationship most visitors have with their host communities remains rather superficial (Curtis, 1997). While much change has occurred in the region, either as a result of government action to improve the environment or because the Spanish tourism industry has aimed to promote more sustainable tourism, only time will tell if rejuvenation has come to the region and an alternative scenario to lose–lose can be applied.

Given these four scenarios, the ideal would be to move towards a win–win situation. While highly laudable, many destination communities will unfortunately remain in their less than favourable situation as the trade-offs needed for change are too overwhelming for tourism to accept. There are, however, some examples of success where a lose–lose scenario has been reversed. Two examples of coastal tourism development in recovery are Benidorm and Majorca (Mallorca) (Curtis, 1997). In the case of Benidorm, renewal in tourism has come about in the late 1990s as a result of product renewal and new marketing initiatives that have changed the image of the destination from a 3-S monoculture to one that is varied, promoting quality and diversity of experience. In contrast, the recovery process in Majorca (Mallorca) has been driven by legislative changes and a 'desaturation' programme, where unsightly tourism infrastructure has been removed to improve its overall image.

Conclusion

In this chapter an attempt has been made to present communities with regards to type, scale, function, structure and the extent of partnership involved. Communities are ultimate metaphysical systems that tend to out-weigh even their physical and anthropological constructs. The understanding that communities are symbolic constructions is perhaps rudimentary with respect to any attempt to launch tourism in various social settings. It has generally been observed that this facet is disdainfully neglected in the pursuit of so-called economic development. Thus, tourism is instituted on the wrong foot and vitiates all planning exercises.

The typology of the resident–tourist interface, presented in the second half of the chapter, bears evidence of this, to a fair extent. It is imperative to note that the win–win, win–lose, lose–win and lose–lose situations illustrated are broad-based and generalized. The accompanying case examples under each scenario are subject to vagaries of time and space. While the efficacy of this typology in being a forecasting mechanism is yet to be researched, its *post hoc* relevance in explaining the successes and failures in community tourism is undeniable. Additional research is required to develop suitable models of host–visitor relationships for the appropriate planning and development of sustainable tourism, especially at the local and regional levels. In sum, this chapter suggests that community is a contested concept and that the elements making up the destination community are as varied as the relationships that exist between them and the tourism experience they afford.

References

Bosselman, F.P., Peterson, C.A. and McCarthy, C. (1999) *Managing Tourism Growth: Issues and Applications*. Island Press, Washington, DC.

Boyd, S.W. and Timothy, D.J. (2001) Developing partnerships: tools for interpretation and management of World Heritage Sites. *Tourism Recreation Research* 26(1), 49–55.

Bramwell, B. and Lane, B. (eds) (2000) *Tourism Collaboration and Partnerships: Politics, Practice and Sustainability*. Channel View Publications, Clevedon.

Burns, P. (1999) Editorial – Tourism NGOs. *Tourism Recreation Research* 24(2), 3–6.

Burr, S.W. (1991) Review and evaluation of the theoretical approaches to community as employed in travel and tourism impact research on rural community organization and change. In: Veal, A.J., Jonson, P. and Cushman, G. (eds) *Leisure and Tourism: Social and Environmental Changes*. World Leisure and Recreation Association, Sydney, pp. 540–553.

Burton, R. (1995) *Travel Geography*. Pitman, London.

Butler, R. and Hinch, T. (eds) (1996) *Tourism and Indigenous Peoples*. International Thomson Business Press, London.

Cater, E. and Lowman, G. (eds) (1994) *Ecotourism: a Sustainable Option?* John Wiley & Sons, Chichester.

Cohen, A.P. (1985) *The Symbolic Construction of Community*. Ellis Horwood, Chichester.

Conlin, M.V. (1996) Revitalizing Bermuda: tourism policy planning in a mature island destination. In: Harrison, L.C. and Husbands, W. (eds) *Practicing Responsible Tourism: International Case Studies in Tourism Planning, Policy and Development*. John Wiley & Sons, Chichester, pp. 80–102.

Curtis, S. (1997) Rejuvenating holiday resorts: a Spanish case study. *Travel and Tourism Analyst* 2, 77–93.

Dahms, F. (1991) St. Jacobs, Ontario: from declining village to thriving tourist community. *Ontario Geography* 36, 1–13.

Drumm, A. (1998) New approaches to community-based ecotourism management – learning from Ecuador. In: Lindberg, K., Wood, M.E. and Engeldrum, D. (eds) *Ecotourism: a Guide for Planners and Managers*. Ecotourism Society, North Bennington, Vermont, pp. 197–213.

Eadington, W.R. (1999) The spread of casinos and their role in tourism development. In: Pearce, D.G. and Butler, R.W. (eds) *Contemporary Issues in Tourism Development*. Routledge, London, pp. 127–142.

Fry, C. (1977) The community as a commodity: the age graded case. *Human Organization* 36(2), 115–122.

Getz, D. (1993) Tourist shopping villages: development and planning strategies. *Tourism Management* 14, 15–26.

Getz, D. (1994) Resident attitudes towards tourism: a longitudinal survey in Spey Valley, Scotland. *Tourism Management* 15, 247–258.

Hall, C.M. (2000) Tourism, national parks and Aboriginal peoples. In: Butler, R.W. and Boyd, S.W. (eds) *Tourism and National Parks: Issues and Implications*. John Wiley & Sons, Chichester, pp. 57–71.

Jansen-Verbeke, M. (1986) Inner city tourism: resources, tourists and promoters. *Annals of Tourism Research* 13, 79–100.

Joppe, M. (1996) Sustainable community tourism revisited. *Tourism Management* 17, 475–481.

Klemm, M. (1992) Sustainable tourism development: Languedoc-Roussillion thirty years on. *Tourism Management* 13, 169–180.

Lawson, R.W., Williams, J., Young, T. and Cossens, J. (1998) A comparison of resident's attitudes towards tourism in ten New Zealand destinations. *Tourism Management* 19, 247–256.

Mason, D. and Cheyne, J. (2000) Resident attitudes to proposed tourism development. *Annals of Tourism Research* 27, 391–411.

Mercer, D. (1994) Native peoples and tourism: conflict and compromise. In: Theobald, W.F. (ed.) *Global Tourism: the Next Decade.* Butterworth-Heinemann, Oxford, pp. 124–145.

Mitchell, C.J.A., Parkin, T. and Hanley, S. (1998) Are tourists a blessing or bane?: Resident attitudes towards tourism in the village of St. Jacobs, Ontario. *Small Town* 28(6), 18–23.

Mitchell, R.E. and Reid, D.G. (2001) Community integration: island tourism in Peru. *Annals of Tourism Research* 28, 113–139.

Morrison, A.M. (1989) *Hospitality and Travel Marketing.* Delmar, Albany.

Murphy, P.E. (1983) Tourism as a commodity industry: an ecological model of tourism development. *Tourism Management* 4, 180–193.

Murphy, P.E. (1985) *Tourism: a Community Approach.* Methuen, London.

Nepal, S. (2000) Tourism, national parks and local communities. In: Butler, R.W. and Boyd, S.W. (eds) *Tourism and National Parks: Issues and Implications.* John Wiley & Sons, Chichester, pp. 73–94.

Pearce, D.G. (1989) *Tourist Development.* Longman, Harlow.

Pearce, P., Moscardo, G. and Ross, G. (1996) *Tourism–Community Relationship.* Pergamon, Oxford.

Prentice, R. (1993) Community-driven tourism planning and residents' preferences. *Tourism Management* 14, 218–227.

Ryan, C. and Montgomery, D. (1994) The attitudes of Bakewell residents to tourism and issues in community responsive tourism. *Tourism Management* 15, 358–369.

Selin, S. (1999) Developing a typology of sustainable tourism partnerships. *Journal of Sustainable Tourism* 7(3/4), 260–273.

Smith, V.L. (ed.) (1977) *Hosts and Guests: the Anthropology of Tourism.* University of Pennsylvania Press, Philadelphia.

Sproule, K.W. and Suhandi, A.S. (1998) Guidelines for community-based ecotourism programs: lessons from Indonesia. In: Lindberg, K., Woods, M.E. and Engeldrum, D. (eds) *Ecotourism: a Guide for Planners and Managers.* Ecotourism Society, North Bennington, Vermont, pp. 215–236.

Stokowski, P.A. (1994) *Leisure in Society: a Network Structural Perspective.* Mansell, London.

Timothy, D.J. (1998) Cooperative tourism planning in a developing destination. *Journal of Sustainable Tourism* 6(1), 52–68.

Timothy, D.J. (1999) Participatory planning: a view of tourism in Indonesia. *Annals of Tourism Research* 26, 371–391.

Timothy, D.J. and White, K. (1999) Community-based ecotourism development on the periphery of Belize. *Current Issues in Tourism* 2(2/3), 226–242.

Torkildsen, G. (1983) *Leisure and Recreation Management.* E.& F.N. Spon, London.

Tosun, C. (2000) Limits to community participation in the tourism development process in developing countries. *Tourism Management* 21, 613–633.

Wells, J. (1996) Marketing indigenous heritage: a case study of Uluru National Park. In: Hall, C.M. and McArthur, S. (eds) *Heritage Management in Australia and New Zealand: the Human Dimension.* Oxford University Press, Melbourne, pp. 222–230.

Wright, J.K. (1966) *Human Nature in Geography.* Harvard University Press, Cambridge, Massachusetts.

COMMUNITY TOURISM DYNAMICS II

The Economics of Tourism in Host Communities   **3**

DIMITRI IOANNIDES

Department of Geography, Geology and Planning, Southwest Missouri State University, Springfield, USA

Introduction

A few years ago, a team of consultants shocked the New York sports community by recommending a relocation of the Yankees baseball team from the Bronx to Manhattan's West Side. Their proposal called for the construction of a multi-purpose arena with a retractable domed roof for baseball, football, concerts and conventions. The estimated cost for the entire facility was a staggering US$1.06 billion. The rationale for the costly relocation of the Yankees was that 'a new ball park along the Hudson River would produce a significant increase in attendance, higher prices for luxury seats and *an enhanced image for New York City*' (*New York Times*, 1996) [emphasis added]. Proponents of the project, including George Steinbrenner, the Yankees' owner, offered a number of reasons for moving the ballpark to Manhattan. Among them was the contention that a downtown location for a major sports facility would reinforce Manhattan's existing entertainment district comprising the Javits Convention Center and the ongoing redevelopment of the 'theater district' on Times Square and 42nd Street by, among others, the giant of the entertainment world, the Walt Disney Corporation (Bressi, 1996).

At the time of writing, the final decision as to whether the New York Yankees will move from their home of many decades had not been reached. Not surprisingly, there has been much opposition to the plan by numerous people and organizations. Nevertheless, George Steinbrenner and the then Mayor of New York City, Rudolph Giuliani, stated that they did not want the Yankees' options for relocating outside the Bronx to be limited and clearly would be more than happy to see the proposed new sports arena in Manhattan.

New York's efforts to retain a sports team and develop a substantial convention/entertainment district replicate trends that have become all too familiar throughout urban America over the last two decades, namely cities' efforts to promote tourism (Judd, 1995). Between 1992 and 1995, US cities spent over US$1 billion in subsidies to entice or retain sports franchises (Lever, 1995). Indeed, as Judd (1999: 45) argues:

> by the end of the 1980s, it could be safely assumed that no owner in any of the professional sports would ever agree to build a stadium with private dollars. Owners have come to expect other subsidies as well, in the form of guaranteed attendance minimums, the construction of luxury boxes, and control of stadium merchandising.

More often than not, new sports stadiums are built near a city's downtown area so they can become part of a broader city centre entertainment complex. Recently, Baltimore enticed the Cleveland Browns (now the Ravens) football team with a publicly funded 70,000-seat stadium located close to its Inner Harbor entertainment complex. Cleveland itself has built a new downtown stadium for a new Browns football franchise.

The ongoing battle for professional sports teams is one of numerous efforts undertaken by communities throughout the USA and worldwide to boost visitor arrivals. Other projects include the development of attractions like museums, aquariums and art galleries. The author's adopted home town of Springfield, Missouri, is currently constructing the 'American National Fish and Wildlife Museum', a US$40 million project designed by Cambridge Seven Associates Inc. Proponents of this publicly funded project believe that once it is completed, it will attract approximately 1.5 million visitors a year and produce US$37.7 million in economic impacts. They base their estimates on the performances of similar facilities designed by the same firm, including the Tennessee Aquarium that attracted 1.5 million visitors in its first year of operation and the Baltimore Aquarium that has drawn an average of 1.4 million visitors a year since opening in 1981 (Cambridge Seven Associates, 2000).

Localities' efforts to draw tourists do not end here. In an attempt to lure the lucrative business travel market, numerous middle-sized and larger cities throughout the country have spent enormous sums of money to compete for meetings and conventions (Judd, 1995). This is hardly surprising considering the size of the 'meetings and conventions' business. Between 1980 and 1987, the number of convention centres increased by 37%, exhibition space rose by 60% and by the end of the decade, the industry generated approximately US$44.5 billion per annum (Zelinsky, 1994). In 1992, various associations collectively spent US$32 billion for 'off premises meetings and conventions' (Judd, 1995: 179). Almost every city with a population above 250,000 now offers convention facilities, often within or near the central business district. Major cities normally have a comparative advantage in attracting major national or international conventions because they offer diverse attractions and supporting tourist facilities. Conversely, smaller towns have the benefit of lower costs and are often successful in attracting lower profile, regional meetings.

Yet another increasingly common form of development that cities use to attract visitors has been the downtown festival mall or waterfront redevelopment project. So many attempts have been made to emulate Rouse's Faneuil Hall (Boston), South Street Seaport (New York), and Union Station (St Louis) in downtowns throughout North America that the terms 'rousification', 'rousilization' and 'faneuilization' have found their way into the urban planning lexicon (Chang *et al.*, 1996). Similarly, John Portman's 'cities within cities' (Judd, 1995: 183), such as Atlanta's Peachtree Center and Detroit's Renaissance Center, have been replicated in cities from Dallas to Minneapolis. Just as in the case of sports stadiums, cities have heavily subsidized these downtown festival malls through programmes like community development block grants, urban development action grants and property tax abatements.

Tourism's rising popularity as an economic growth strategy is not limited to large cities, however. Over the last few years more small communities have become major destinations on the tourist trail. Places like Pigeon Forge, Tennessee; Branson, Missouri; and Jackson, Wyoming; each having a resident population of less than 5000, but attracting more than five million tourists annually. Even though rapid tourism growth has burdened these communities with undesirable environmental and social effects, the industry's impressive economic performance has reinforced the desire of community leaders in hundreds of other small towns around the nation to pursue tourism.

The examples discussed in the preceding paragraphs indicate that policy makers, planners and community leaders throughout the USA and the world have begun to pay serious attention to tourism as an economic panacea. The question is why? What accounts for tourism's growing popularity as an economic growth strategy, particularly over the last two decades? Why are civic leaders ready to spend hundreds of millions of dollars, often without conducting rigorous cost–benefit analyses, to attract visitors? Perhaps, more important is the following question: do the economic impacts of all these programmes justify the huge outlays of funds? These are the focus of this chapter, and the following sections examine these questions in some detail. Moreover, an attempt is made to examine the economic impacts of tourism in destination communities within the broader framework of sustainable development.

Why Tourism? The Economic Rationale for the Industry

Fainstein and Gladstone (1999) argue that, other than tourism, cities nowadays have few options for economic development. Compared to most sectors, including extractive industries and manufacturing, tourism-related investments hold the perceived promise of rapid returns. Tourism is an attractive sector for policy makers primarily because of its wealth- and job-creating potential, not to mention that 'ordinary residents have often benefited from tourism-related investments, both financially and through improved amenities' (Fainstein and Gladstone, 1999: 24–25). The revenues associated with the sector can be used to improve a destination's infrastructure and services (e.g. roads, airports, sewage systems and fire protection) and other facilities (e.g. greenways, playing fields, parks and theatres), all of which ultimately benefit the local population. The tourism-related improvements can also boost a community's image for potential investors seeking locations to establish their business or attract new residents in search of a locality with a high quality of life (Law, 1992).

Communities will often adopt tourism as a means of diversifying their economic base, particularly in situations where they may be heavily dependent on a narrow range of activities. In recent years Leadville, Colorado, and Leavenworth, Washington, a mining and a logging community, respectively, have adopted programmes to attract visitors, hoping to stem their economic decline. According to Leavenworth's web site, 'for more than thirty years [the town] lived on the brink of extinction' following the shut down of its sawmill, until the 1960s when its leaders recast it as a 'Bavarian village' (Leavenworth, 2000). The web site indicates that the transformation has worked, stating that 'since the change to a Bavarian motif, Leavenworth has become a pillar of the tourism industry in the Pacific Northwest. Today, more than a million tourists come to Leavenworth each year'.

On a grander scale, the deindustrialization of western societies and global economic restructuring have led to numerous localities competing for increasingly mobile capital (Britton, 1991; Hall and Hubbard, 1996). In response to this situation, cities that were once centres of traditional manufacturing or major mercantile powers have recast their industrial plants, warehouses, railway stations, harbours and market spaces into what Urry (1990) has called out-of-the ordinary objects of the tourist gaze. Liverpool's Albert Docks, a symbol of a bygone era when that city was one of the world's major ports, have now been converted into a space for tourist consumption that includes the Liverpool Tate Gallery, the Merseyside Maritime Museum and the Beatles' Story. By the same token, cities like Pittsburgh, Pennsylvania, once famous for steel production, now seek to enhance their image among tourists and residents by creating '24-hour downtowns', city centres where residents work, shop, dine and live (CNN.Com, 1999).

The downtowns of large and small cities are particularly attractive for tourism-related initiatives because these areas often possess a large proportion of a community's historical resources and lack the dull uniformity that characterizes suburban areas, particularly in the USA (Kunstler, 1993; Fainstein and Stokes, 1995; Beauregard, 1998). It is not surprising, therefore, that some of the most successful visitor destinations throughout the world are communities that possess a revitalized historic core. Among the reasons for the ascendancy of tourism development programmes and related entertainment attractions during the late 1980s and early 1990s, at least within the USA, was the economic downturn that characterized the property market and particularly the overcapacity of downtown office spaces following years of speculative construction in downtown areas (Fainstein and Stokes, 1995). Fainstein and Stokes argue that local governments have been quite eager to sponsor the development of facilities such as sports arenas and convention centres by using public money, especially since such investments promise a constant revenue stream unlike spending on other public goods such as schools and roads. Because money for major tourism facilities in the USA, like museums and aquariums, often comes from state and not local governments, policy makers are keen to sponsor such programmes, especially as they do not appear to inflict a direct burden on local taxpayers. Furthermore, it is important to note that because many tourism-related facilities and events can be reproduced in numerous areas, community leaders are more likely to compete to attract a facility such as a major hotel or an aquarium instead of a manufacturing plant; just because a Sheraton or a Hilton was constructed in one community does not mean that they cannot be constructed in another. By the same token, even though a city may not be granted an international event like the Olympic Games or a World's Expo one year it does not mean that a second bid will be unsuccessful (Fainstein and Stokes, 1995).

The worldwide perception of tourism as a growth sector stems from the fact that, unlike most consumer services (e.g. retailing), it can be considered an export or basic industry (Law, 1992), albeit an odd one, because the consumer must visit the place of production as opposed to the goods being transported to the market (Debbage and Daniels, 1998). Localities can use tourism as an invisible export in the same way they may use the production of tangible manufactured or agricultural goods to attract necessary foreign exchange and fulfil their overriding economic goals of wealth creation, employment generation and enhancement of the host population's living standards. Unlike other sectors, tourism usually 'requires little, by value, in imports for every unit of foreign exchange which it generates [and] thus a greater proportion of the foreign exchange earnings of tourism can be used for investment in the development of manufacturing industries or in reducing the foreign earnings debt' (Mathieson and Wall, 1982: 45). Mathieson and Wall also maintained

that policy makers favour the development of tourism instead of concentrating on the export of agricultural or mining products, since communities seldom have control over the prices for the latter commodities.
Furthermore, tourism is an attractive development option for many
localities because it is characterized by a high-income elasticity, meaning
that a substantial increase in the number of visitors and tourist dollars
can result, despite a fairly moderate increase in the disposable income of
tourists.

Beyond its promise of wealth creation, tourism is seen as a way to create
a labour pool with a certain modicum of human capital. Even though, as
discussed in more detail later, there is considerable debate as to the quality
of the jobs created (the 'good jobs' versus 'bad jobs' argument), the heart
of the matter is that tourism can provide a source of employment in
situations where options are limited (Fainstein and Gladstone, 1999). The
argument can also be made that barriers to entry in the tourist sector are
low and the cost of job creation is considerably less (one eighth) of that in
manufacturing (Urry, 1990). As Mathieson and Wall (1982) contend, the
same investment in tourism as in the petroleum industry will normally
create more jobs. Since many jobs in tourism require minimal skills, it is
possible to absorb a large proportion of the required workforce from other
sectors without the major investments in training programmes that are
often required by other industries.

Most analysts agree that the promotion of tourism in a certain community or region has an impact on local entrepreneurial activity, although
the precise nature of this impact has not yet been fully explored (Timothy
and Wall, 1997; Shaw and Williams, 1998; Timothy and White, 1999).

According to Mathieson and Wall (1982: 82), the extent to which the
tourist sector can establish linkages with local entrepreneurs depends
upon:

- The types of suppliers and producers with which the industry's
  demands are linked.
- The capacity of local suppliers to meet these demands.
- The historical development of tourism in the destination area.
- The type of tourist development.

One of the most cited studies relating tourism to entrepreneurial
activity is the now dated study by Lundgren (1973, cited in Mathieson and
Wall, 1982) that proposed an evolutionary model of entrepreneurship
related to the development of Caribbean hotels. Through his model,
Lundgren suggested that the establishment of a hotel sector on an island
economy leads to three consecutive stages of local entrepreneurial activity.
Although during the early stages the hotels may depend heavily on foreign
suppliers for items like food, eventually these establishments will manage to

create a relationship with local entrepreneurs such as farmers (Telfer and Wall, 1996). In other words, Lundgren contends that tourism's evolution in an area eventually stimulates the production of local agricultural commodities and use of other local resources. A handful of similar studies have sought to explore the relationship of tourism development to sectors such as the construction industry (e.g. Bond and Ladman, 1982, cited in Shaw and Williams, 1994). Overall, however, the topic of entrepreneurial activity in tourist environments remains a research lacuna that warrants further examination (Ioannides, 1995; Dahles, 1997).

Tourism's Multiplier Effects: Realities and Myths

The preceding section highlighted some of the key economic reasons that have led communities worldwide to embark on tourism-related development strategies. Nevertheless, despite the apparent popularity of tourism as a tool for attracting economic growth, the industry has also received heavy criticism for various reasons. In *Devil's Bargains: Tourism in the Twentieth-Century American West*, Rothman (1999: 10) paints a pessimistic picture of tourism's role in community development:

> despite its reputation as a panacea for the economic ills of places that have lost their way in the postindustrial world or for those that never found it, tourism typically fails to meet the expectations of communities and regions that embrace it as an economic strategy . . . Tourism transforms culture into something new and foreign; it may or may not rescue economies.

Rothman and others (e.g. Britton, 1978; Britton, 1982) criticize tourism from an economic standpoint, arguing that only a few locals, including a handful of major landowners and developers, benefit from the industry's growth.

All too often the tourist sector in various communities depends heavily on outside interests (e.g. hotel chains or tour operators, expatriate owners) and has little control over its fate (Timothy and Ioannides, 2002). For instance, tour operators based in major tourist markets can act as key gatekeepers in determining the flow of visitors to various destinations. Seeking to minimize their risks, these players regularly market holiday type (e.g. holiday in the sun or golfing holiday) rather than actual destinations. Thus, major tour operators can always substitute destinations within the same product line without incurring heavy costs. If, for example, one destination declines in popularity because it has become too overcrowded, tour operators can relatively easily substitute this with another more attractive venue. Because of their desire to minimize risks, tour operators also commonly negotiate generous cut-off days with hoteliers in host destinations and rarely, if ever, pre-pay for the rooms they reserve. This situation places the operators of lodging establishments, particularly the independent entrepreneurs of small-scale establishments, in a weak bargaining position *vis-à-vis* the tour operators (Ioannides, 1998). By the same token, major hotel companies also commonly transfer the risk of doing business to establishments in the destination community. They achieve this by involving themselves in the hotel industry of a certain area through franchise agreements, lease or management contracts rather than practising equity participation. Since they rarely own the hotels they control, these major companies can easily remove their operations from an area and find a more profitable substitute destination. The owner of the establishment in the original host community is left to rue the loss of business (Ioannides, 1994).

One topic about which there has been considerable debate is the issue of tourism multipliers. Generally, there appears to have been an overall change of heart in the manner in which tourism's promises of economic multipliers are regarded by policy makers and academics. In the 1950s, the pervasive feeling reflected in documents like the Zinder report (1969) was that tourism-related development could induce significant income and employment multipliers in host societies. This attitude appears to have been tempered considerably since the 1970s, when more rigorous analyses of tourism's impacts on destinations throughout the world indicated that claims concerning the sector's multiplier phenomenon must be treated with a high degree of scepticism (Bryden and Faber, 1971). Among others, Mathieson and Wall (1982) criticized the Zinder report for not making a major allowance for leakages and assuming that the multiplier for all the eastern Caribbean islands was the same.

The measurement of multipliers is one of three principal methods available to economists for estimating tourism's economic impact on host societies. The other two are regional input–output analyses and various impact studies at the local level (Ryan, 1991). Although the popularity of multiplier studies has waned considerably since the 1970s, partly because of the practical difficulties of measuring income flows and employment creation, Ryan (1991: 70–71) argues that 'with the emergence of tourism as a means of helping to regenerate inner city areas in both Europe and North America there has been some renewed interest in the use of such techniques'. One reason behind this resurgence of attention is that in many communities, especially in countries like the UK, local authorities must justify the spending of taxpayers' money for tourism-related projects.

The concept of the multiplier is based on the work of the economist John Maynard Keynes who, in the 1930s, developed the macroeconomic theory 'that emphasizes the importance of changes in autonomous expenditures (especially investment, government spending, and net exports) in determining changes in output and employment' (Samuelson and Nordhaus, 1989: 978). According to this approach, two types of flows condition any change to the gross regional product (GRP) of a particular region: injections flowing into the region and leakages flowing outwards. The equation for calculating the GRP is:

$$GRP = C + I + G + E - M$$

where: C = consumption; I = investment; G = local government spending; E = exports; and M = import purchases.

Since tourism is a basic or export sector, the injection of additional tourist dollars (E) into the economy (all other things being equal) will lead to regional economic growth (Davis, 1990). If, however, the growing demands of the tourist industry for supplies (e.g. building materials or luxury items like exotic food) cannot be entirely satisfied by local producers, the need to import various goods (M) will inevitably dampen the industry's positive impact on the economy. Take, for instance, a hypothetical seaside community that attracts luxury tourists. While these tourists bring much-needed foreign exchange into the area, money also leaks out since the expensive tastes of these individuals mean that many of the food products they demand cannot be found locally. Moreover, items such as the air-conditioners, spas and swimming pool filter systems may also have to be imported as they are not manufactured locally, leading to even heavier leakages from the local economy. In addition to imports, income taxes and the savings of the local population and institutions lead to leakages because they all cause a certain amount of money to be removed from circulation (Puczko and Ratz, 2001). This means that for tourism to contribute to the economic growth of a locality, the total amount of leakages (M) will have to be less than the sum of C + I + G + E (see equation above) (Ryan, 1991). Generally speaking, the smaller the economic base of a region or community, the higher the leakages and, thus, the multiplier will be lower (Mathieson and Wall, 1982). In other words, in a regional economy where there is a highly diversified industrial base and links between sectors are strong, it is unlikely that tourism will lead to an excessive reliance on imported goods. By contrast, an isolated agrarian community seeking to develop high impact mass tourism without diversifying the rest of the community will inevitably have to rely heavily on imported goods and services. Moreover, it is important to note that multipliers tend to be higher at the national level than they are at the community or regional levels (Murphy, 1985).

The best way to indicate how the multiplier phenomenon works in a regional economy is through a simplified example. Suppose that in a resort community the total spent by visitors amounts to US$10,000. This money will go to providers of services like lodging establishments, petrol stations, restaurants and attractions. Of this total amount, suppose that the providers of these services all have a marginal propensity to consume (MPC)[1] equal to two-thirds of their income (i.e. US$6666.67) on other goods and services. If the providers of these goods and services also have an MPC of two-thirds, they will end up spending US$4444.44 (2/3 of US$6666.67). Hypothetically speaking this process can take place until all new rounds of additional spending have been exhausted. The total value of the income multiplier in this scenario can be calculated by the equation:

$$IM = 1/(1 - MPC) = 1/(1 - 2/3) = 3$$

where: IM = income multiplier; and MPC = marginal propensity to consume.

This means that in this case the original spending of US$10,000 by the visitors actually created a total income of US$30,000 (10,000 × 3) in the local economy. Obviously, then, the size of the multiplier in a certain community will depend on how large the marginal propensity to consume is. The greater the extra consumption is (and the less the propensity to save) the greater will be the multiplier (Samuelson and Nordhaus, 1989).

In all, there are three different kinds of income multiplier: direct expenditure, indirect spending and induced spending (Mathieson and Wall, 1982). Direct expenditure is the money paid directly by the tourists to the providers of visitor-related services such as hoteliers. Indirect spending arising from this initial round of expenditure is the money paid for wages and salaries to local workers of tourist-related establishments and the amount required for replacing their inventories (e.g. food, drinks, merchandise). Finally, Mathieson and Wall (1982: 65) describe induced spending in this manner: 'As wages and salaries within an economy rise, consumption also increases and this provides an additional impetus for economic activity.' Generally speaking a multiplier of 1.3 implies that for every dollar that is spent a further 30 cents are created through indirect and induced effects (Williams, 1998).

One of the most extensive recent studies of tourism's economic impacts was done by Braun (1992). By examining the impact of conventions on Orlando, Florida, for 1989, Braun was able to estimate that the total expenditure of 1.6 million meeting attendees came to over US$1 billion. Using input–output analysis, he calculated that the income multiplier from the convention trade amounted to 1.7.

---

[1] The marginal propensity to consume (MPC) is an economic term indicating the proportion of every additional dollar a family receives as disposable income which is spent on additional consumption (Samuelson and Nordhaus, 1989).

Even though most studies pay attention to income multipliers (Williams and Shaw, 1988), there are other types of tourism multipliers[2] (Archer, 1977; Mathieson and Wall, 1982). Another important multiplier that may be considered, especially in communities where tourism is introduced to reduce unemployment, is the employment multiplier. The most common way of measuring employment multipliers is by estimating 'the ratio of direct and secondary employment generated by additional tourism expenditure, to direct employment alone' (Mathieson and Wall, 1982: 65). The jobs created through visitor spending in places like hotels and restaurants can be considered direct employment. Tourism-related jobs not created directly through visitor spending (e.g. laundries and banking) are known as indirect employment. The jobs created in the rest of the community through the spending of the tourist employees' income are described as induced employment (Puszko and Ratz, 2001).

There are numerous studies relating to employment multipliers even though researchers have focused primarily on direct employment creation. While it is relatively straightforward to calculate the number of jobs created directly in tourism sectors like lodging establishments it is notoriously hard to estimate what proportion of jobs in other sectors like construction and transportation may have resulted because of investment in the tourist sector. Moreover, there is considerable debate concerning the accuracy of employment multipliers because different tourism activities produce a variety of jobs (from hotel porters to waiting staff and from chamber-maids to back-office personnel), some of which are more labour intensive than others. Although a luxury hotel will have a high ratio of workers per room, it is likely that the self-catered apartment sector will have a low proportion of employees to each room (Puczko and Ratz, 2001).

Most tourism employment multiplier studies relate to full-time jobs. However, tourism is also commonly a seasonal activity often leading to the employment of a high number of part-time or seasonal workers who are hard to measure. In certain tourist environments (e.g. the Greek islands), tourist industry entrepreneurs depend heavily on their relatives to help out during periods of peak demand. It is quite usual, for instance, in some destinations to have teenage children who are home from school helping out in the family-owned hotel without receiving remuneration. Also, it is not uncommon in many communities for people who work as school-teachers or farmers during part of the year to hold a second job in the tourist sector. Often they do so as part of the informal sector, meaning that

---

[2] In addition to income multipliers arising from tourism, Mathieson and Wall (1982) discuss another three types of multiplier: employment multiplier, sales multiplier and output multiplier. Randall and Warf (1996) used an input–output matrix to estimate, among others, the output multiplier arising from American Association of Geographers' national conferences over a 12-year period.

they are not officially registered as tourism workers and do not pay taxes and social security on their earnings.

A major criticism of tourism-related employment is that a large proportion of the jobs created in tourist environments are low-skilled and poorly paid, often highly feminized, and part-time. Randall and Warf's (1996) study of the economic effects of American Association of Geographers' (AAG) conferences seems to confirm this situation. Although the convention trade creates numerous employment opportunities in urban areas of the USA, many of the jobs are low quality. Thus, one has to 'question the equity in the distribution of benefits from tourism investments' (Randall and Warf, 1996: 282). An earlier study of tourism's role in the British economy also revealed the questionable nature of many of the generated jobs:

> a study of tourism accommodation along the East Anglia coast found that 44 per cent of all employment constituted part-time, seasonal jobs for women. Just under 20 per cent of the total number of jobs were permanent and full time, with a further 27 per cent being seasonal full time jobs.
>
> (Williams and Shaw, 1988: 92)

The 'good jobs versus bad jobs' argument concerning tourism's contribution to local and regional economies will undoubtedly go on for some time. Regardless of the outcomes of this debate, certain authors have suggested that rather than disparaging tourism for creating poorly waged jobs and other negative effects in host communities, the sector's 'critics would do better to insist that subsidies for tourism promotion be balanced by provisions for higher minimum wages, local participation in the supply of services, and job placement and training programs' (Fainstein and Gladstone, 1999: 25). Moreover, analysts have to recognize that the outcome of tourism's performance in terms of job creation in a particular locality is contingent on the way the sector is organized and structured.

Questions to be asked when examining the employment impact of tourism include: What proportion of the tourism-related jobs are unionized? Do the tourism workers (even part-time employees) receive benefits? How do rates of pay in tourism sectors compare to other industries like agriculture? After all, in some settings, especially in less developed regions, workers may be lured into tourism from primary sectors like agriculture and fishing precisely because the industry holds the promise of better working conditions at a higher rate of remuneration. Though in some western societies, including the USA, tourism is often looked down upon in terms of the quality of jobs it creates, it is not unusual for people in other parts of the world (e.g. the Greek islands) to make a career in the sector even in 'lower level' activities such as serving in restaurants. In some popular Mediterranean destinations tourism's rapid rate of growth has led to extreme employment shortages in other sectors like farming and construction. This situation often results in the inflation of these destinations' wage structure and, in many cases, the need to import workers from other areas (Williams, 1998).

The apparent inconsistency in the findings of previous studies indicates that just because tourism may have minimal positive economic impacts in certain localities, this should not be an excuse for dismissing the sector as irrelevant for further attention. Ryan (1991) contends there is no guarantee that in areas where tourism has very low employment and income multipliers other activities (e.g. manufacturing) will be any more successful. 'Weak multipliers from tourism may be no more than a reflection of deficiencies in such economic systems. If labour is comparatively unskilled, if there are shortages of assets and infrastructure, then almost by definition any economic activity will suffer' (Ryan, 1991: 86).

Tourism, the Economy and Sustainable Development

The preceding sections have highlighted some economic impacts associated with the promotion of tourism in various localities. Despite the lack of a firm consensus as to whether these effects are positive or negative, community leaders frequently regard tourism as a relatively speedy and obstacle-free way to engender economic growth compared with other sectors. However, the promotion of tourism development in many contexts often takes place without balancing short-term economic priorities with longer-term environmental and sociocultural objectives. This phenomenon remains the status quo in most societies and is the major stumbling block towards attaining sustainable development in tourist environments.

The achievement of sustainable development within any context, including a tourist destination, implies a delicate balance between conflicting economic, environmental and social equity objectives. In other words, reaching the goal of sustainability in a tourist environment would indicate that the economy's growth is distributed equitably, and the effects of these actions on the natural and built environment are minimized (Campbell, 1996; Ioannides, 2001). In theory, however, even though the concept of sustainable development within tourist environments sounds simple, it is difficult to implement for many reasons including that at any destination there are many stakeholders with conflicting agendas.

> Players who prioritize concrete economic growth objectives are often focused
> on short-term goals compared to those who may give preference to less
> tangible social justice and environmental protection goals . . . Profit-oriented
> developers are usually concerned about reaping a fast reward from their
> investment and will not be too worried about the environmental or societal
> ramifications of their actions. Unless forced by statutes and other regulatory

instruments, these players rarely, if ever, wish to admit responsibility for the externalities generated by their projects.

(Ioannides, 2001: 57)

Moreover, the tourist industry's fragmented nature makes it a hard sector to plan and develop in a balanced manner. In most destinations, the tourist sector is made up of numerous businesses, all of which may have minor impacts of their own. To implement a sustainable development agenda, the message must be relayed to the operators of these individual establishments that they should be concerned about the cumulative effects that 'take place when the impacts of many . . . developments are aggregated' (Bosselman *et al.*, 1999: 43). Unfortunately, however, it is precisely the tourism entrepreneurs' inability or unwillingness to comprehend the collective results of their individual actions that limits any genuine efforts to adopt balanced growth strategies.

In many tourist destinations, the implementation of a growth management regime often appears as an afterthought following the realization that the very resources attracting the visitors originally may be under threat from excessive development (Ioannides, 2001). In such cases, an overwhelmingly boosterist approach to tourism development may be gradually replaced by an increasingly regulatory system designed to protect the remaining natural resources and enhance the quality of the built environment. It is becoming common in destinations facing a threat to their competitive advantage because of uncontrolled development for representatives of the tourist industry (e.g. tour operators and hoteliers) to adopt the sustainability banner. Nevertheless, although a handful of government officials and industry representatives are genuinely concerned about the negative impacts of their sector on the physical and sociocultural environments, one has to question the true motives behind the embrace of the 'sustainability' label, especially by the private sector. After all, most tourist-related enterprises are primarily concerned with maximizing their profits and 'the profit maximization motive does have a tendency to subvert and subjugate other considerations, ethical and environmental' (Mowforth and Munt, 1998: 199). More likely, many tourist companies' efforts to embrace a greener image and back the conservation of natural resources reflect these organizations' desire to protect their profit margins (Timothy and Ioannides, 2002).

The fact that economic objectives remain the top priority of private businesses, as well as most public agencies, can be illustrated by the following example. In an effort to curb the negative impacts of rapid tourism development, many islands in the Mediterranean, including Cyprus and Malta, have recently implemented strategies oriented towards attracting luxury-oriented visitors instead of large numbers of low-spending package travellers. Their rationale is that a few high-spending individuals will pose a smaller threat to the environment than many budget travellers but still bring in large amounts of foreign exchange. However, the manner in which these island communities have sought to target these presumed high spenders is questionable and demonstrates their limited understanding of sustainable development. Realizing, for example, that high-spending tourists demand luxury facilities, Cypriot authorities have approved the construction of golf courses, facilities that can hardly be thought of as nature-friendly and which certainly make little sense in the semi-arid Mediterranean environments. By the same token, the high-end hotels with heated pools, air-conditioning and other luxury facilities commonly demanded by high spenders are usually far more energy intensive than budget-oriented facilities (Ioannides and Holcomb, 2001).

The preceding example paints a pessimistic picture concerning the prospects of achieving balanced growth in tourist environments. As long as environmental and societal concerns remain subservient to the more tangible priority of economic growth generation, then it is unlikely that the broader vision of intra- and inter-generational equity as envisioned in a sustainable development scenario will be achieved.

Conclusion

Worldwide, communities have embraced tourism because of its perceived promise of economic growth generation. Undoubtedly, there are numerous economic effects on host regions arising from the development of the sector although there is no clear consensus regarding the nature of these impacts. For example, there is still much debate in the literature concerning tourism's income and employment multipliers. While community leaders and industry analysts regularly seek to underline the benefits of the tourism multiplier phenomenon, other commentators advocate caution by stressing that the promises of income and employment generation are undermined by factors such as leakages or poorly paid jobs. It generally appears, however, that this debate has failed to dampen the enthusiasm with which local leaders chase schemes to attract more visitors. Indeed, many of the tourism projects that have appeared in numerous US localities have not been backed by rigorous assessments like cost–benefit or environmental impact studies. The lack of sophisticated analyses to assess the impacts of tourism development is to do with the emphasis that many officials place on the sector as a means of promoting their community's image and the industry's failure to take responsibility for the cumulative effects of its actions.

The absence of rigorous analysis concerning tourism's impacts, including its economic effects, does not bode well for those observers advocating the promotion of balanced development forms in destination communities. This inadequacy in methodology is reflected by the fact that many of the strategies which communities have recently adopted under the guise of sustainable development have been flawed. Limited understanding of tourism's impacts and the overshadowing of a community's societal and environmental objectives by profit-making objectives mean that the overarching goal of sustainable development within touristic environments will remain unattainable.

References

Archer, B.H. (1977) *Tourism Multipliers: the State of the Art.* University of Wales Press, Cardiff.

Beauregard, R.A. (1998) Tourism and economic development policy in US urban areas. In: Ioannides, D. and Debbage, K.G. (eds) *The Economic Geography of the Tourist Industry: a Supply-side Analysis.* Routledge, London, pp. 220–234.

Bond, M.E. and Ladman J.R. (1982) A strategy for developing tourism. *Research in Tourism* 2(2), 45–61.

Bosselman, F.P., Peterson, C.A. and McCarthy, C. (1999) *Managing Tourism Growth: Issues and Applications.* Island Press, Washington, DC.

Braun, B. (1992) The economic contribution of conventions: the case of Orlando, Florida. *Journal of Travel Research* 30(3), 32–37.

Bressi, T.W. (1996) Reveille for Times Square. *Planning* 62(9), 4–8.

Britton, R.A. (1978) International tourism and indigenous development objectives: a study with special reference to the West Indies. PhD thesis, University of Minnesota, Minneapolis, Minnesota.

Britton, S. (1982) The political economy of tourism in the Third World. *Annals of Tourism Research* 9, 331–358.

Britton, S. (1991) Tourism, capital, and place: toward a critical geography of tourism. *Environment and Planning D: Society and Space* 9, 451–478.

Bryden, J. and Faber, M. (1971) Multiplying the tourist multiplier. *Social and Economic Studies* 20, 61–82.

Cambridge Seven Associates (2000) http://www.c7a.com/studio/ studio.htm

Campbell, S. (1996) Green cities, growing cities, just cities? Urban planning and the contradictions of sustainable development. *Journal of the American Planning Association* 62(3), 296–312.

Chang, T.C., Milne, S., Fallon, D. and Pohlman, C. (1996) Urban heritage tourism: exploring the global–local nexus. *Annals of Tourism Research* 23(2), 284–305.

CNN.Com (1999) Rust Belt cities rejuvenate downtowns (accessed 9 September) http://cnn.com/TRAVEL/NEWS/9909/20/life.downtown.reut/

Dahles, H. (ed.) (1997) *Tourism, Small Entrepreneurs, and Sustainable Development: Cases from Developing Countries.* European Association for Tourism and Leisure Education, Tilburg, The Netherlands.

Davis, H.C. (1990) *Regional Economic Impact Analysis and Project Evaluation.* University of British Columbia Press, Vancouver.

Debbage, K.G. and Daniels, P. (1998) The tourist industry and economic geography: missed opportunities. In: Ioannides, D. and Debbage, K.G. (eds)

The Economic Geography of the Tourist Industry: a Supply-side Analysis. Routledge, London, pp. 17–30.

Fainstein, S.S. and Gladstone, D. (1999) Evaluating urban tourism. In: Judd, D.R. and Fainstein, S.S. (eds) *The Tourist City.* Yale University Press, New Haven, Connecticut, pp. 21–34.

Fainstein, S.S. and Stokes, R. (1995) Spaces for play: the impacts of entertainment development on New York City. Paper presented at the annual meeting of the Association of Collegiate Schools of Planning, Detroit, Michigan, 18–22 October.

Hall, T. and Hubbard, P. (1996) The entrepreneurial city: new urban politics, new urban geographies? *Progress in Human Geography* 20(2), 153–174.

Ioannides, D. (1994) The state, transnationals, and the dynamics of tourism evolution in small island nations. PhD thesis, Rutgers University, New Brunswick, New Jersey.

Ioannides, D. (1995) Strengthening the ties between tourism and economic geography: a theoretical agenda. *Professional Geographer* 47(1), 49–60.

Ioannides, D. (1998) Tour operators: the gatekeepers of tourism. In: Ioannides, D. and Debbage, K.G. (eds) *The Economic Geography of the Tourist Industry: a Supply-side Analysis.* Routledge, London, pp. 139–158.

Ioannides, D. (2001) Sustainable development and the shifting attitudes of tourism stakeholders: toward a dynamic framework. In: McCool, S.F. and Moisey, R.N. (eds) *Tourism, Recreation and Sustainability: Linking Culture and the Environment.* CAB International, Wallingford, pp. 55–76.

Ioannides, D. and Holcomb, B. (2001) Raising the stakes: implications of upmarket tourism policies in Cyprus and Malta. In: Ioannides, D., Apostolopoulos, Y. and Sönmez, S. (eds) *Mediterranean Islands and Sustainable Tourism Development: Practices, Management, and Policies.* Continuum, London, pp. 234–258.

Judd, D. (1995) Promoting tourism in US cities. *Tourism Management* 16, 175–187.

Judd, D. (1999) Constructing the tourist bubble. In: Judd, D.R. and Fainstein, S.S. (eds) *The Tourist City.* Yale University Press, New Haven, Connecticut, pp. 35–53.

Kunstler, J.H. (1993) *The Geography of Nowhere: the Rise and Decline of America's Man-Made Landscape.* Touchstone, New York.

Law, C.M. (1992) Urban tourism and its contribution to economic regeneration. *Urban Studies* 29, 599–618.

Leavenworth (2000) The history of Leavenworth. (Official web site, accessed 8 October) http://www.leavenworth.org/history.html

Lever, P. (1995) Stadium mania puts cities over a barrel. *Planning* 61(12), 22.

Lundgren, J.O.J. (1973) Tourism impact/island entrepreneurship in the Caribbean. Paper presented to the Conference of Latin American Geographers.

Mathieson, A. and Wall, G. (1982) *Tourism: Economic, Physical, and Social Impacts.* Longman, London.

Mowforth, M. and Munt, I. (1998) *Tourism and Sustainability: New Tourism in the Third World.* Routledge, London.

Murphy, P.E. (1985) *Tourism: a Community Approach.* Methuen, London.

New York Times on the Web (1996) West Side Yankees? Report details benefits of move (5 April).

Puczko, L. and Ratz, T. (2001) *The Impact of Tourism: an Introduction*. Häme Polytechnic, Hämeenlinna, Finland.

Randall, J.E. and Warf, B. (1996) Economic impacts of AAG conferences. *The Professional Geographer* 48(3), 272–284.

Rothman, H.K. (1999) *Devil's Bargains: Tourism in the Twentieth-Century American West*. University Press of Kansas, Lawrence.

Ryan, C. (1991) *Recreational Tourism: a Social Science Perspective*. Routledge, London.

Samuelson, P.A. and Nordhaus, W.D. (1989) *Economics*, 13th edn. McGraw-Hill, New York.

Shaw, G. and Williams, A.M. (1994) *Critical Issues in Tourism: a Geographical Perspective*. Blackwell, Oxford.

Shaw, G. and Williams, A.M. (1998) Entrepreneurship, small business culture and tourism development. In: Ioannides, D. and Debbage, K.G. (eds) *The Economic Geography of the Tourist Industry: a Supply-side Analysis*. Routledge, London, pp. 235–255.

Telfer, D.J. and Wall, G. (1996) Linkages between tourism and food production. *Annals of Tourism Research* 23, 635–653.

Timothy, D.J. and Ioannides, D. (2002) Tour operator hegemony: dependency, oligopoly and sustainability in insular destinations. In: Apostolopoulos, Y. and Gayle, D.J. (eds) *Island Tourism and Sustainable Development: Caribbean, Pacific, and Mediterranean Experiences*. Praeger, Westport, Connecticut pp. 181–198.

Timothy, D.J. and Wall, G. (1997) Selling to tourists: Indonesian street vendors. *Annals of Tourism Research* 24, 322–340

Timothy, D.J. and White, K. (1999) Community-based ecotourism development on the periphery of Belize. *Current Issues in Tourism* 2(2/3), 226–242.

Urry, J. (1990) *The Tourist Gaze: Leisure and Travel in Contemporary Society*. Sage Publications, London.

Williams, A.M. and Shaw G. (1988) Tourism: candyfloss industry or job generator? *Town Planning Review* 59(1), 81–103.

Williams, S. (1998) *Tourism Geography*. Routledge, London.

Zelinsky, W. (1994) Conventionland USA: the geography of a latterday phenomenon. *Annals of the Association of American Geographers* 84, 68–86.

Zinder, H. (1969) *The Future of Tourism in the Eastern Caribbean*. Zinder and Associates, Washington, DC.

Tourism and Local Society and Culture

4

Michael Fagence

Department of Geographical Sciences and Planning, University of Queensland, Brisbane, Australia

Introduction

Evidence from numerous assessments of tourism impact reveals that tourism activity and development have both positive and negative impacts on local communities and their cultures. Some studies purport to demonstrate that tourism can make a positive contribution to the sustainability of local communities, especially by increasing levels of economic welfare and well-being, and by focusing attention on the intrinsic value of local cultures. Other studies seem to suggest that the interaction of tourism with the common activities of local communities is potentially harmful, not least by trivializing culture, by drawing local economies into a dependence on the whims of consumers (the tourists), and by creating a diversity of unwelcome social pathologies and behaviours. The seriousness of any detrimental impact seems to be heightened in the case of tourism activity in less developed societies and economies, and indigenous and isolated communities in remote areas, where the opportunity for alternative development is low. However, as the case described later in this chapter reveals, there are significant challenges to vulnerable communities and cultures even in developed societies.

Even a cursory review of the literature reveals that most studies of the impacts of tourism in destination communities and their cultures focus on less developed societal and economic contexts. The circumstances of impact on the communities in 'more developed' contexts have been subject to less scrutiny, or perhaps more accurately, to less moralizing, posturing and rhetoric. One reason for this might be the expectation that developed communities lie within economic and social contexts that can more easily adapt to, and cope with, the challenges, and for substitute economic activities and some protection for the sensitive cultures to be put in place. However, as a recent compilation of case studies in Europe has revealed (Boissevain, 1998), there may be consequences of action at the broader national, regional scale that can do little to protect and sustain vulnerable communities once the level of tourism development has put at risk some of the social and cultural elements that were the foundation of the original tourism attraction.

This chapter considers some of the principal underlying assumptions about the interaction of tourism development and the circumstances of local communities and their culture. In particular, the objectives are:

- To review those aspects of local communities and their culture that have potential as tourist attractions.
- To examine the nature of the principal social and cultural interactions of hosts and guests.
- To examine the social and cultural transformations that result from the development of the attraction.
- To consider strategies that may contribute to the management of any consequential impacts of the tourism gaze on sensitive and vulnerable communities and cultures.

Theory and Practice

The literature considering both the theoretical and practical aspects of interactions between tourism development and the circumstances of local communities is extensive. Even so, there are degrees of imbalance in, for example, the geographical spread of case studies, the basic context (with a preponderance of assessments of less-developed countries and indigenous communities), and the idiosyncratic nature of extrapolations of any lessons learned from the experiences recorded. An attempt is made in this section to unravel some of the complications arising from such imbalances.

Sources of attraction

In a review of culture and tourism in Europe (Richards, 1996), attention was drawn to the progressive convergence of tourism and culture. Both have responded to the developing patterns of consumption so that one facilitates and supports the other. This circumstance is particularly true as the 'culture industry' has moved into the marketplace to compete for attention with the recreational attractions of, for example, theme parks, cinemas, entertainment centres, recreational shopping and so on. The outcome has been a culture industry that is less dependent on the support of elite patrons and more on the patronage of a mass audience. One of the principal responses of local communities has been to assess their range of potential tourism products and to match them against realizable client interest, especially where potential visitors consider that the culture of a particular region or destination is 'exotic' when compared to that of their home and origin.

As a consequence, many regions and destinations may owe their tourism attractiveness to culture, cultural activities and the evidence of a different (or exotic) cultural ambience. This situation has particular social and community implications.

What is cultural tourism and what are the attractions that fit into the ambit of this particular interest? Discussions and reviews conducted by MacCannell (1976), Cohen (1988), Craik (2001), and the compendious inventories in government reports (e.g. Government of Ontario, 1993) and in national and international studies (e.g. Munsters, 1996; Richards, 1996; Foo and Rossetto, 1998) have tended to confuse (even surprise) rather than clarify what is meant by 'cultural tourism'. An exacerbation of this situation has been caused by the interpretations given to some of the sub-classes of cultural tourism such as ethnic tourism, heritage tourism and urban tourism, and the difference between attractions that are considered 'high culture' and those that are more common and classified as 'low culture', with modern patterns of tourism consumption tending towards 'low culture'. Commonly, there are three major groupings – high, institutionalized culture; folk, popular culture; and ethnic symbols (see Table 4.1).

However, some commentators have viewed the differentiation and categorization of cultural tourism attractions in destination communities suspiciously. For example, Schouten (1995) questioned the real intention of visitors to cultural sites and settings, considering that the 'real' attraction of the cultural facility may have more to do with its novelty (even 'exoticness'), convenience of location for a general recreational visit, or even its convenience for shopping visits, than with its intrinsic cultural value.

Table 4.1.   Categories of cultural tourism.

Category	Examples
High, institutionalized culture	Museums, exhibitions, visual arts, historic sites, theatre, performing arts, literature, science and technology centres
Folk, popular culture	Film, entertainment, sport, mass media, shopping, events, food, produce, crafts, customs, traditions
Ethnic symbols	Folkways, vernacular architecture, education, transport, religion, dress, language, work patterns

Even so, no matter what the 'real intention' of visitors, or the range of tourism resources that attract them, once at the destination, there are particular interactions between visitors (or guests) and the local community (or hosts), which generate identifiable impacts. These various interactions deserve some examination.

Host–guest interactions

A number of generalizations may be made at this point. First, there are difficulties in understanding the host–guest interaction because of, for example, the inconsistency of the impact and the lack of universals (everywhere-the-same), the difficulty of filtering specific host–guest effects from other socializing influences (such as repatriate visits, global television, worldwide print media), the impact of visiting friends and relatives (VFR) movements, the general adaptation and evolutionary processes of destination communities, the characteristics of the visitors and residents, the different forms of tourism, and so on. Secondly, there is a tendency to identify and then concentrate on the negative influences at the expense of any positive impacts. Thirdly, as in most observational and interpretive research, there are problems of observation and measurement, the predilections of the researchers, and the responses of those interviewed. Despite these difficulties, there is considerable value in isolating the impacts on destination communities, and especially in unravelling the influences on social change and the conservation of local cultural resources.

Visitor–resident interactions and encounters occur in three 'domains', each with its own peculiarities (see Table 4.2). The three domains are space, time and responsibility/respect. In the spatial domain, tourists and residents often share the same space while engaging in routine or recreation-related activities, such as shopping, using public transport and walking on the beach. The temporal dimension reflects the consistent and current use of the tourism-related space, and the seasonal fluctuations where at some time, the space may be occupied by both groups, and at other times by only the host community. In addition, the temporal dimension acknowledges the transient nature of the tourist occupation of space. This transience underpins the respect and responsibility dimension; the degree of respect for and responsibility towards the local environment can be expected to be highest among the residential community, not least because it is they who may be responsible for underwriting the costs of the services, amenities, infrastructure and maintenance. The recompense for this lies in the accumulation of facilities and amenities for local use, which reflects the aggregate population of residents and visitors, rather than the local population alone.

Table 4.2. Host–guest interaction domains.

Domain	Explanation
The spatial domain	For example: in the shared use of commercial services (e.g. shops), in transport, at entertainment venues, the shared use of community services (such as the demands made on police, hospital and emergency services), the joint use of spaces for parking, at the beach, etc.
The temporal domain	For example: there are transitory encounters where the guests/tourists are temporary users and transient users of services, facilities, amenities and spaces which the hosts use regularly or consistently; in addition, some locations and services are dominated by the presence of guests/tourists during the visitor season, causing the hosts to avoid those locations or to choose their visits so as to avoid the congestion associated with visitor peak concentrations
The domain of responsibility and respect	For example: guests tend to assume little responsibility for maintaining the destination visited, with hosts assuming both the responsibility for maintenance and the costs of the maintenance. One ongoing benefit for hosts lies in the availability of resources, facilities, amenities and so on, once the guests have left

Measurement of interaction: indices of irritation and development life cycle

A small body of theory exists, which attempts to interpret, even to 'measure', some of the outcomes of these interactions and encounters. These 'measures' are speculations about residents' reactions to tourists, reflecting host perceptions, attitudes and responses to the presence of guests. Such measures are often referred to as indices of irritation (Doxey, 1976), extending from an accommodation and acceptance of visitors, through a gradation to apathy, annoyance, aggravation and antagonism towards them. The reactions to visitors are based on generalized perceptions about them and their value systems, and some degree of personal experiences of encounter and exasperation. Some of the common perceptions of residents, as reported in many studies (e.g. Ap, 1990; Tsartas, 1992; Brunt and Courtney, 1999; Snaith and Haley, 1999), include the following:

• A heavy concentration of tourists tends to create a negative attitude towards tourism by residents and their communities, an attitude which may be lessened if the clear economic benefits (jobs, incomes, image of place, level of services and amenities) of tourism can be seen.

- Residents prefer tourism attractions and facilities to be concentrated rather than dispersed throughout the community.
- Residents blame visitors for raised prices, levels of criminal activity and reduced moral standards.
- In terms of the impact on culture, destination residents tend to blame tourists for reducing the significance of local culture by trivializing it or by causing it to be commodified and packaged for easy consumption (and even transportability in the form of souvenirs).

Some of the problems in assessments of this type lie in the general poor development of sociocultural modelling, poor databases from which assessments are made, and the deployment of management and planning strategies that are aimed least at reducing the degree of detrimental impact.

Almost as a companion 'measuring' device is the tourism and resort life cycle. Both this index and that of Doxey (1976) are indicative rather than precise. Originally conceptualized to study the growth of tourism destinations (Butler, 1980), the indicative measure of the life cycle has provided a graded yardstick to interpret both the sequential phases of growth of a resort area and the associated forms, scope and intensity of tourism development. At its most basic level, the development life cycle indicates a temporal phasing of growth and development, reflecting the responses of tourism entrepreneurs, agencies, tourists and local communities to the availability of tourism resources (attractions). There are four initial growth phases (exploration, involvement, development and consolidation), each with its 'typical' stakeholder responses; the challenge occurs after consolidation, with the destination needing to determine what will happen next – stagnation, decline or rejuvenation. At each phase are environmental, economic, political, social and cultural implications. Generalizations from disparate cases may be unwise, but there seems to be a tendency for growth, expansion, redevelopment and re-visioning strategies so that existing capital investment can be sustained and maximized. In many instances, decisions are made based on economic and political criteria instead of substantial public consultation processes. One outcome of this is that it is seldom the local community that determines the level of tourism development, and the use of social and cultural resources (see Timothy and Tosun, Chapter 10 this volume). However, there are cases where both careful community consultation and management strategies have been deployed which contribute positively to community sustainability (in social and cultural terms). The case study in the next section is one such example.

Social pathologies and cultural transformations

The principal concerns about the vulnerability of local communities and their culture are derived from the differences in value systems, behaviours and attitudes towards sociocultural issues that distinguish residents from visitors, and even among the stakeholder groups in the host communities. These concerns are heightened where the target communities are tight-knit, unsophisticated (compared to tourists), tradition-bound and where the manifestations of visitor affluence may be seductive, especially to the younger age groups. Some of the challenges include:

- sustaining daily lifestyles in the face of visitor intrusion;
- coping with tourist numbers (a measure of carrying capacity);
- coping with the pressure for change;
- retaining the meaning of the traditions and ceremonies;
- retaining authenticity; and
- containing the tendency towards commercialization.

Vulnerability may be encapsulated in the combined interpretations of such key terms as transformation, modification, modernization, exploitation and stereotyping. Any developmental action that might be interpreted as contributing to any of these circumstances may bring about the progressive neutralization and generalization of the local culture and its host community, reducing its distinctive identity and, thereby, its special attractiveness. The implications of these various issues have been raised dramatically by, for example, MacCannell (1973, 1976) and Cohen (1979). Another aspect of the vulnerability is the tendency for only the marketable elements to be targeted; this may accelerate the neutralization of these elements and the fossilization of those that remain untargeted and bypassed. Such action may cause the 'museumization' of those untouched elements and the creation of a 'fake culture' where some elements are replicated simply because they are clearly attractive to potential visitors and users. An outcome is that tradition becomes entertainment, and the symbolism of actions becomes commercialized. Some of the action and host community response (from the various stakeholder groups), whether positive or negative, is dependent upon the expectations of the tourists, the experiences they are seeking, the numbers and types of tourists, and the availability of resources locally to meet the expectations. These issues were examined by MacCannell (1973) in his interpretation of the 'staged sets' of the presentation of local culture to tourists, the 'front' (or public) and the 'back' (or private) tourist spaces. There is an element of this distinction in the case study presented here, where, whether deliberately or coincidentally, the conservative Amish groups seem to be able to protect their 'back' spaces and, thereby, their basic lifestyles, while some of the more liberal Amish and Mennonite groups are participants in the 'front' space, meeting the tourists' expectations of Amish culture.

Experience has revealed that there is a range of common outcomes of tourism development (or further development). These include some challenges to economic, social and cultural structures (Table 4.3).

Table 4.3. Outcomes of tourism development.

Changes	Family and community levels
To economic structures	• At the family level, with changes to the status of the various income earners • At the community level, with changes to investment priorities, sources of financing, employment structures, ownership patterns, role of government
To social structures	• At the family level, with changes to responsibility levels, decision-making roles, influence on the family, employment opportunities • At the community level, with changes to the significance of local leaders, the influence of government, the influence of 'external' stakeholders, new political structures
To cultural structures	• At the family level, with hosts imitating guests' behaviour, with hosts indulging in 'cultural prostitution' (as the communities interpret their role as servants, entertainers, objects of the tourist gaze), with the manifestations of the 'demonstration effect' and the emulation of visitor behaviour • At the community level, with local cultures being manipulated to meet the expectations of tourists, with the homogenization and symbiosis of culture (assimilation and reflection of guest behaviour) leading to 'cultural drift' as the community starts to lose its special identity, with the packaging and commodification of selected attributes of local culture (at the expense of the culture as a whole)

The impact of the 'demonstration effect' has achieved most attention in the literature on social and cultural influences on vulnerable communities. This phenomenon is usually expressed as the impact of foreign ways on a host community in terms of value systems, standards of behaviour, and attitudes towards people, property, culture and spaces. Common manifestations of this effect include the importation of foreign goods, changes in approaches to service, creation of alien services and facilities (e.g. casinos, discos, entertainment), emulation of visitor acquisitiveness and personal possessions (e.g. cameras, video and computer equipment), and the loosening of loyalties to place and people. The consequences of these changes of attitude and behaviour in the destination community may lead to frustration and community unrest, strategies to 'get rich quick', the out-migration of young adults, and a range of social pathologies including increased levels of criminal activity (e.g. vandalism, theft, personal assault), drug use, a black market in imported/substitute goods, gambling and prostitution. Although not all of these consequences can be attributed wholly to tourism development and the presence of visitors, some may well be. There seems to be some psychological slippage when the host community fails to recognize that the behaviour of tourists on holiday or at times of recreation is not their normal behaviour, so that any effort to emulate or imitate the tourists is not a replication of their typical behaviour. Particular community consequences of residents responding to the demonstration effect include ongoing health hazards, possible child abuse (in the workplace), changes to language, revisionism and commercialization of culture so that only marketable elements are sustained, and loosened respect for kinship and community. Among the positive consequences are increased employment and income possibilities, a clear rationale for the maintenance of local customs and traditions (to be offered to inquisitive tourists), the sustainability of local crafts and art, community income to support the improvement of local services and infrastructure, and a heightened community profile.

There is a subset of issues within the demonstration effect that is influenced by the assimilation potential of the guests, which is affected by the degree of difference between the local community and the tourists, the differences in tourist type, and the respective approaches towards each other of the locals and tourists. For example, as the case study below reveals, it is the distinctiveness of the destination community that is of particular tourist appeal. One of the principal problems for host communities is derived from the uncertainty of tourist carrying capacity; small numbers of visitors (as is evident in the life cycle and irritation indices) pose few problems, but mass visitation levels, especially where the number of visitors greatly exceeds the host population, may cause severe local dislocation. This may be influenced by the types of tourists involved, with some types (e.g. explorers, elite special interest tourists) adapting well to local conditions while others (typically the mass tourist, charter groups) being more intrusive to local communities. This intrusion may not be deliberate; it may simply be a consequence of the imbalance in numbers between hosts and guests. In a circumstance similar to that considered below in the case study, Buck (1978) examined how some members of the local community may construct a boundary zone in which they are willing to provide public evidence of their lifestyle to meet the basic expectations of the visitors – a process of staged authenticity. This action provides some degree of sanitization of the demonstration effect. In addition, the personal attributes and attitudes of the two groups, the nature and maturity of the host community, and the willingness of both groups to meet the behavioural expectations of the other will influence the degree of assimilation and accord.

In summary, the social and cultural consequences of visitors to vulnerable host communities may be detrimental or they may be positive. The outcome is likely to be determined particularly by matters such as:

• Tourist carrying capacity of the destination community.

- Resilience of the local community and its capacity to withstand the pressures of 'alien' behaviour.
- Resilience of the local culture and its capacity to withstand the pressures of market-led promotion and demand for packaged and commoditized culture.
- Types of tourists.
- Adaptability of the visitors.
- Introduction of suitable management strategies, which may include spatial segregation into dedicated host and guest precincts, and strategies to distract visitors from communities, sites and settings that may be particularly vulnerable to any level of visitation.

A Case Study of Sociocultural Implications

The case study considered here highlights some of the important basic issues encountered in the previous section. While it is not a 'mainstream' case study, its particular contribution to an appreciation of the interaction of local communities, their culture and tourism development lies partly in its novelty. The communities considered here are almost anachronistic in the context of modern lifestyles; they are located in a well-developed national and regional economy (Pennsylvania, USA), yet reveal an attachment to a lifestyle which, in its purest form, seeks to be detached from modern conditions. It is this separateness, and also exoticness, which lies behind the touristic attractiveness. However, just as modern tourism generally responds to a plethora of motivations, so too the communities considered in this case study are responding to a diversity of tourist motivations – the general recreational tourist, the special interest tourist, the day or weekend excursionist. As some commentators have suggested, the attraction of the communities as a cultural resource may be incidental to the real purposes of the visitors.

Research methods

The research reported in this study is based on three periods of fieldwork conducted in Pennsylvania (USA) and Ontario (Canada) in the late 1990s. Before and since those visits, conventional desk research has been undertaken to establish the background situation and the parameters of the study, and to achieve corroboration and verification of the accumulating information by using published papers and reports. Some of this database was tested in field locations during consultations with members of the Amish and Mennonite communities, public officials, media commentators, and other intermediaries who had access to the conservative community members and who were willing to relay the outcome of those dialogues to this author. At various points in this study, reference is made to 'anecdotal' sources. These are the conservative community members (either directly, or through the intermediaries), public officials (at, for example, the planning commission, a number of local government agencies, and the principal tourism marketing agency), and researchers at Mennonite and local historical societies. These are treated as anecdotal because they have not yet been verified from other scientifically credible sources. However, these sources have traditionally been used as surrogates for the very conservative Old Order members of the community, because those members are tacitly unwilling to participate in public scrutiny and examinations of what they consider to be their private domain. They are content to let 'the English' (their generic description of any non-Old Order person) draw their own conclusions about what they see and hear.

Background

The selected communities lie within a diffuse group referred to generically as Anabaptist, comprising the Amish, the Mennonites and a few other subgroups identifiable by their particular social and religious codes and behaviour (Hostetler, 1968; Kraybill, 1989). These groups evolved in the period of social and religious chaos during the 17th century in Europe, developing unique ideas about the church, the state, the family and the person. This led to the development of a particular code of behaviour regarding dress, conduct, association with people outside of the community, the maintenance of a peculiar language, and led the groups to high levels of skill and self-sufficiency in rural crafts and food production. It also contributed to a fortress mentality of separation from mainstream society. Various groups of Anabaptists migrated across Europe in the 18th century seeking a safe haven for their practices, some eventually travelling to North America with several arrival points on the east coast of the USA and Canada. Since the early arrivals in the 18th century, the Anabaptists have spread out across the continent, with distinct concentrations in, for example, Pennsylvania and Ohio in the USA, and Ontario and Manitoba in Canada. They have developed a diverse social structure with a detectable gradation from strict observance of the behavioural code brought with them from Europe (whose members are usually referred to as 'Old Order'), to more liberal codes that merge almost imperceptibly into mainstream society. It is the Old Order and similar strict observance groups that are of particular interest to tourists.

From different points of entry into North America, these groups have tended to become concentrated in rural areas that lie within a few hours' drive of major urban centres like New York, Boston, Baltimore,

Washington DC and Toronto. This ease of access and proximity to large population centres has contributed to their becoming targets for visitors because of their distinctiveness and 'exoticness', their reputation for high-quality agricultural produce and domestic crafts including furniture and other furnishings, and because of their convenient location within day excursion travel from major metropolitan centres.

This case study examines the extent to which some of the principal issues considered in the previous section are evidenced, and which may be generalized. In particular, attention will be given to such matters as:

- Potential for tourist interest in these communities – the sources of tourism attractiveness.
- Evidence of host–guest interaction and encounters.
- Indices of interaction.
- Evidence of the tourism development life cycle.
- Evidence of social pathologies and cultural transformations.

Reference is made to the vulnerability of the Anabaptist culture, and the impacts of this vulnerability on the communities.

Sources of tourism attraction

The features of touristic interest in these communities range across a broad spectrum of attractions, including, for example, a recreational countryside, state parklands, historic villages and heritage trails, major designer-label shopping centres, commercial entertainment and theme parks. However, it is not this range of attractions that is solely responsible for the particular tourist interest in these communities and their regional setting. Rather, it is the subset of the cultural features listed earlier (see Table 4.1). These attractions include village sites and settings, folk and popular cultural features, and ethnic symbols (see Table 4.4).

Host–guest interaction

There are no published scientific assessments of host–guest interactions between Old Order communities and mass tourism. The literature record of interactive assessments in general of Old Order communities and visitors (not necessarily engaged in tourism) are largely anecdotal or the outcome of participant observation studies; there are problems of comparability between cases, and only occasionally do the studies include tourism as one of the points of interaction. Interpretations have been made of the possible implications of host–guest interaction, largely based on the extrapolation of the general responses of Old Order members to non-members

Table 4.4. Cultural tourism attractions in Anabaptist regions.

Categories	Sub-categories
The village sites, and their countryside setting	
The folk and popular culture features	• Quilts and other furnishings • Wood and other craft items • Quality garden and farm produce (available in local stores and restaurants) • Traditional behaviour in dress, transport, religious observance (see under ethnic symbols)
The ethnic symbols	• Sombre dress code of plain colours, free of decoration and embellishment, with a style reminiscent of the puritanical forms of the 17th century • Horse and buggy transport • Focus on agrarian, and agrarian-related skills • Pursuit of simple agricultural practices (such as the use of horse-drawn farm machinery, and the avoidance of chemical fertilizers) • The isolated 'Dutch barn' farmsteads • Simple architectural forms for farm buildings (sometimes described as the Dutch barn) and houses, with the readily identifiable additions to farm-house structures to accommodate an increase in family members and especially the grandparents • Communal telephone boxes • Lack of electricity power cables • Ingeniously substituted engineering devices to generate power, distribute water and so on • The peculiar language • The 'churches' or communal worship 'meeting places'

by commentators such as Hostetler (1968), Kraybill (1989) and others. In addition, some of these commentators have attempted to unravel the implications of these interactions for local economies, and for the sustainability of the peculiar cultural regime of the Anabaptist groups. The interpretation recorded here utilizes these sources.

For most tourists, the subtleties of difference between the degrees or levels of Anabaptists are of little significance. What is sought, especially through the visual image, is evidence of the presence of Old Order members, and practical expressions and evidence of their crafts and lifestyle. That the Old Orders are largely exclusive and do not engage in formal interaction with non-members is of little concern to most tourists.

Anecdotal and some recorded evidence indicates that the tourists seek only to engage in interaction with those members of the religious group willing to meet with them. It is then the imagination of the tourist that extrapolates to generalized meetings with 'genuine' Old Order members. For tourism, it is fortunate that the communities are aware of what the tourist seeks, and therefore oblige by dressing for the part, and engaging in appropriate behaviour. Members of strict orders, which do not wish to become involved with visitors, behave as though the intruders are not evident or even present; they conduct their lifestyle without interruption, largely ignoring the many visitors who peer at them, and point their cameras at them. There is evidence that some groups have been disturbed by the penetration of visitors into the special domains of the 'meeting places', and that the tourist gaze is at least visually disturbing if it upsets routine rural activities and domestic regimes.

Such interaction as occurs between local communities and visitors is driven by the intention of the less strict orders to engage the tourists in commercial exchange. Spatial interactions take place in, for example:

- local convenience stores;
- stores which retail Anabaptist crafts;
- farmers' markets, especially for rural produce;
- commercially sponsored shopping villages with a particular focus on Anabaptist goods and services;
- alleged Amish attractions, such as buggy rides;
- museums or static displays of Amish heritage, including farmsteads, meeting rooms and school rooms; and
- information centres, souvenir stores and bookshops which retail or exchange information on Anabaptism.

The tradition of independence, self-sufficiency, attention to quality, and integrity tends to increase the admiration of the tourists for the output of these communities, and leads to heightened degrees of inquisitiveness. The less strict orders in the communities are willing participants in interactive practices not least to benefit economically from visitors' fascination with exotic behaviour and products. Some commentators (e.g. Olshan, 1994) have described the resultant cottage industries and services as the potential Trojan horse for Amish society.

Other spatial encounters occur in, for example, the narrow lanes of the farming areas, the general highway system (in which care has to be exercised in negotiating the passage of the relatively slow-moving buggies), and the parking areas of shopping villages, although the horse-and-buggy travellers usually have dedicated parking spaces, or hitching rails. In most Amish areas the geographical pattern of rural communities is such that the visitor population is dispersed through the region, yet concentrated into a number of distinct villages, each with its own special identity and range of attractions. There is one linear concentration astride a major state and federal highway. Recent growth has tended to concentrate into defined precincts, whether along the highway or at the periphery of existing villages.

In terms of temporal encounters, few tourists commit their time to understanding the intricacies of the Anabaptist way of life, and most would seem to be content that someone dressed as Amish or Mennonite similar to the Old Order is present at the time of the exchange or service. Some commentators have raised concerns that non-members take advantage of the tourists' perceptions and present themselves as Old Order (particularly in dress) even though they are not. This is alleged to occur especially at farmers' markets with the sale of crafts and farm produce. There is a regular tourist season (particularly the period from May to late September) in which the encounters are at a peak. However, outside of this season, weekend and especially holiday weekend secondary peaks are created by day excursions by residents of, or visitors to, the major metropolitan centres which are within 3 or 4 hours' driving time. With the potential scope of tourist interest, Luthy (1994: 129) argues that any sizeable Amish settlement within several hours' driving time of large cities is being affected by tourism.

Some of the transitory encounters are intrusive. For example, visitors tend to congregate around religious meeting places to experience the gathering and exodus of the worshippers on Sundays; they park at farm gates to photograph Old Order members at work in the fields or farm buildings; they wait near communal telephone boxes to witness users and use-levels; they lurk in the aisles of farmers' markets or even at roadside stalls to hear the peculiar language spoken.

Scientific evidence of the impact of host–guest interactions is scarce. Most of what exists is largely anecdotal, and refers to general circumstances rather than directly to the impact of tourism. Some commentaries refer to Old Order families migrating away from the tourist regions to peripheral areas in part to reduce the potential for contact with non-members of the community. However, on closer analysis, most evidence points to this outward migration being induced more by real estate development and suburban extension into traditional farmland areas than by tourism development *per se*. One outcome of this possible displacement of Old Order families has been the resort through planning schemes to tourist enclaves, thereby formalizing a type of spatial segregation of uses and users.

Several circumstances seem to conspire to frustrate the assessment of measures of interaction, and especially of potential irritation of hosts with guests in the form hypothesized by Doxey (1976). First, the strictest orders of Anabaptism try to avoid direct contact with visitors and intruders, thereby defusing potential interactive irritation. Secondly, the underlying philosophy of these groups is intrinsically non-confrontational. Thirdly, the

Old Order groups are unwilling to become involved in secular studies and data collection exercises. Fourthly, the Old Orders will not normally engage government in the planning for and management of their territory. Fifthly, the more liberal groups that participate in the common interactive encounters of commercial exchange are scarcely different from other tourist destination communities, in part considering the tourists as contributors to their general economic well-being (in terms of employment, income, aggregate services and facilities). For the more liberal groups, the common perceptions of visitors remain consistent in this case.

Life cycle assessment

A life cycle assessment of tourism development in Lancaster County has been conducted by a locally based geographer (Hovinen, 1981, 1982). His assessment revealed progressive changes in the county through four decades. In the 1930s, the Amish territory was considered to be 'quaint', accommodating a peculiar 'plain people' who were very different from 'typical' rural Americans. The growing interest was curtailed by the Second World War, but with the growth of holiday travel in the 1950s, the non-Old Order community became willing participants in activity which improved the level of economic well-being in the region, particularly as the fascination of visitors with the crafts and produce of the region provided a useful profile, marketing tool and additional source of economic development. Significant capital investment in tourism-related development and infrastructure in the next decade or so established the reputation of the region as a tourist destination, which was augmented by the immigration of chain hotels, entertainment venues and cosmetic Amish-like theme attractions. Hovinen (1981, 1982) rejects the Butler (1980) phases of consolidation and stagnation, preferring to use the appellation of a phase of 'maturity', extending from the mid-1970s, incorporating phases of tourists' repeat visits. This interpretation is substantiated by recent evidence, which is indicative of the targets of attraction to the region being augmented to include the designer-label shopping malls, the state parkland areas, the heritage trails and villages, and the new entertainment venues. The ongoing outcome is the forestalling of any decline in attractiveness by the embarkation on strategies of diversification and distraction which have in part refreshed the profile of the region while sustaining visitor interest in the original motivation for travel to the area (Hovinen, 1997; Fagence, 1999).

The social consequences of high visitor levels

The principal concerns about the vulnerability of local communities and their culture are derived from the differences in value systems, behaviour and attitudes between hosts and guests. In the case described here, the vulnerability of the host community is heightened by three factors. First, the strictest orders do not wish to become involved with guests. Secondly, their non-confrontational philosophy may put at risk their ability to withstand intrusion and disruption (and particularly their unwillingness to use conventional government forces to offer them protection). Thirdly, there is the ease with which non-member groups can replicate those facets of the exotic culture to achieve commercial gain, even if authenticity is lost.

The particular challenges of exposing the Old Order and the less strict member communities to the vagaries of tourism include:

- Disruptions to daily routines.
- Questioning, especially by the younger age groups, of the rationale for the customary behaviour, especially when it seems to miss out on providing some of the accoutrements of a developed lifestyle (as evidenced by the visitors).
- The focus of visitors' attention on only selected aspects of the local culture, and particularly those features which have commercial value, or which are novel and exotic.
- The rapidity of change in fashion (of the visitors, especially in dress, vehicles, preferences for culture-dependent goods and services).
- The preference for superficial understanding of local culture, and the inclination to seek to witness or participate in the highest profile activities.
- The casual approach to authenticity, and the willingness of tourists to accept substitution.
- The superficiality of commercialization.

While the well-established Old Order Amish and Mennonite groups can withstand some of these challenges, in part by disassociating and detaching themselves from them, the wider community of hosts (i.e. the less strict orders) and the non-Anabaptist community, and the tourists seem, by their actions, to be determined to 'reshape' the Anabaptist symbols to meet their own preferences. For example, the references include the following:

- If Amish symbolism is being used in advertising the product or service, then it can be assumed that the goods or services are not genuinely Amish.
- If the manifestations of modern commercial exchange (such as the use of credit cards) are being facilitated, then the enterprise is not embraced by the Old Order.
- If the 'inside story' is being revealed to tourists (such as by tour guides), then the interpretation is derived from a member of a less strict order than the Old Order.

- If the goods for sale are craft-like, but appear to be mass produced, then they are commoditized products, perhaps stereotypical rather than genuinely typical.

These actions are evidence of the focus of attention being on the marketable elements of Old Order symbolism. An outcome has been a focus of attention by tourists on a narrowed range of products (especially in woodcrafts and quilts), which has flowed back to the production end of the process, with replication replacing the traditional creativity of the communities. Two by-products are noticeable: one is the importation of mass-produced replicas, sometimes with an Asian origin; the second is the accumulation of stereotypical, mass-produced items, set out on store forecourts as in a car sales yard. Other outcomes include the creation of entertainment venues exhibiting Amish symbols, presenting dramatized histories of Amish development. Most commentaries, especially by Anabaptists of less strict sects than the Old Order, explain that these dilutions and modifications pander to the brief attention spans of tourists, and suggest to the more gullible members of the sects that the serious pursuit of the symbolism and meaning is of little consequence 'in the real world'. This satisfaction of tourists with superficiality and commoditized culture contributes to a special form of demonstration effect in the host community (see Table 4.5, compare to Table 4.3).

Some of the difficulties for the Old Order in facing the challenges of the tourist gaze and penetration into their area are derived from the responses of these groups to the question 'how much tourism is enough (or too much)?' The Old Orders hold a very low threshold of psychological carrying capacity. The impacts of visitor numbers on, for example, standards of health and hygiene, have not been studied rigorously, and remain conjectural. There is a similar dearth of quantifiable evidence on the impact of tourism on kinship ties and the retention by these strict orders of the young age groups. There has not been a dramatic reduction in the retention rates, and there is both anecdotal and physical evidence (for example in the extensions to the farm houses) that the family units persist through consecutive generations. There is evidence of the reduction in land ownership by Old Order communities, and their 'forced' migration away from the concentration of tourism activity, although this may be as much to do with a response to general real estate development and suburban expansion as with the direct impact of tourism development. The sequence of changes to local language styles as a consequence of the impact of tourism development and tourists has not been studied rigorously in this region, and even the longitudinal study of changes in Mennonite groups in Canada (e.g. Hamm, 1987; Redekop et al., 1994) has not sought to isolate the likely impact of tourism on those changes. The Old Order communities are reluctant to comment directly on the commercialization of their traditional

Table 4.5. Impacts of demonstration effect.

Level	Impact
At the community level	• Investment is attracted to those services which may provide inducement to visitors (such as improved roads, car parks, shopping villages) at the expense of needed community services for the hosts • Ownership (of property) gravitates towards those uses which are tourist-focused at the expense of traditional farming enterprise (even if self-sufficient) • Partnership with government (once considered almost anathema by Old Order members) and non-Anabaptist members (especially to secure major commercial development) • Trend towards homogenization of cultural features
At the family level	• Some emulation of tourist behaviour, especially focusing on acquisitiveness of material goods at the expense of the symbols of genuine Anabaptist meaning • Some preference for commitment only to those occupations which contribute to a financial return, and to remuneration levels which enable acquisition of material goods • Preference of some members of the family to leave the community to learn what they consider to be necessary life skills • Changes to family responsibility levels, with some re-ordering of seniority and respect (based in part on income levels and economic contribution to the family)

crafts, and the substitution of imported and 'fake' items for the genuine Amish crafts.

In summary, the social and cultural consequences of visitors to the Amish regions are being influenced by matters such as:

- The perceptions of visitor carrying capacity.
- The internalized social and religious resilience of the Old Orders.
- The distaste for but acknowledgement of the importation and substitution of 'manufactured' goods, services and experiences.
- The diversity of tourist aspirations and experiential expectations.
- The responsibility assumed by the Old Orders to protect their lifestyle, and the acquiescence of tourists in that task.
- The isolation and independence of the Old Orders, and their unwillingness to compromise their lifestyle.
- The pursuit of the economic and social opportunities due to tourism by the less strict orders, which may be largely indistinguishable from the general populace.

- The involvement of government stakeholders in the creation of diversionary strategies.

Conclusions

In summary, the generalizations from this chapter include:

- The underlying 'message' is that the introduction of tourism into even vulnerable communities may not be detrimental to them and to their cultures if it is managed efficiently.
- The key to the compatibility of local communities with tourism is linked particularly to the degree of participation of all the stakeholders in the strategy process and its operation.
- If the 'custodians' of any of the principal resources wish to withdraw from that process, then that is their right, and any resultant strategy should acknowledge and accommodate that right.
- The aspirations of the hosts and 'custodians' of the tourism resources and the diverse expectations of the tourists will need to be integrated in the tourism-mix and the tourist-mix.
- This integration may need a diversionary sub-strategy to deflect detrimental tourism intrusion from sensitive cultural areas.
- Any social pathologies which are coincident with the development of tourism may not have tourism as their principal cause.
- The influence of the 'demonstration effect' is inevitable, but its local significance will be determined largely by the strength of the philosophy and code which binds the community (and especially vulnerable groups) together.
- Some of the flamboyant trappings of tourism are inevitable in most tourism areas, so that forms of spatial segregation and precincting may be necessary as a measure of physical and aesthetic control.

Local responses to cope with visitor interest: ways and means of managing

The various stakeholder groups will approach the accommodation of tourism into a vulnerable cultural setting in a number of different ways. Within the community, it is likely that, as in this case, some vulnerable groups will consider their best strategy to be to retreat behind a psychological boundary in the 'back country' of the tourism region to avoid contact with the visitors. Other groups in the community, including those which may be more liberal in their cultural attachments and non-members of the cultural group may seek to explore conventional entrepreneurial opportunities by creating businesses that service the tourism market and its associated activities (e.g. retailing, transport, provisioning, land development, entertainment). The various levels of government will become involved in responding to visitor interest, in part to derive economic and political benefit, but also in meeting the infrastructure requirements of the communities as they come under pressure from increased visitation.

What may emerge, either by design or by coincidence, may be a pastiche of strategies that have the effect of facilitating the development of tourism and providing protection and sustainability of the 'exotic' cultural resource. This pastiche is dependent upon partnerships between stakeholders, with each stakeholder group accepting responsibility for integrating its sub-strategy into a holistic programme of actions, which achieve the highest degree of visitor satisfaction and the highest degree of cultural conservation for the host communities. Previous work by this author (Fagence, 1999) on this issue in the case-study region has identified eight possible partnership strategies (see Table 4.6). The overriding aim is to develop a local partnership of sympathetic interests that can address and respond to the multifaceted pressures of visitor–host interaction and pursuit of their various interests.

Research needs

A number of issues, revealed through this chapter, warrant further research attention. The fundamental research needs are for improvements to the databases on social and cultural circumstances, and for improvements to social cultural modelling to facilitate appropriate interpretations. Within the specific context of this chapter there are five particular research needs.

1. There needs to be clarification of whether the circumstances of potential tourism development in the so-called developed and less-developed 'environments' are similar or different.
2. Planning tools need to be developed that are compatible with the interests of vulnerable groups who need protection and cultural resources that deserve to be exposed to the tourist gaze.
3. It will be helpful to planners to have a better understanding of perceptual and psychological carrying capacity to heighten awareness of the pressures being experienced by vulnerable groups and cultures.
4. Related to 3. above, it is necessary to develop a deeper understanding of the implications of visitor–host interaction, especially to identify the characteristics that may heighten tension, and to clarify the generalizability of indices of irritation.
5. It may be useful to be able to separate the 'demonstration effects' and social pathologies that are attributable to tourism and those that are the outcomes of more general societal changes.

Table 4.6. Possible development strategies.

Strategy	Purpose
1. Image	To meet the visitor expectations of seeing the symbols of the region's identity, acknowledging that strict authenticity may not be as important to the tourist and the tourism industry as to the custodians of the culture
2. Protection	To control the disturbance of the custodians' territory through planned practices of physical segregation
3. Deep meaning	To protect the deep meaning of the culture by restricting direct confrontation, by providing appropriate interpretation for visitors, and by confirming for the younger members of the cultural group the advantages of their own lifestyle (compared to that of the visitors)
4. Authenticity	To 'allow' replication of the symbolism of the cultural group (which may be difficult to counter if it is not protected by licence or copyright), in part as a contribution to the image of the region
5. Spatial frameworks	To develop nodal or linear concentrations of distinctive and symbolic cultural heritage features, thereby protecting visitor penetration into protected back country
6. Diversification	To provide a diversity of tourism attractions and facilities to meet the variety of expectations and motivations of the many different tourist types, and as a means of deflecting some pressure from the cultural attractions
7. Codes of practice	To develop codes of planning practice with specific codes, regulations, controls, strategies which can afford some protection to vulnerable cultural resources and which can provide incentives to sustain them
8. Organization	To develop a locally based organization of the different stakeholders so that each party to the development or conservation decision can play a distinctive and positive (rather than obstructionist or rampant development) role

Experience gleaned from recorded literature and anecdotal evidence suggests that the intrinsic value of culture is becoming increasingly commercialized, with the progressive collapse of the distinction between culture as an aesthetic, intellectual commodity and the product of social development, and culture as a resource that can be exploited for commercial purposes. The research questions are multitudinous; so far, the answers, and the standard of tourism planning practice, have been found wanting in many cases. Even so, there is evidence that the potential to devise strategies for cooperation, mutual support and sustainability lies within the creative capacity of stakeholder groups in regions where there is tourist interest in the communities and their culture.

References

Ap, J. (1990) Residents' perceptions research on the social impact of tourism. *Annals of Tourism Research* 17, 610–616.

Boissevain, J. (ed.) (1998) *Coping with Tourists.* Berghahn Books, Providence, Rhode Island.

Brunt, P. and Courtney, P. (1999) Host perceptions of sociocultural impacts. *Annals of Tourism Research* 26, 493–515.

Buck, R. (1978) Boundary maintenance revisited: tourist experience in an Old Order Amish community. *Rural Sociology* 43, 221–234.

Butler, R. (1980) The concept of a tourist area cycle of evolution: implications for management of resources. *Canadian Geographer* 24, 5–12.

Cohen, E. (1979) Rethinking the sociology of tourism. *Annals of Tourism Research* 6, 18–35.

Cohen, E. (1988) Authenticity and commoditization in tourism. *Annals of Tourism Research* 15, 371–386.

Craik, J. (2001) Cultural tourism. In: Douglas, N., Douglas, N. and Derrett, R. (eds) *Special Interest Tourism.* John Wiley & Sons, Brisbane, pp. 113–139.

Doxey, G. (1976) When enough's enough: the natives are restless in Old Niagara. *Heritage Canada* 2(2), 26–27.

Fagence, M. (1999) Sustaining cultures in the face of tourism. Paper presented to Tourism Industry and Education Symposium, Jyväskylä, Finland, September.

Foo, L. and Rossetto, A. (1998) *Cultural Tourism in Australia.* Bureau of Tourism Research, Canberra.

Government of Ontario (1993) *The Cultural Tourism Handbook.* Government of Ontario, Toronto.

Hamm, P. (1987) *Community and Change Among Canadian Mennonite Brethren.* Wilfred Laurier University Press, Waterloo, Ontario.

Hostetler, D. (1968) *Amish Society.* Johns Hopkins University Press, Baltimore.

Hovinen, G. (1981) A tourist cycle in Lancaster County. *The Canadian Geographer* 25(3), 283–286.

Hovinen, G. (1982) Visitor cycles: outlook for tourism in Lancaster County. *Annals of Tourism Research* 9, 565–583.

Hovinen, G. (1997) Lancaster County, Pennsylvania's heritage tourism initiative. *Small Town* 28(3), 4–11.

Kraybill, D. (1989) *The Riddle of Amish Culture.* Johns Hopkins University Press, Baltimore.

Luthy, D. (1994) The origin and growth of Amish tourism. In: Kraybill, D. and Olshan, M. (eds) *The Amish Struggle with Modernity.* University Press of New England, Hanover, pp. 113–129.

MacCannell, D. (1973) 'Staged authenticity': arrangements of social space in tourist settings. *American Journal of Sociology* 79, 357–361.

MacCannell, D. (1976) *The Tourist: a New Theory of the Leisure Class.* Schocken Books, New York.

Munsters, W. (1996) Cultural tourism in Belgium. In: Richards, G. (ed.) *Cultural Tourism in Europe.* CAB International, Wallingford, pp. 109–126.

Olshan, M. (1994) Amish cottage industries as Trojan Horse. In: Kraybill, D. and Olshan, M. (eds) *The Amish Struggle with Modernity.* University Press of New England, Hanover, pp. 133–146.

Redekop, C., Krahn, V. and Steiner, S. (eds) (1994) *Anabaptist/Mennonite Faith and Economics.* University Press of America, Lanham, Maryland.

Richards, G. (ed.) (1996) *Cultural Tourism in Europe.* CAB International, Wallingford.

Schouten, F. (1995) Improving visitor care in heritage attractions. *Tourism Management* 16, 259–264.

Snaith, T. and Haley, A. (1999) Residents' opinions of tourism development in the historic city of York, England. *Tourism Management* 20, 595–603.

Tsartas, P. (1992) Socio-economic impacts of tourism on two Greek islands. *Annals of Tourism Research* 19, 516–533.

Heritage, Identity and Places: for Tourists and Host Communities

5

GREGORY J. ASHWORTH

*Faculty of Spatial Sciences, University of Groningen, Groningen,
The Netherlands*

Introduction

It is clearly evident from much of the content of this book that over the past
20 years a growing literature has focused on the impacts of tourism upon
destination areas whether as an economic activity or as social behaviour. In
particular there has been a growing interest in the tourism industry and
tourists as agents of cultural change in the communities frequented by
tourists. It is equally evident that much of this interest originally stemmed
from a defensive concern among anthropologists and others who studied,
or who identified with, communities around the world that were con-
fronted suddenly by tourism. The nature, scale and speed of the introduction of tourism was seen as threatening what was viewed as undesirable
tourism-induced change of various sorts. More recently the tourism industry and the public sector organizations responsible for its planning and
management at the local level have begun to reflect such concerns in their
policy documents. In particular the idea of sustainable development has
been extended and applied to a social or community sustainability to be
pursued through 'responsible' policies not least in tourism. This is seen as
providing both a means of defining the goals of local policy but also as contributing the instruments through which such goals might be attained. It is
not the intention here to reiterate such concerns, illustrate their soundness
nor to investigate the validity of the use of the concept of sustainability as a
policy instrument in this way. Rather it is the purpose here to investigate
some aspects of the relationship between tourism and local communities
through questioning the universality of some of its common assumptions.

©CAB *International* 2003. *Tourism in Destination Communities*
(eds S. Singh, D.J. Timothy and R.K. Dowling)

The idea of heritage, that is the contemporary uses of the past, will be used here partly to limit an otherwise wide discussion and partly as a means of linking people and places through heritage as the vehicle for the creation and transmission of place identities. This is of course a variant on the well-known 'whose heritage?' question and equally well-known multiple answers to it. The relevance here is that heritage is intrinsically 'multivocal' (Graham, 1997: 3) that is, it is inevitably reflecting and transmitting the many different voices that have ascribed meanings to it; it is thus equally polysemic in conveying different messages, including in this case different place identities, either sequentially or synchronously. The introduction of tourism into this discussion adds two dimensions. First, heritage is both a resource for important tourism products and prime determinant of place specificity, which sells tourism destinations. Secondly, heritage has long been related to an idea of 'community' where objects, activities and people become transformed into the concepts of 'vernacular', 'craft' and 'folk'. Thus tourism becomes an additional user and creator of place identities shaped by a multi-sold heritage.

Exploring Assumptions

The argument cursorily outlined above contains a number of assumptions – not all of which are openly expressed but all of which can be questioned to some degree. These include assumptions about the nature of community, the nature of tourism and the nature of the goals for the destination management policies that may be devised.

Assumptions about community and place identity

Community has already been defined in many ways in this book and many of its dimensions explored. It remains here, therefore, only necessary to reiterate two points about its relationship to places. First, if communities are multiple and complex rather than unidimensional and inclusive, then tourism becomes one more ingredient in the mix, not merely an external influence. If community identities more resemble the nesting hierarchies of Russian dolls rather than a bank of mutually exclusive pigeon-holes then questions of priority arise. Simply which community of many is being considered, who represents it and do its interests conflict with those of other communities?

For example, there is an annual media event at Stonehenge, a megalithic monument in southern England, that could no doubt be replicated at other locations around the world that have become endowed with symbolic value for diverse interests (Chippendale, 1990). Various sundry interest groups including latter-day 'Druids', 'New Age travellers', 'extra-terrestrial believers' and many other religious or ideological groups express the wish to occupy the same physical space at the same time on Midsummer's Day. Various communities thus identify with the same sacralized heritage space. Those currently responsible for managing the site are a national public agency of a state that post-dates the structure by two millennia and regards it as an archaeological rather than religious object. They favour 'genuine' historical investigators and 'proper' tourists both of whom would be physically inconvenienced by the other groups. There is in addition the community of residents both local and national, who are politically represented, and whose interest may be the existence of the monument but not necessarily its active use by anyone. Clearly choices have to be made and priorities established on the basis of unclear criteria and undefined goals. The conflict that results in this case may be trivial but elsewhere in similar situations, for example at the Ayodhya temple/mosque site in India, in 1992, it led to riot and death.

Secondly, it cannot be assumed that there is a fixed unchanging relationship between community and location; between a cohesive social group and a physical setting with which they identify. Admittedly this may have been the norm since the introduction of settled agriculture but it cannot be assumed to be a universal condition. There are many communities without places, including those expressing a 'Diasporic' rather than place-bound nationalism (Kearns, 1998). Jews, at least before 1948, and currently Roma are obvious non-place bound communities as are, more mundanely, growing numbers of voluntary expatriates in an increasingly global labour market. The opposite idea of places existing without community and thus without identity results in the 'placelessness' described by Relph (1976) which is space without place, assuming that place is a community-induced identification with space.

More interesting for the argument here is that if the relationship between community and place is unstable through time then displacement is possible. The inherent mobility of both people and much of their heritage often results in their separation. This is the existence not of 'non-place', in the above sense but of the wrong place. There are two ways that this may occur. Either there is a change in the physical location of the community or there is a change in the nature of the place such that the community no longer identifies with it.

The relevance of the above discussion to tourism in particular is the underlying assumption that tourism is the active component in the relationship and conversely that local communities are passive reactors to tourism-induced change. Tourism is thus viewed as an exogenous variable exerting various influences upon otherwise stable communities. It may be that tourism can act as a mirror to local communities reflecting back to them a local identity that they can then adopt in some form. Indeed logically an isolated community will have no sense of the uniqueness or peculiarity of its own culture until the first visitor arrives and recognizes its distinctiveness. This extreme position is now relatively rare but tourism can still enhance and develop local cultures and senses of identity through its discovery and valuation of previously locally unappreciated aspects of the locality.

Assumptions about tourism and host communities

Underlying almost all discussion of the relationships between tourists and residents is the assumption that they are significantly different and there-fore generate different place identities, which allows competition to occur between them. However, this assumption can be questioned from two, admittedly contradictory, directions. First, tourism creates its own heritage and thus its own places. If it is accepted that heritage is a modern product created by the current users of it for their contemporary purposes then logically tourism creates the heritage it consumes. Consequently tourism places are created for and by the tourist. The assumption here is that tourists are in search of, and can only be sold, their heritage, which can be incorporated into their pre-existing mental constructs about the past. Conversely, the pasts required for the construction of heritage for con-sumption by local communities in fulfilment of their contemporary needs is not only quite different but results in a product which tourists are likely to find incomprehensible, irrelevant or in post-colonial contexts even distaste-ful, hostile and thus eminently rejectable. Consequently, as the consumer decides what is heritage, then in so far as tourists and local residents are assumed to be different in various ways then so will be the heritage. If the tourist is consuming a different product than the local users, even if created from the same resources from the past, then there is a parallel existence, even in the same physical space, of multiple places. Thus, compe-tition should not occur but plainly it does (see Robinson and Boniface's book (1998) significantly entitled *Cultural Conflict and Tourism*). Therefore it must be competition not for the same place but possibly for the same space in which to locate different places.

A second argument is that over the assumption that change occurs because tourists are different from residents and indeed that the wider the differences, the more serious the induced changes and the greater is the concern. However, again this may not be a universal or necessary condition of foreign tourism. Intra-European tourism accounts for most foreign tourism visits within the world system and economic, social and cultural differences between Europeans are matters of detail. Admittedly what remains are differences in behaviour and attitude between normal, or work situations, and leisure situations rather than fundamental differences of culture or economy. It can even be argued that the rise in importance of special interest tourism, which is in essence the continuing on holiday of activities and hobbies pursued at home, means that the tourist is often now merely a resident in a different place. If there are no substantial differences in living standard or lifestyle between tourist and host, or these are declining, then the argument of tourist-induced change either collapses or is diminished in significance. Indeed it is indicative that the cases generally chosen for investigation of such changes are those where such differences are most pronounced, which may be exceptional rather than typical.

Assumptions about the goals of local policy

Sustainable or responsible local policies are frequently defensive and even restorative. There are implied answers to the question, 'whose culture is it?' and its heritage variant, 'who owns the past?' It is assumed that not only can host communities and their interests be identified but that in multi-use competition with tourism they have an assumed priority.

It has now become almost a conventional wisdom among the custodians of heritage resources that local communities have an ethically superior claim to pasts and that previously prevalent policies for collection, display and interpretation of artefacts represent a form of cultural colonialism. Local cultures may even be seen as having been expropriated and not only 'stolen' but also often misused through misinterpretation or just lack of suitable respect for locally symbolically valued objects. It is further asserted that this should be modified or even corrected through the empowerment of local communities. In practice this may mean almost anything from just local consultations and cooperation with local communities in matters of interpretation, to returning artefacts, museums and sites to complete local community control. The logic of the argument is that heritage should not only be returned to local people but that it should be housed, cared for and interpreted by them and for their own purposes.

The implications of this growing respect for a community claim to the past to tourism uses is enormous, and is indeed only a part of a much wider community claim to control over almost all tourism resources. It has now become commonplace in tourism policy documents to accept the paramountcy of the local claim and to argue that tourism development will be permitted only in so far as it does not challenge such a claim. For example, the recent 'code of ethics' for museum presentations in the UK states, 'in spite of the general right to public access to museum collections, consider restricting access to certain specified items where unrestricted access may cause offence or distress to actual cultural descendants' (Museum Association, 1999: 4). In other words, an absolute right of veto on the accessibility of others should be given to anyone claiming a cultural descent, however that is determined, from the artefact. Such local policies are echoed internationally by ICOMOS/UNESCO conventions on 'repatriation' or 'de-Elginization' (in effect 're-nationalization') which expressly subordinates global claims, including that of tourism, to the local.

Given the now almost universal acceptance of the primacy of claims of the local community to 'their' culture and past, it may seem unacceptable to many to even question this assertion. However it does have a number of drawbacks. It may be merely passing control of the past from an international or national cultural elite to a local one which is not self-evidently more democratic or responsible. Secondly, what are the limits to destination community control over local heritage resources and do these extend to a monopoly of interpretation or access? Presumably host communities value heritage resources differently from others for if not then the return to community control would seem to have only a symbolic value with no implications for policy. Such differences may lead to different treatments and interpretations in a way that restricts or denies the claims of those outside such communities. Ultimately, and this problem has arisen, heritage could also be concealed or disposed of by them as being 'theirs to destroy', not 'ours to preserve'. It is perhaps worth remembering that iconoclasm is just the exercise of a local option to destroy cultural artefacts that offend local community values.

The obvious relevance to tourism of these assumptions inherent in much local cultural policy is that its role in the multi-use of heritage or consumption of place identities is reduced to that of a marginal development option. Tourism may be tolerated for its economic advantages only in so far as it does not compromise the local priority use.

Model

A more flexible and dynamic relationship between local and tourism senses of place could be modelled as a series of stages (Fig. 5.1).

First, there is assumed to exist a probably unreal, initial state of stable equilibrium in which local cultural identities are being constantly expressed through, and reinforced by, their local iconography, notably in the built environment. Then assume that tourists discover or are attracted to the area by its communicated sense of place. Tourism as it develops induces change. Tourism is inevitably selective of those easily recognizable, reproducible and sellable components of the place identity, which it simplifies, homogenizes and stereotypes. Local cultural artefacts are globalized through the 'creolization' process described by Schimany (1997). This may be seen as clarifying and strengthening the distinctive character of places for a wider market or as a loss of subtlety and variation in the sense of

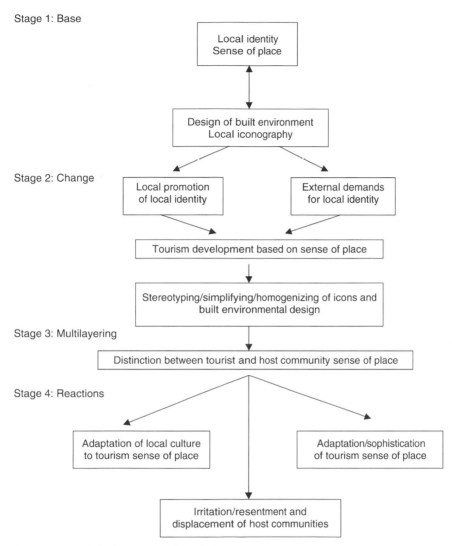

Fig. 5.1. Model of tourism-induced change.

place. This process of change leads to a gap developing between the sense of place projected to, and consumed by, tourists and that required by locals for their place identification.

The third hypothesized phase is the emergence of at least two quite different senses of place, one for tourist and the other for local consumption. These may coexist in mutual spatial or functional isolation (in marketing terminology the markets are segmented and separated). The final stage hypothesizes three possible adjustments to this situation. First, destination communities can adjust their place images to that of the tourists as they come to accept and incorporate in their own self-image the identity projected to them by visitors. They assume the identity that has been sold and is now reflected back to them. A process of imitation and identification leads to adaptation and acculturation (Schimany, 1997). Secondly, however, if tourism continues to develop then the tourist sense of place can, over time, become more diversified and nuanced, reselecting much that was previously rejected or overlooked. It becomes more 'authentic', powered by the need within tourism to constantly diversify the product as a reaction to both the volatile fashion-prone character of tourism markets as well as the increasing sophistication of visitors to this destination. The tourist search for the 'authentic' is rewarded by a sense of place perceived as being much closer to that of the residents. The third reaction is when these different place identities lead to a form of heritage dissonance (Tunbridge and Ashworth, 1997). The multilayering of identities may not matter but may, in certain circumstances, result in the cultural, economic and, even on occasion, physical, displacement of locals who no longer feel 'at home' in the tourist place. The seriousness of this is likely to be determined by the coincidence of difference in place identity with other differences in the economic or political fields. These may have little relation to the activity of tourism, which thus becomes a symbol and focus of more far-reaching economic or political problems.

The existence and policy implications of such hypothesized processes will now be examined in some case studies.

Three Case Studies

The arguments and model outlined above could be tested almost anywhere. Three examples are selected here which differ widely in size and situation but share the characteristics of a strongly developed tourism sense of place. None of the cases described below are complete descriptions of either tourism development or of local host communities but focus upon a single specific point relevant to this argument. On the island of Newfoundland a relatively homogeneous local community which had changed little for 400 years became redefined largely through the tourism image projected to others. In the state of New Mexico a more complex multilayered local society sold an image of itself to tourists and then largely adopted that image. Finally, in the Kazimierz district of the city of Kraków quite recent heritage tourism development has been based upon the heritage of a locally defunct community, which raises the possibility of conflict between exclave heritage tourism and local identity.

Newfoundland

The historical context for the development of tourism on the island of Newfoundland can be cursorily summarized. Four centuries of European settlement resulted in an economic and social monoculturalism. The dependence upon fishing of a culturally homogeneous and socially conservative society prompted official attempts at modernization, which was broadly defined as economic and social diversification and globalization. Tourism was seen as a crucial instrument in this modernization process and was expected to deliver not only new economic benefits but also new social attitudes.

The introduction of railway and ferry routes at the end of the 19th century made the markets of industrial-urban societies accessible at just the time when their populations were obtaining the means and desire to experience precisely the tourism products that Newfoundland could provide (Stuckless, 1986).

Two resources could be commodified for tourism and in both the previously commonplace was recognized as exceptional. First, the physical geography viewed by the inhabitants of 'The Rock' as a negative barrier was transformed into the marketable 'wilderness'. This wilderness also consisted of the rocky coastline and inland 'Barrens' together with their wildlife, which were previously viewed by locals as an obstacle to be ignored or a resource and food source to be exploited. It now became something to be conquered (sport hunting and fishing), defied (wilderness survival and trekking), or just looked at (romantic environmentalism) by tourists. It was marketed as a product to be traversed, felt, viewed, eaten or just preserved to be known about. Secondly, the mundane paraphernalia, settlement patterns and social conventions of fishing communities became 'the timeless tradition of simple fisherfolk' (Overton, 1988: 12). The social isolation of fishing communities, their musical, linguistic, craft and attitudinal survivals was the resource for the invention of 'Newfoundland tradition', a sort of 'rural fundamentalism' in the 'last stronghold of non-industrial values' (Mowat, 1972).

Tourism for a small wealthy elite at the end of the 19th century was expanded in the inter-war period by The Newfoundland Tourism Commission (founded in 1925) of the self-governing Dominion and after 1949 by the Department of Tourism, Culture and Recreation of the Canadian Province. Its economic success was patchy (Province of Newfoundland and Labrador, 1992, 1994, 1996), its attempt to become 'Canada's Ocean Playground' was contested, especially by Nova Scotia, but a strong image of an unspoilt wilderness inhabited by unspoilt people was successfully promoted (Overton, 1980). This has been expressed by a series of popular novels on the romance of the Newfoundland outport such as Mowat (1972, 1989),

MacFarlane (1991) and Proulx (1993), the last currently generating a 'Proulx tourism'.

The successful creation of the Newfoundland tourism image had a social impact that was not only unexpected but also quite contrary to the original social modernization programme. The local community became the 'Newfies' sold to tourists. The fishing outport that modernizing governments had tried to eliminate has become not only the valued tourism product (Ashworth, 1998) but also the symbol of Newfoundland identity. The tourism identity has proved unhelpful in attracting other economic activities or encouraging social change. Romantic wilderness becomes inconvenient isolation and quaint cultural survivals become old-fashioned backwardness. 'In trying to escape the capitalist consumer bubble and the world of staged authenticity and mass tourism, many seek simpler lifestyles and real culture in places like Newfoundland. What exists in such backwaters, however, is poverty, unemployment, inequality and desperation' (Overton, 1996: 168). The image has locked the island into a traditionalism from which it has proved very difficult to escape.

The case of Newfoundland therefore contradicts some of the assumptions discussed above. There was little local self-awareness until tourism developed and tourism-induced social and economic change was an explicit objective of such development. However, the image promoted for tourists was largely adopted by Newfoundlanders with profound, unexpected and generally unwelcome local economic and social consequences.

New Mexico

The state of New Mexico in the south-west USA is inhabited by at least three major ethnic/cultural communities. First, there are the Native Americans, or Indians (Tiwa, Tewa, Hopi, Navajo and Zuni) who pre-date European settlement, and whose distinctive pueblo settlements are 'adobe' (i.e. sun-dried mud and straw) houses grouped together in irregular stepped 'high-rise' clusters often as much as six or seven storeys high. Secondly, the Hispanic explorers, gold seekers, missionaries and settlers date from the 16th century. They created distinctive 'praesidio' government towns (e.g. Santa Fé 1610, Socorro 1615, Albuquerque 1705) and isolated haciendas along the broad valley of the Rio Grande and its tributaries. Finally, the 'Anglo' settlers, traders, fur trappers and adventurers arrived from the north-east after Mexican independence, using the Santa Fé Trail from Kansas after 1822 (Brown, 1988), conquering and annexing the territory between 1846 and 1848.

Tourism developed mainly from the very end of the 19th century when the coming of the railways allowed the myths of 'the west' to be visited by North Americans (Bryan, 1988; Howard and Pardue, 1996). In New Mexico it was powered specifically by a combination of art, climate and perceived 'Latin' lifestyles. Artists and connoisseurs were attracted by the light and climate of the plateau around Santa Fé and Taos at the end of the 19th century. They became themselves a part of the attraction for both other artists and tourists who incorporated art into their sense of place and found the presence of artists a validation of their own decision to visit. The art and crafts of both the Indians and Hispanics proved a source of cultural inspiration, and this, together with the relaxed way of life, created a potent range of tourism products for sale on US markets. The local Anglo merchants and political leaders were not slow to recognize the value of this place image to tourism and other economic activities. The result was substantial tourism development selling a commodified hybrid of Spanish/Indian designs and lifestyles, as viewed through the creations of the New Mexico 'school of art'. The period 1920–1940 was the heyday of practising artists personified in Georgia O'Keeffe (O'Keeffe, 1939) whose house at Abiquiu is a major tourist attraction. This effectively created what became known as the Santa Fé style of architecture and design (Wilson, 1996).

This was in part a preservation movement and in part a reconstruction or rediscovery of what had been, or might have been. The most visible, memorable and reproducible manifestations of the style are in vernacular architecture and civic design. There was the legacy in the town plan itself with the 'Plaza' as the central multifunctional space (Rodríguez, 1994), as in Santa Fé, Taos or Albuquerque, generally flanked by the symbolic government buildings (notably the 'Palace of the Governors', Santa Fé). The church whether in the towns or the missions among the Indians (such as St Francis Assisi, Taos or San Miguel Mission, Santa Fé) and the rural haciendas (e.g. Martinez Hacienda, Taos) form distinctive and prominent symbolic landscape elements. The buildings are increasingly designed, or decorated, in a self-conscious adobe style with rounded walls and parapets, flat roofs and protruding roof beam supports. The establishment of the Old Santa Fé Association in the 1920s, and later the Historic Santa Fé Foundation, was a powerful force for conformity with this style. Museums and galleries (e.g. The Santa Fé Museum of Fine Art, 1917; The Wheelwright Museum of the American Indian, 1937) were also initiated as were such events as Hispanic fiestas and Indian markets. Themed hotels such as the La Fonda in Santa Fé opened in the 1920s. The architecture accommodates and reflects a lifestyle seen as vaguely both Latin and Native American with an emphasis upon 'authentic' crafts and customs that are seen as having both aesthetic and moral value. There is thus a combination of a folk heritage idea with *La Vie Boheme* and a perceived relaxed Mediterranean lifestyle.

In the course of time these images and expressions of a local culture, originally promoted for others, became themselves adopted by local communities as part of their own self-identity. The dynamic interaction between local and tourism cultures continues. The adoption by locals of what was originally intended for tourism, particularly the fiestas and markets, further authenticates the tourism experience for the visitor. Tourists meanwhile, in search of the ever more authentic, 'discover' or are sold by locals, aspects of the local culture hitherto unknown by either group, which in turn may be subsequently locally adopted as part of an expanding vernacular. This sense of place could be seen as a compromise or hybridization, in so far as it contains elements drawn from the major cultural groups and is marketed to both tourists and residents. The dominant established place image of contemporary New Mexico for internal and external consumption is neither Spanish colonial nor American western but a distinctive Santa Fé Style (see Arreola, 1995 for a similar discussion of the 20th century creation of a hybrid 'Tex-Mex' San Antonio). The process through which it was created makes it very difficult, and probably pointless, to separate tourist from local community heritage let alone adjudicate on which came first or which should be awarded primacy of concern.

Kraków-Kazimierz

Relating local communities to local heritage and further introducing tourism into the equation becomes especially complex when considering the Jewish Holocaust. Who should own, preserve, interpret and manage, in whose interest, the heritage of ghettos, stetls and camps? This raises wider issues including the sensitivity needed when managing atrocity heritage for tourist entertainment. However, especially relevant in this argument are the situations of community without heritage and heritage without community.

The first case is where local communities deliberately disinherit themselves or are disinherited by others. Allied and later German authorities systematically demolished and concealed potential heritage and sites associated with the Nazi regime either because local communities did not wish it to be part of their place identity or because of concerns that other, later, undesirable ideological communities would use it to sacralize places as symbolically valuable to them. Policies of deliberately induced collective amnesia, the obverse of collective memory, may be essentially benign and in the perceived interests of the local community or part of a heritage cleansing designed to undermine the identity of a local community (van der Kooij, 1993). In both cases, however, the introduction of heritage tourism would be highly unwelcome to either the local community or the governing authorities.

The second case is where heritage is created for a local community that no longer exists in that locality. The result is to create an exclave heritage divorced from local inhabitants. The increasing use of holocaust heritage as tourism resources has brought this issue into sharper focus in many parts of Europe. There are intrinsic difficulties in using the heritage of atrocity for the creation of entertainment products in a leisure industry. These difficulties are exacerbated when it is not clear which pasts, and whose pasts, are to be interpreted by whom and to whom. These difficulties are repeated in numerous memorialized camps, cemeteries, synagogues and sites of former ghettos across Europe (Charlesworth, 1994).

The Kazimierz district of Kraków (Fig. 5.2) was one of the largest and oldest districts of legalized continuous Jewish settlement in a Poland that accommodated the largest Ashkenazi Jewish community and provided the largest number of victims of the 'final solution'. Jews achieved some legal recognition and self-government in a walled ghetto in the 15th century and the town became a major centre of Jewish religious and cultural life in Central Europe. It was, however, never exclusively Jewish, housing many other often socially or economically marginal groups. For most of its history the majority of the population was Christian and consequently the most spectacular heritage buildings are Christian churches. German occupation

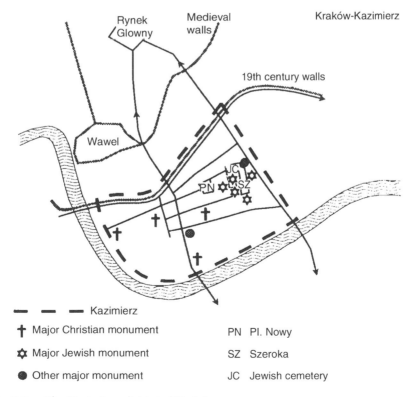

Fig. 5.2. The Kazimierz district of Kraków.

in 1939 led first to a concentration of the Jewish population, estimated to number 65,000 (Gilbert, 1997) and finally deportation and elimination in March 1943.

Kraków had a long established cultural tourism industry that burgeoned after the 1990 relaxation of travel and the return of the cities of Central Europe to the European art city tourism circuits. The numbers of foreign visitors doubled to 500,000 between 1987 and 1992. Small numbers of visitors made their way into Kazimierz in the 1960s and 1970s, generally seeking out the remnants of Jewish occupation motivated by a direct family link (Guber, 1992). Although the Kazimierz district lacked tourism facilities or even much interpretative marking until recently, it was well located to reap some spillover effects from the expanding Kraków tourism. The popularization of Keneally's book by Spielberg's 1993 film, *Schindler's List*, which was filmed in Kazimierz although it described historical events that had occurred at Pozgodze on the other bank of the Vistula, was the catalyst for rapid tourism development focusing specifically upon Kazimierz. A worldwide notoriety for the district led to a demand for 'Schindler tourism' focused especially on the evocatively photogenic cluster of synagogues, cemeteries and now also Jewish restaurants in the north-east of Kazimierz (Fig. 5.2). It is also significant that the Auschwitz camp is nearby and one of the main tourism excursion destinations of visitors to Kraków so that ghetto and camp can be combined in a single 'Auschwitzland' package (Hartmann, 1998).

The question, 'what is the contribution of this heritage, and the tourism it generates, to place identity?' can be answered from the position of at least three communities. First, the worldwide Jewish community provides most of the tourists, especially from the USA and Israel. It has also contributed much of the financing for the restoration of the remaining synagogues and cemeteries and for the Jewish Cultural Centre. The presence of Jewish tourists and the marketability of holocaust heritage to non-Jewish visitors has encouraged the establishment of some Jewish restaurants, souvenir and information sites, public exhibitions and signage. The fundamental difficulty for the local authority is how to restore a Jewish settlement without Jewish inhabitants. The result is a clear case of 'exclave heritage' where what is perceived as someone else's heritage is inserted in response to exogenous demand, into a district.

Secondly, the wider Polish nation can see Kazimierz heritage as either commemoration of longstanding Polish tolerance in a multi-religious city or as atonement for their active or passive collaboration in genocide. Poles, or more specifically Catholic Poles, can be viewed as fellow victims or as associate perpetrators. Selling Kazimierz to Poles, whether as tourists or as residents, raises these interpretation issues and also the question of which Kazimierz, Christian or Jewish, is to be sold?

Finally, the reaction of the existing local inhabitants to the exclave heritage is largely negative. This is not just a revival of anti-semitism among economically deprived Christians, provoked by the re-insertion of a rich foreign implant, and rich foreign visitors, into their locality. The present inhabitants are among the poorest groups in the city and many are re-housed migrants displaced from the eastern territories lost in 1945. The houses, public utilities and spaces are in poor condition and in obvious need of renovation. Resentment at the concentration of resources upon the heritage of a group that no longer exists is compounded by the fear of displacement through the return of expropriated property to the heirs of previous owners. The presence of a resuscitated Jewish heritage raises not only the question of 'whose heritage?' but also more immediately threateningly 'whose property?'

The important lesson from Kraków-Kazimierz is that host communities cannot be awarded an automatic paramount claim to local heritage, for if they were, then Jewish Kazimierz would not now exist. The heritage of the Holocaust is not the exclusive property of the present local inhabitants nor even of the geographically distant descendants of its victims. The complex ethical dimensions of the problem are compounded by mundane economic and social realities. The local authority welcomes the windfall economic gains that foreign tourists offer and the stimulus that tourism provides for local investment. However there is also a recognition that the urban renewal needed to transform near valueless property into valuable real estate gains little from tourism and is actively hindered by potential Jewish claims for property restitution. Most of the present inhabitants do not have the financial resources to renovate the area and the gentrification that might encourage private investment in this historic and centrally located district derives few gains from its Jewish identity. The 'gentrifying' Polish middle class are unlikely to relate to the Jewish heritage and the tourism it generates and may well be reluctant to invest in, and populate, a reconstructed 'ghetto' whose heritage is memorialized atrocity and conflict.

The development plan produced with international cooperation (ECOS, 1995) recognized many of the difficulties outlined above, identified the investment needs, and suggested scenarios for cultural tourism development in the context of local urban renewal. Implementation however has involved many other actors, from Kraków and elsewhere, with more varied motives and interests. The fundamental issues of heritage, identity and community make even quite trivial and routine local management measures contentious and provocative. In particular the management of tourism as a catalyst for local change demands such an extreme sensitivity in detail that this plan has not yet been implemented (Ashworth, 1996; Ashworth and Tunbridge, 1999).

Conclusion: the Limits and Possibilities of Policy

The cases discussed above are unique in the detailing of their problems and policy solutions, but the issues they raise are echoed widely elsewhere. The only universal conclusion to this discussion of heritage, tourism, identities and communities is perhaps the need to be aware of simplistic assumptions and beware of simplistic policy solutions.

The case studies speak for themselves and should not be summarized here. It remains only to attempt to dispel any lingering feeling of the powerlessness of policy in the face of these complex, multifaceted and intractable issues, where the introduction of tourism into an already fraught relationship of local communities with local place identities compounds an already convoluted situation. Two more optimistic management lifelines are offered here. These are labelled for convenience, the 'Disneyland effect' and the 'replication of Venice' although each is a general condition applicable beyond the eponymous places.

The Walt Disney Corporation can be taken to be the creator of the archetypal recreational theme park and is more usually associated with the entertainment than the heritage industry. However, it has long pioneered the re-creation of historical experiences such as the 'Wild West', which have been very influential in shaping popular visions of the past. Take, for example, the Disney invention of 'Mainstreet USA', a pastiche of buildings and facilities, that might have been found on the main street of a US town before such environments, the lifestyles and values they reflected, were destroyed by the auto-dominated suburb. The success of this exhibit in evoking a popular nostalgia and establishing in the popular imagination the existence of a past much to be desired led directly to 'Mainstreet' town planning programmes in North America that attempted to recreate such physical environments. A product created for tourism became a desirable past for local communities to be recreated in support of local identities. This raises the more generally applicable point that tourism, far from always posing a threat to local identities, can create heritage, which later becomes centrally significant for local communities. The 'Disney effect' demonstrates the effectiveness of deliberate planning action

A second condition, the 'replication of Venice', illustrates the point that problems of local conflict between users of place identities may often be self-inflicted and are thus easily resolvable. In the well-documented case of Venice, a substantial tourism industry is highly concentrated into a small part of the lagoon city. City managers and tourism researchers alike (Costa and van der Borg, 1993; van der Borg, 1998) define the problem as an excess of demand over supply, leading to conflict between users, displacement of local communities and serious damage to both the physical resources and the quality of the place experience.

Policy solutions therefore have focused on ways of prioritizing users and limiting demand according to predetermined carrying capacities. Meritorious users include local residents, 'serious' students of art or architecture and high-spending visitors. Policies to favour these at the expense of the others are operationalized through controlling access both to and within the lagoon city, determining the types and costs of tourism facilities available and influencing the flows of information. However, the problem arises because the essential Venice has been defined as the spatially restricted area around Piazza San Marco and the routes across the Accademia and Rialto bridges across the Grand Canal to Piazza Roma. Venice can be enlarged and more Venices created if this area were to be expanded into the currently largely unvisited, neighbouring 'campos', on to other lagoon islands and beyond to the Venetian colonies from Chioggia, through Capodistria, Ragusa and across the Eastern Mediterranean. The principal objection to doing this comes from those who argue that there can only be one unique Venice, which is located only where they say it is. Thus, the authenticators of the heritage and the 'markers' of the tourism resources claim to be the sole arbiters of what is, or is not, 'real' Venice. They therefore restrict, for their own motives, the place-product and then volubly express their concern for the well-being of these products when they are inevitably overused. The conflict has thus been created by the very custodians of the resources of the past who are most vociferous in their complaints about tourism use. If place identities can be created then it follows that places are reproducible and tourism places are more easily replicated than most.

If the answer to the question, 'which community is using which heritage to shape which identity?' is 'many' then multiple place identities responding to the needs of multiple communities are quite inevitable. Conflict, however, is neither inevitable nor unresolvable as identities, and the heritage that expresses and supports them, are community creations. That which was created by deliberate intervention can equally be managed by it.

References

Arreola, D.D. (1995) Urban ethnic landscape identity. *Geographical Review* 85, 518–534.

Ashworth, G.J. (1996) Jewish culture and holocaust tourism: the lessons of Kraków-Kazimierz. In: Robinson, M., Evans, N. and Callaghan, P. (eds) *Tourism and Culture: Towards the 21st Century.* University of Northumbria, Newcastle, pp. 1–13.

Ashworth, G.J. (1998) The Newfoundland outport: the unsaleable tourism product. *Trident* Spring, 4–5.

Ashworth, G.J. and Tunbridge, J.E. (1999) Old cities, new pasts: heritage planning in the cities of Central Europe. *Geojournal* 49, 105–116.

Brown, W.E. (1988) *The Santa Fé Trail.* Patrice Press, St Louis.

Bryan, H. (1988) *Wildest of the Wild West: True Tales of a Frontier Town on the Santa Fé Trail.* Clearlight Publishers, Santa Fé.

Charlesworth, A. (1994) Contesting places of memory: the case of Auschwitz. *Environment and Planning A* 12, 579–593.

Chippendale, C. (1990) *Who Owns Stonehenge?* Batsford, London.

Costa, P. and van der Borg, J. (1993) *The Management of Tourism in Cities of Art.* University of Venice, Venice.

ECOS (1995) *Kazimierz Action Plan.* Viator, Kraków.

Gilbert, M. (1997) *Holocaust Journey.* Phoenix, London.

Graham, B.J. (1997) *Modern Europe: Place, Culture, Identity.* Arnold, London.

Guber, R.E. (1992) *Jewish Heritage Travel: a Guide to Central and Eastern Europe.* John Wiley & Sons, New York.

Hartmann, R. (1998) Dealing with Dachau in geographic education. In: Briodsky, H. (ed.) *Land and Community: Geography in Jewish Studies.* University Press of Maryland, Bethesda, pp. 125–137.

Howard, K.L. and Pardue, D.F. (1996) *Inventing the South West.* Northland, Flagstaff, Arizona.

Kearns, L. (1998) Nationalism and identity. Paper presented at International Conference of Historical Geographers, Queen's University, Belfast.

MacFarlane, D. (1991) *Coming from Away.* Macfarlane, Walter and Ross, Toronto.

Mowat, F. (1972) *A Whale for the Killing.* McClelland and Stewart, Toronto.

Mowat, F. (1989) *The New Founde Land: a Personal Voyage of Discovery.* McClelland and Stewart, Toronto.

Museums Association (1999) *Codes of Ethics.* Museums Association, London.

O'Keeffe, G. (1939) *About Myself: Catalogue to Georgia O'Keeffe Exhibition.* Georgia O'Keeffe Exhibition, New York.

Overton, J. (1980) Promoting the real Newfoundland: culture as tourist commodity. *Studies in Political Economy* 4, 115–137.

Overton, J. (1988) Is there a Newfoundland culture? *Journal of Canadian Studies* 23(1), 5–22.

Overton, J. (1996) *Making a World of a Difference: Essays on Tourism, Culture and Development in Newfoundland.* Memorial University, St John's.

Proulx, E.A. (1993) *The Shipping News.* Touchstone, New York.

Province of Newfoundland and Labrador (1992) *Strategic Economic Plan.* Government of Newfoundland, St John's.

Province of Newfoundland and Labrador (1994) *A Vision for Tourism in Newfoundland in the Twenty-first Century.* Department of Tourism, Culture and Recreation, St John's.

Province of Newfoundland and Labrador (1996) *Tourism Strategy.* Department of Tourism, Culture and Recreation, St John's.

Relph, E. (1976) *Place and Placelessness.* Pion, London.

Robinson, M. and Boniface, P. (1998) *Tourism and Cultural Conflicts.* CAB International, Wallingford.

Rodríguez, S. (1994) Subaltern historiography on the Rio Grande: on Gutiérrez's 'When Jesus came, the corn mothers went away'. *American Ethnologist* 21, 892–899.

Schimany, P. (1997) Soziokulturelle Auswirkungen des Tourismus. *Papiere zur Sozialwissenschaft* 16, 34–46.

Stuckless, A. (1986) *The Tourism Industry in Newfoundland and Labrador.* The Queen's Printer, St John's.

Tunbridge, J.E. and Ashworth, G.J. (1997) *Dissonant Heritage: Managing the Past as a Resource in Conflict.* John Wiley & Sons, Chichester.

van der Borg, J. (1998) Tourism management in Venice, or how to deal with success. In: Tyler, D., Guerrier, Y. and Robertson, M. (eds) *Managing Tourism in Cities.* John Wiley & Sons, Chichester, pp. 125–135.

van der Kooij, G. (1993) Archaeologie en maatschappij in de zuidelijke Levant: de keuze van een verleden. *Archaelogisch Informatie Cahiers* 5, 60–68.

Wilson, C. (1996) *The Myth of Santa Fé: Creating a Modern Regional Tradition.* University of New Mexico Press, Albuquerque.

Politics and Place: an Analysis of Power in Tourism Communities

6

C. Michael Hall

Department of Tourism, Otago University, Dunedin, New Zealand

Introduction

The concept of community has been significant in tourism, and tourism planning in particular, for over 20 years. Indeed, the central role of the 'community' in tourism planning has come to be recognized as one of the tenets of sustainable and socially responsible tourism. However, while community-based planning is an important driver in academic and bureaucratic approaches to tourism development (Murphy, 1985, 1988), it is important to recognize that such an approach does not automatically lead to either sustainable tourism development or even a reduction in the amount of conflict surrounding tourism development. Instead, as Hall (2000) argued, a local focus allows for the dynamics of the planning process to be altered as stakeholders face their interdependencies at a place-specific level. A key point being that the local should not be romanticized, as so often seems to be the case in discussions of tourism planning. As Millar and Aiken (1995: 629) observed:

> Communities are not the embodiment of innocence; on the contrary, they
> are complex and self-serving entities, as much driven by grievances, preju-
> dices, inequalities, and struggles for power as they are united by kinship,
> reciprocity, and interdependence. Decision-making at the local level can be
> extraordinarily vicious, personal, and not always bound by legal constraints.

Nevertheless, a community-based approach provides the possibility that the necessity to consult over the use of shared resources and the needs of neighbours opens the way for resolution over tourism conflicts. Perhaps more significantly with a reduction in the extent of formal government procedures in much of the Western world as part of a push towards 'smaller government' and 'public–private partnership', a community-based process of management and conflict resolution may provide for greater informality in personal relationships between stakeholders in which trust is able to develop (Hall, 2000). When examining the role of the community in tourism it is impossible to separate the social, economic and political processes operating within a community from the conflict which occurs between stakeholders. Conflict and disagreement between members of a community over the outputs and outcomes of tourism are, in fact, the norm. As Millar and Aiken (1995: 620) commented:

> Conflict is a normal consequence of human interaction in periods of change, the product of a situation where the gain or a new use by one party is felt to involve a sacrifice or changes by others. It can be an opportunity for creative problem solving, but if it is not managed properly conflict can divide a community and throw it into turmoil.

Tourism planners therefore typically have to find accommodation between various stakeholders and interests in tourism development in an attempt to arrive at outcomes acceptable to stakeholders within the wider community (Hall, 2000). Indeed, much of the recent burst of activity in the tourism literature regarding cooperation and collaboration in tourism destinations is a direct response to the need to find mechanisms to accommodate the various interests that exist in tourism development (e.g. Selin, 1993, 1998; Selin and Chavez, 1994; Jamal and Getz, 1995; Timothy, 1998). However, this then raises a number of very important questions regarding the processes that occur within communities, particularly with respect to which stakeholders have the greatest ability to achieve their aims and why. It is for this reason that the role of politics and power in tourism needs to be studied.

Politics and Power

The study of politics is inexorably the study of power. Politics is about power, who gets what, where, how and why (Lasswell, 1936). Decisions affecting tourism, the nature of government involvement in tourism, the structure of agencies responsible for tourism development, management, marketing and promotion, the nature of tourism in tourism development, and the identification and representation of tourism resources and attractions, such as heritage, within communities all emerge from a political process. This process involves the values of actors (individuals, interest groups and public and private organizations) in a struggle for power. As Lindblom (1959: 82) noted, 'One chooses among values and among policies at one and the same time'. Similarly, Simmons *et al.* (1974: 457) noted that, 'It is value choice, implicit and explicit, which orders the priorities of government and determines the commitment of resources within the public jurisdiction.'

Politics denotes the struggle over scarce resources, the domination of one group over another and the potential exercise of state control. Mainstream tourism research has either neglected or ignored the inherently political nature of tourism. However, in recent years, the political issues associated with heritage representation have increasingly come into focus, particularly with respect to indigenous peoples and control of their heritage (Hewison, 1987; Hollinshead, 1992). Nevertheless, with few exceptions, questions regarding the political dimensions of tourism and place and the power of certain interests within a community to dominate over other interests have not received the attention they deserve (Hall, 1994; Hall and Jenkins, 1995; Morgan and Pritchard, 1998). As Thrift and Forbes (1983: 247) declared, 'any satisfactory account of politics and the political must contain the element of human conflict; of groups of human beings in constant struggle with each other over resources and ideas about the distribution of resources'.

The study of politics and power arrangements is therefore vital in the analysis of the political dimensions of tourism at the community level because power governs 'the interplay of individuals, organizations, and agencies influencing, or trying to influence the direction of policy' (Lyden *et al.*, 1969: 6). Within the processes of tourism development and management, certain issues may be suppressed, relationships between parties and stakeholders altered, or inaction may be the order of the day. Critical to this may be the design and structure of institutional or organizational arrangements for tourism (Hall and Jenkins, 1995). 'All forms of political organization have a bias in favour of the exploitation of some kinds of conflict, and the suppression of others, because organization is the mobilization of bias. Some issues are organized into politics while some others are organized out' (Schattsneider, 1960: 71). Those who benefit from tourism development may well be placed in a preferred position to defend and promote their interests through the structures and institutions by which communities are managed. Significantly, the influential models of community tourism promoted by Murphy (1985) clearly fail to address issues of power and representation in a community approach. Indeed, the appendix at the end of Murphy's (1985) book provides the example of Tourism Victoria in Canada in which the organization of the community interest in tourism is clearly seen in relation to the tourism industry rather than the wider community.

The very notion of 'power', one of the cornerstones of political analysis, is an 'essentially contested' concept (Gallie, 1955–1956). Power may be conceptualized as, 'all forms of successful control by A over B – that is, of A securing B's compliance' (Lukes, 1974: 17). The use of the concept of power is inextricably linked to a given set of value assumptions, which predetermine the range of its empirical application. Lukes has constructed a typology of power and related concepts in an effort to clarify their meaning and relationship (Table 6.1).

Lukes (1974) identified three different approaches, or dimensions, in the analysis of power, each focusing on different aspects of the decision-making process:

- One-dimensional view emphasizing observable, overt behaviour, conflict and decision-making.
- Two-dimensional view, which recognizes decisions and non-decisions, observable (overt or covert) conflict, and which represents a qualified critique of the behavioural stance of the one-dimensional view.
- Three-dimensional view, which focuses on decision-making and control over the political agenda (not necessarily through decisions), and which recognizes observable (overt or covert) and latent conflict.

The third dimension of power bears significant parallels to the work of Foucault (1972) on power. However, the agency exerting power is located

Table 6.1. Typology of power and related concepts. Sources: Bachrach and Baratz (1970: 24, 28, 30, 34) and Lukes (1974: 17).

Concept	Meaning
Authority	B complies because he/she recognizes that A's command is reasonable in terms of his/her own values, either because its content is legitimate and reasonable or because it has been arrived at through a legitimate and reasonable procedure
Coercion	Exists where A secures B's compliance by the threat of deprivation where there is a conflict over values or course of action between A and B
Force	A achieves his objectives in the face of B's non-compliance
Influence	Exists where A, without resorting to either a tacit or overt threat of severe deprivation, causes B to change his course of action
Manipulation	Is an 'aspect' or sub-concept of force (and distant from coercion, power, influence and authority) since here compliance is forthcoming in the absence of recognition on the compiler's part either of the source or the exact nature of demand upon him
Power	All forms of successful control by A over B – that is, of A securing B's compliance

locally in the work of Lukes (1974), in that Lukes is readily able to identify local agency, citing the example of Crenson (1971), and more globally in the writings of Foucault, where broader knowledge is regarded as operating.

Each of the three dimensions arises out of, and operates within, a particular political perspective as the concept of power is 'ineradicably value-dependent' (Lukes, 1974: 26). For example, a pluralist conception of the tourism policy-making process, such as that which underlies the notion of community-based tourism planning (e.g. Murphy, 1985, 1988; Haywood, 1988), will focus on different aspects of the decision-making process, than structuralist conceptions of politics, which highlight social relations within the consumption of tourist services (e.g. Urry, 1990a,b; Britton, 1991). These distinctions are significant for our understanding of tourism. As Britton (1991: 475) recognized:

> we need a theorization that explicitly recognizes, and unveils, tourism as a predominantly capitalistically organized activity driven by the inherent and defining social dynamics of that system, with its attendant production, social, and ideological relations. An analysis of how the tourism production system markets and packages people is a lesson in the political economy of the social construction of 'reality' and social construction of place, whether from the point of view of visitors and host communities, tourism capital (and the 'culture industry'), or the state – with its diverse involvement in the system.

However, given the need to understand the dominant groups and ideologies operating within the political and administrative system that surrounds heritage tourism, it seems reasonable to assume that the use of a wide conception of power, capable of identifying decisions, non-decisions and community political structure, will provide the most benefit in the analysis of the political dimensions of tourism (Hall, 1994; Hall and Jenkins, 1995).

One-dimensional views of community decision-making

A somewhat romantic and naive view of community tourism holds that everyone has equal access to power and representation. To an extent this has been one of the driving elements behind utilizing the community as an appropriate framework for planning for tourism development as there appears to be an inherent assumption that it is somehow 'closer to the people'. The one-dimensional view is closely related to a pluralist notion of power which contends that power is diffused and balanced in modern societies so that there is no one group or class which dominates decision-making and planning and that decisions are ultimately legitimized through electoral and legal processes. In addition, the pluralist perspective, originally associated with Dahl (1961) through his studies of community decision-making, contends that 'conflicts' can be dealt with through the 'checks and balances' of the political system. However, public participation in tourism planning has long been recognized as imperfect. For example, Dowling (1993: 53) noted 'research into community attitudes towards tourism is reasonably well developed, although incorporation of such views into the planning process is far less common'. Jenkins (1993) identified seven impediments to incorporating public participation in tourism planning.

1. The public generally has difficulty in comprehending complex and technical planning issues.
2. The public is not always aware of, or understands, the decision-making process.
3. The difficulty in attaining and maintaining representativeness in the decision-making process.
4. The apathy of citizens.
5. The increased costs in terms of staff and money.
6. The prolonging of the decision-making process.
7. Adverse effects on the efficiency of decision-making.

Nevertheless, a one-dimensional view of power in communities suggests that even though imperfect, the community decision-making process is at least visible. An example of how such visibility may be interpreted would be in relation to a tourism development proposal that goes through the standard local government planning tribunal decision-making process in which a proposal is mooted, comments and input called for from those with an interest. A decision is then made by a planning tribunal, often by a vote, in which discussions regarding the decision have been made in a setting in which anyone is able to observe and listen to proceedings and the arguments presented. The decision may then be in complete favour of the proponent, or may suggest modifications to the development proposal, or it may be rejected outright.

Yet power is not evenly distributed within a community and some groups and individuals have the ability to exert greater influence over the tourism planning process than others through their access to financial resources, expertise, public relations, media, knowledge and time to put into contested situations (Hall and Jenkins, 1995). Therefore, in some circumstances, the level of wider public involvement in tourism planning can be more accurately described as a form of tokenism in which decisions or the direction of decisions has already been prescribed by local government by virtue of other policies and decisions. For example, that which led to the election of certain representatives over others. Communities rarely have the opportunity to say 'no' in the longer term, nor can decisions be easily undone.

Two-dimensional views of community decision-making

Two-dimensional views of community decision-making focus on decision-making and non-decision-making and observable (overt and covert) conflict (Bachrach and Baratz, 1970). A non-decision is a means by which demands for change in the existing allocation of benefits and privileges in the community can be suffocated before they are even voiced; or kept covert, or killed before they gain access to the relevant decision-making arena; or, failing all these things, maimed or destroyed in the implement-ation stage of the policy process (Lukes, 1974). Examples of two-dimensional views abound in communities around the world. For example, in some jurisdictions voting for local government is restricted to property owners, while in others barriers to voter registration may exist which tend to reduce the ability of poorer people to vote. Another classic example of non-decision-making is when electors are given a number of options with respect to development proposals. However, other potential options, such as to reject a development altogether, may not be made available.

An area that has generated considerable interest by commentators on tourism in relation to non-decision-making is that of public–private part-nerships. Harvey (1989: 7) recognized that 'the new entrepreneurialism of the smaller state has, as its centerpiece, the notion of a "public–private part-nership" in which a traditional local booster is integrated with the use of local government powers to try [to] attract external sources of funding, new direct investments, or new employment sources'. For example, in the case of the UK many of the partnerships established between government and business in the 1980s and 1990s as part of urban and regional development programmes were heavily criticized for their narrow stakeholder and insti-tutional base. In a classic restatement of non-decision-making, Goodwin (1993: 161) argued that in order to ensure that urban leisure and tourism development projects were carried out, 'local authorities have had planning and development powers removed and handed to an unelected institution. Effectively, an appointed agency is, in each case, replacing the powers of local government in order to carry out a market-led regeneration of each inner city'. In this case, partnership does not include all members of a community, those who do not have enough money, are not of the right lifestyle, or simply do not have sufficient power, are ignored. The institu-tional arrangements for supposed community development were therefore able to ignore the demands of some members of that community. For example, in referring to Derwentside in the UK, Sadler (1993:190) argued:

> The kind of policy which had been adopted – and which was proving increas-ingly ineffective even in terms of its own stated objectives . . . rested not so much on a basis of rational choice, but rather was a simple reflection of the narrow political and intellectual scope for alternatives. This restricted area

did not come about purely or simply by chance, but had been deliberately encouraged and fostered.

Community political issues therefore have an organizational aspect. Thus, research on tourism's political dimensions at the community level needs to connect the substance of policy, i.e. the general focus on data, with the process of policy-making including the relationship between power structure, including that of institutional arrangements, and ideology (Hall and Jenkins, 1995). Clearly, there are 'politically imposed limitations upon the scope of decision-making', such that community level 'decision-making activities are channeled and directed by the process of non-decision-making' (Crenson, 1971: 178), often by dominant business interests. As Crenson recognized, pluralism is 'no guarantee of political openness or popular sovereignty', and 'neither the study of [overt] decision-making' nor the existence of 'visible diversity' will tell us anything about 'those groups and issues that may have been shut out of a town's political life' (Crenson, 1971: 181). Studies of the political aspects of community tourism should therefore attempt to understand not only the politically imposed limitations upon the scope of decision-making and community representation, but also the political framework within which the research process itself takes place (Hall, 1994).

Within many current discussions in the tourism literature of the establishment of collaborative networks and partnership arrangements (see Hall, 2000), including those in community tourism and destination promotion (e.g. Kotler *et al.*, 1993), tourism policy networks are typically portrayed as interdependent, co-equal, patterned relationships (Klijn, 1996). However, different political actors occupy different positions and can carry different weight within such networks. Some sit in positions with extensive opportunity contexts, filling 'structural holes' (Nohria, 1992: 10), while others may be reluctant participants or may not even be able to participate at all. Organizations and actors also differ with respect to resource dependencies (Rhodes, 1981), leading to differences in their relative power to influence decision-making processes. As Clegg and Hardy (1996: 678) remind us, 'We cannot ignore that power can be hidden behind the facade of "trust" and the rhetoric of "collaboration", and used to promote vested interest through the manipulation of and capitulation by weaker partners.'

Three-dimensional views of community decision-making

At first glance, examination of a three-dimensional view of power in community decision-making may appear to be quite problematic. After all, how can one study, let alone explain, what does not happen? Nevertheless, as Crenson (1971: vii) recognized, the way 'things do not happen' is as important as what does: 'the proper object of investigation is not political activity but political inactivity'.

Heritage provides an opportune setting in which to investigate the third dimension of power. It has long been acknowledged that heritage tourism is an essential element in the representation of the winners' view of history (Hewison, 1987; Hollinshead, 1992; Hall, 1997; Timothy and Boyd, 2003). Communities reconstruct the past and reinterpret the present within the context of tourism development. However, community representations and reconstructions of heritage are often not fully inclusive. Particular ideologies represent themselves to the gaze of the tourist through museums, historic houses, historic monuments and markers, guided tours, public spaces, heritage precincts and tourist landscapes. The gaze of the tourist is not value neutral, and the representation of heritage may act to legitimate current social and political structures. As Norkunas (1993: 5) recognized, 'The public would accept as "true" history that is written, exhibited, or otherwise publicly sanctioned. What is often less obvious to the public is that the writing or the exhibition itself is reflective of a particular ideology'. Similarly, Papson (1981: 225) commented, 'tourism depends on preconceived definitions of place and people . . . government and private enterprise not only re-define social reality but also recreate it to fit those definitions. This process is both interactive and dialectical. To the extent that this process takes place, the category of everyday life is annihilated'.

In most Western communities, positive imaging and heritage is a primary focus of governance with respect to tourism. In some urban areas, the outcome has been described as 'the city as theme park' in which the architecture of the inner-city utilizes historic facades 'from a spuriously appropriated past' to generate consumption within an atmosphere of nostalgia and display. 'The result is that the preservation of the physical remnants of the historical city has superseded attention to the human ecologies that produced and inhabit them' (Sorkin, 1992: xiv).

Monterey, California provides a valuable example of the political nature of tourism at the community level in relation to heritage. Monterey has a substantial heritage tourism industry that is based on the historic significance of the region in terms of US expansionism, with a literary and industrial heritage in the form of Cannery Row (made famous by Steinbeck) and Fisherman's Wharf. Different tourist landscapes, such as those in Monterey, whether they are historic or commercial, can be read as distinct cultural texts, a kind of outdoor museum, which display the artefacts of a community and society. Each of these tourist cultural texts reveals certain ideological assumptions and power relationships, which underlie the tourist environment as a form of cultural production. Indeed, Norkunas (1993: 10) notes that the 'ideology of the powerful is systematically embedded in the institutions and public texts of tourism and history'.

   The rich and complex ethnic history of Monterey is almost completely absent in the 'official' historic tours and the residences available for public viewing. In Monterey, as in many other parts of the world, heritage is presented in the form of the houses of the aristocracy or elite. Historically significant houses are also highlighted from this perspective. History is 'flattened' or conflicting histories suppressed, thereby creating a simplified generalized image, which is consumed by the visitor. In a restatement of Lukes' third dimension of power from a tourism perspective, Norkunas (1993: 36) notes, 'This synopsis of the past into a digestible touristic presentation eliminates any discussion of conflict; it concentrates instead on a sense of resolution. Opposed events and ideologies are collapsed into statements about the forward movement and rightness of history'. Such a situation occurs with very little or no overt conflict over heritage representation despite the clear presence of potentially alternative perspectives on heritage in the form of ethnic and minority groups, which have a long-standing history and relationship to Monterey. Heritage is not contested in the public sphere. Despite the presence of 'democratic' institutions and channels for the representation of diversity in the community, conflicts and issues are ignored in the public history of Monterey. Therefore, what gets reproduced 'is the image of elite Americans of European descent who control, and have always controlled the destiny of the city . . . public history texts as well as tourist texts are involved in a form of dominance, a hegemonic discourse about the past that legitimates the ideology and power of present groups' (Norkunas, 1993: 26).
   The recent industrial past has also been de-emphasized in the heritage product of Monterey. As in many Western urban industrial communities, economic restructuring within the new global economy has led to the demise of many industrial operations, such as canning. The industrial waterfront has now become a leisure space combining shopping and entertainment with residential and tourist development. Industrial heritage is typically an essential component of waterfront redevelopment. Heritage precincts are established which tell the reader the economic significance of the area, not of the lives of those who contributed to wealth generation. Narratives of labour, class and ethnicity are typically replaced by romance and nostalgia. Previous overt conflict in the community, whether between ethnic groups, classes or, more particularly, in terms of industrial and labour disputes are either ignored or glossed over in 'official' tourist histories. The overt conflict of the past has been reinterpreted by local elites to create a new history in which heritage takes a linear, conflict-free form. In the case of Monterey, the past is reinterpreted through the physical transformation of the canneries. 'Reinterpreting the past has allowed the city to effectively erase from the record the industrial era and the working class culture it engendered. Commentary on the industrial era

remains only in the form of touristic interpretations of the literature of John Steinbeck' (Norkunas, 1993: 50–51).

The Monterey experience is repeated time and time again throughout the world. From Victoria and Vancouver in British Columbia to Liverpool and the London Docklands in the UK, and from Hobart and Sydney in Australia to Auckland and Wellington in New Zealand, the urban heritage waterfront has been developed as a means of rejuvenating inner-city areas and of solving urban problems such as the environment and overcrowding. However, the political dimensions of heritage representation and the simplification of place have been little considered. As Boyer (1992: 199) observed:

> In both the tourist industry and historic preservation, there seems to be an attempt (not wholly successful) to unify and heighten the sense of the present by emphasizing the break with the past and with tradition, or to justify a particular aspect of the present by emphasizing a related aspect of the past. In the reconstructed seaport, do we concentrate on the ingenuity of the mechanics or the exoticness of the imports, on the wealth of the merchants or the poverty that led seamen to indenture themselves? Everything is significant. Museums, historic zones, and city tableaux present highly particular staging(s) of the past.

Communities and Tourism: the Politics of Place

The creation and representation of place is a social process. By its very nature tourism is explicitly related to notions of place through tourism promotion and development. However, whether it be in the developed world or in the less developed countries, tourism development has tended to be dominated by sectional interests and by an institutional ideology that inherently represents tourism as a 'good' form of economic development. As has been argued above, such a process is inherently political. As Harvey (1993: 8) stated, 'The question immediately arises as to why people accede to the construction of their places by such a process.' In many cases they of course do not, communities may resist the change inherent in tourism development. For example, 'political battles between residents and specially created redevelopment authorities have punctuated the urban renewal of Australian waterfronts' (Kelly and McConville, 1991: 91). However, while short-term opposition did save the physical fabric of many Australian inner-city communities, it is worthwhile noting that the social fabric has been changed through gentrification and touristification of many areas leaving only heritage facades. Surely a community is more than a collection of buildings.

Significantly, Harvey (1993, 2000) noted that resistance by members of some communities has not checked the overall process of place competition. A mixture of coercion and co-optation centred around maintenance of real-estate values, assumptions regarding employment and investment generation, and an assumption that growth is automatically good, has led to the creation of local growth coalitions in many communities.

> Coercion arises either through inter-place competition for capital investment and employment (accede to the capitalist's demands or go out of business; create a 'good business climate' or lose jobs) or more simply, through the direct political repression and oppression of dissident voices, from cutting off media access to the more violent tactics of the construction mafias in many of the world's cities.
>
> (Harvey, 1993: 9)

The central concerns of politics and power are sometimes apparent in tourism at the community level, but more often they are not. Ideology and power relations are inscribed not only in space through the uneven development of the qualities of places (Lefebvre, 1991), but also through their representation. This is particularly so in relation to tourism promotion and imaging and heritage. As Norkunas (1993: 97) described with respect to heritage tourism in Monterey:

> The ruling class carefully controls the form and content of historical re-creations and tourist landscapes, legitimizing itself by projecting its own contemporary socio-cultural values upon the past. This struggle, the tension between groups with power and groups with varying but lesser degrees of power, is replayed in the many spheres in which the public enactment of identity is staged. The erection or non-erection of statuary is a physical manifestation of that tension; nostalgic reinterpretations of socially condemnatory fiction, which results in a humorous caricature of poverty is yet another manifestation of this struggle. Dominance is expressed not in terms of physical coercion but as rhetoric.

Tourism continually redefines social and political realities at the community level. 'Policies which are used to attract tourists, lengthen their stay, and increase their expenditures . . . function to redefine social realities. As definitions are imposed from without, the socio-cultural reality which arises out of everyday life becomes further consumed' (Papson, 1981: 233). Tourism development, marketing, routing and zoning, and the very notion of serving tourists affects notions of belonging, place and community (Morgan and Pritchard, 1998) no matter where in the world tourism is occurring. The most effective starting point in seeking to make community tourism development work therefore is to make the process as transparent as possible. There is no such thing as a perfect planning process. However, arguably, the more people can see a process in operation the more able they will be to negotiate and plan in their own interests. Tourism planning is therefore as much about developing social and intellectual capital as it is about managing economic and natural capital.

From a political perspective, the representation and maintenance of communities therefore needs to be understood in a far wider context than has generally hitherto been the case. The application of models of community participation in tourism planning which assume the pluralistic allocation of power within a community may unwittingly serve to reinforce existing power structures to the exclusion of oppositional and contrary perspectives. These include not only those of many ethnic and working class communities who face the extinction of their past but also those who simply do not want tourism in their community.

References

Bachrach, P. and Baratz, M.S. (1970) *Power and Poverty: Theory and Practice.* Oxford University Press, New York.

Boyer, M.C. (1992) Cities for sale: merchandising history at South Street Seaport. In: Sorkin, M. (ed.) *Variations on a Theme Park: the New American City and the End of Public Space.* Hill and Wang, New York, pp. 181–204.

Britton, S.G. (1991) Tourism, capital and place: towards a critical geography of tourism. *Environment and Planning D: Society and Space* 9, 451–478.

Clegg, S.R. and Hardy, C. (1996) Conclusion: representations. In: Clegg, S.R., Hardy, C. and Nord, W.R. (eds) *Handbook of Organization Studies.* Sage Publications, London, pp. 676–708.

Crenson, M.A. (1971) *The Un Politics of Air Pollution: a Study of Non-decisionmaking in the Cities.* Johns Hopkins University Press, Baltimore and London.

Dahl, R.A. (1961) *Who Governs?* Yale University Press, New Haven.

Dowling, R.K. (1993) Tourism planning, people and the environment in Western Australia. *Journal of Travel Research* 31(4), 52–58.

Foucault, M. (1972) *The Archeology of Knowledge.* Pantheon, New York.

Gallie, W.B. (1955–1956) Essentially contested concepts. *Proceedings of the Aristotelian Society* 56, 167–198.

Goodwin, M. (1993) The city as commodity: the contested spaces of urban development. In: Kearns, G. and Philo, C. (eds) *Selling Places: the City as Cultural Capital, Past and Present.* Pergamon Press, Oxford, pp. 145–62.

Hall, C.M. (1994) *Tourism and Politics: Power, Policy and Place.* John Wiley & Sons, London.

Hall, C.M. (1997) The politics of heritage tourism: place, power and the representation of values in the urban context. In: Murphy, P. (ed.) *Quality Management in Urban Tourism.* John Wiley & Sons, New York, pp. 91–102.

Hall, C.M. (2000) Rethinking collaboration and partnership: a public policy perspective. In: Bramwell, B. and Lane, B. (eds) *Tourism Collaboration and Partnerships: Politics, Practice and Sustainability.* Channel View, Clevedon, pp. 143–158.

Hall, C.M. and Jenkins, J. (1995) *Tourism and Public Policy.* Routledge, London.

Harvey, D. (1989) From managerialism to entrepreneurialism: the transformation in urban governance in late capitalism. *Geografiska Annaler B* 71, 3–17.

Harvey, D. (1993) From space to place and back again: reflections on the condition of postmodernity. In: Bird, J., Curtis, B., Putnam, T., Robertson, G. and Tickner, L. (eds) *Mapping the Futures: Local Cultures, Global Change.* Routledge, London, pp. 3–29.

Harvey, D. (2000) *Spaces of Hope.* University of California Press, Berkeley.

Haywood, K.M. (1988) Responsible and responsive tourism planning in the community. *Tourism Management* 9, 105–118.

Hewison, R. (1987) *The Heritage Industry: Britain in a Climate of Decline.* Methuen, London.

Hollinshead, K. (1992) 'White' gaze, 'red' people – shadow visions: the disidentification of 'Indians' in cultural tourism. *Leisure Studies* 11, 43–64.

Jamal, T.B. and Getz, D. (1995) Collaboration theory and community tourism planning. *Annals of Tourism Research* 22, 186–204.

Jenkins, J. (1993) Tourism policy in rural New South Wales – policy and research priorities. *GeoJournal* 29(3), 281–290.

Kelly, M. and McConville, C. (1991) Down by the docks. In: Davidson, G. and McConville, C. (eds) *A Heritage Handbook.* Allen & Unwin, North Sydney, pp. 91–114.

Klijn, E. (1996) Analyzing and managing policy processes in complex networks. *Administration and Society* 28(1), 90–119.

Kotler, P., Haider, D.H. and Rein, I. (1993) *Marketing Places: Attracting Investment, Industry, and Tourism to Cities, States, and Nations.* Free Press, New York.

Lasswell, H.D. (1936) *Politics: Who Gets, What, When, How?* McGraw-Hill, New York.

Lefebvre, H. (1991) *The Production of Space.* Basil Blackwell, Oxford.

Lindblom, C.E. (1959) The science of muddling through. *Public Administration Review* 19, 79–88.

Lukes, S. (1974) *Power: a Radical View.* MacMillan, London.

Lyden, F.J., Shipman, G.A. and Kroll, M. (eds) (1969) *Policies, Decisions and Organisations.* Appleton-Century-Crofts, New York.

Millar, C. and Aiken, D. (1995) Conflict resolution in aquaculture: a matter of trust. In: Boghen, A. (ed.) *Coldwater Aquaculture in Atlantic Canada,* 2nd edn. Canadian Institute for Research on Regional Development, Moncton, pp. 617–645.

Morgan, N. and Pritchard, A. (1998) *Tourism Promotion and Power: Creating Images, Creating Identities.* John Wiley & Sons, Chichester.

Murphy, P. (1985) *Tourism: a Community Approach.* Methuen, London.

Murphy, P.E. (1988) Community driven tourism planning. *Tourism Management* 9, 96–104.

Nohria, N. (1992) Is a network perspective a useful way of studying organizations? In: Nohria, N. and Eccles, R. (eds) *Networks and Organizations: Structure, Form and Action.* Harvard Business School Press, Boston, pp. 1–22.

Norkunas, M.K. (1993) *The Politics of Memory: Tourism, History, and Ethnicity in Monterey, California.* State University of New York Press, Albany.

Papson, S. (1981) Spuriousness and tourism: politics of two Canadian provincial governments. *Annals of Tourism Research* 8, 220–235.

Rhodes, R.A.W. (1981) *Control and Power in Central–Local Relations.* Gower, Aldershot.

Sadler, D. (1993) Place-marketing, competitive places and the construction of hegemony in Britain in the 1980s. In: Kearns, G. and Philo, C. (eds) *Selling Places: the City as Cultural Capital, Past and Present.* Pergamon Press, Oxford, pp. 175–192.

Schattsneider, E. (1960). *Semi-sovereign People: a Realists View of Democracy in America.* Holt, Rinehart and Wilson, New York.

Selin, S. (1993) Collaborative alliances: new interorganizational forms in tourism. *Journal of Travel and Tourism Marketing* 2(2/3), 217–227.

Selin, S. (1998) The promise and pitfalls of collaborating. *Trends* 35(1), 9–13.

Selin, S. and Chavez, D. (1994) Characteristics of successful tourism partnerships: a multiple case study design. *Journal of Park and Recreation Administration* 12(2), 51–62.

Simmons, R., Davis, B.W., Chapman, R.J.K. and Sager, D.D. (1974) Policy flow analysis: a conceptual model for comparative public policy research. *Western Political Quarterly* 27(3), 457–468.

Sorkin, M. (1992) Introduction: variations on a theme park. In: Sorkin, M. (ed.) *Variations on a Theme Park: the New American City and the End of Public Space.* Hill and Wang, New York, pp. xi–xv.

Thrift, N. and Forbes, D. (1983) A landscape with figures: political geography with human conflict. *Political Geography Quarterly* 2, 247–263.

Timothy, D.J. (1998) Cooperative tourism planning in a developing destination. *Journal of Sustainable Tourism* 6(1), 52–68.

Timothy, D.J. and Boyd, S.W. (2003) *Heritage Tourism.* Prentice Hall, Harlow.

Urry, J. (1990a) *The Tourist Gaze: Leisure and Travel in Contemporary Society.* Sage Publications, London.

Urry, J. (1990b) The 'consumption' of tourism. *Sociology* 24(1), 23–35.

Self-determination: Exercising Indigenous Rights in Tourism

7

ALISON M. JOHNSTON

International Support Centre for Sustainable Tourism, Lillooet, Canada

Introduction

Worldwide there is growing discussion of indigenous peoples' involvement in tourism (e.g. Sofield, 1993; Butler and Hinch, 1996; Notzke, 1999; Whitford *et al.*, 2001). Many of the questions being raised pertain to ethics in business, and considerable attention is being directed in the political and legal fields to issues of self-determination and property rights (e.g. Anaya and Williams, 2001; Strelein and Behrendt, 2001). Most indigenous peoples whose lives and communities are affected by tourism face highly negative, if not exploitative, experiences. Yet globally, a variety of indigenously owned and managed small-scale enterprises, and joint ventures based on these innovations, now stand out as success stories (e.g. Price, 1996; Hatton, 1999; Timothy and White, 1999). This contrast says much about the distance left to cover in achieving sustainable tourism; however, it also points to the emergence of promising new partnerships and leadership alliances. In order for this recent foundation of innovation to be strengthened, it will be necessary for agencies and individuals working to identify best practices at the policy and community levels to understand the major issues of concern to indigenous peoples. This chapter discusses human rights and indigenous rights, and how current debates on these subjects relate to indigenous communities involved in tourism.

Human Rights

General human rights issues related to tourism

The tourism industry has undergone several performance audits in recent years. The subject of human rights has become a recurring theme in these formal and informal reviews. Advocacy groups working in partnership with representative local communities have succeeded in drawing attention to exploitative industry practices, ranging from sub-standard labour codes in 'offshore' destinations, to the sexual predation of women and children. Organizations like the Ecumenical Coalition on Third World Tourism (Hong Kong) and Tourism Concern (UK) conduct ongoing campaigns to pressure for industry reform.

It is generally accepted now that a correlation exists between indicators for development and the ability of those living within a community to exercise their fundamental rights and freedoms. Where extreme poverty exists, it is usually accompanied by racism, repression or corruption, or a not so subtle combination of these. Individuals subject to this systemic discrimination will normally contribute to the growth of national economic indexes, while experiencing increasing hardship in their own home, family and/or community life. None the less, many government ministries responsible for economic development and other aspects of social welfare continue to define their mandate in the context of narrow fiscal objectives.

In the tourism sector, there are mixed messages and outcomes *vis-à-vis* what governments refer to as development (see Telfer, Chapter 9 this volume). This is especially true within isolated indigenous communities of the South, where tourism companies and their local agents are subject to less international scrutiny of their conduct. What is promised is seldom delivered. Through the United Nations (UN) and other more regional or local public processes, indigenous peoples and non-governmental organizations (NGOs) that monitor tourism trends and the implications for host communities are reiterating concerns over the impacts of corporate and consumer behaviour on human rights. Problems identified include those discussed below.

The distorted notion of rights among consumers

In the North, holiday time is legislated and compensated for, making travel a right as opposed to a privilege in the mind of most consumers. From a sustainability perspective, feeding these holiday fantasies is a costly business. Ecological thresholds are routinely crossed by the tourism industry, and in many destinations, international human rights standards are violated daily. Indigenous peoples are particularly vulnerable to this market-driven tourism, losing access to their customary lands and resources, their right to religious freedom at sacred sites, and as a result, their capacity for self-sufficiency. They also face accelerated cultural voyeurism, as tour companies search for new niches. Although most tourists simply want to buy Aboriginal art from galleries or see a 1-hour dance performance (Zeppel, 1998), there is a sizeable market segment that seeks the 'hidden'. Third-party commercialization is now focusing on more private elements of culture, for example, knowledge of medicinal plants, or spiritual ceremonies like the sweat lodge and other cleansing practices, including hot rocks massage techniques now copied in health spas worldwide.

The wilful ignorance of consumers

The majority of tourists view holidaying as an opportunity to sample a lifestyle more lavish than their own, regardless of whether their level of consumption is sustainable. They will resist seeing the dynamics that facilitate affordable travel in the South, and select cocooned holiday environments to avoid confronting questions such as what constitutes a fair exchange or full-fare travel. Only about 5% of tourists seek out explicitly educational travel opportunities. Of this market segment, it is a small fraction that wants more than a surface interpretation of local experiences and perspectives. Most tourists, therefore, would remain unaware of whether they are within the traditional territory of indigenous people or the situation of the 'real' host people, even if their holiday includes an explicit cultural component. The exception would be 'reality tours' coordinated directly by indigenous organizations like Maya'Iq of Mexico or the Rethinking Tourism Project of Minnesota.

The high demand for 'affordable' travel

While household incomes in the North are declining, sales projections for the global tourism industry continue to grow, indicating not only 'business as usual', but an increasingly competitive business environment. In this age of warehouse and Internet merchandizing, the consumer mind is set on discount prices and 'buy now/pay later' options. This attitude poses a serious threat to most destination communities in the South, given that industry prices already lag far behind any realistic accounting of tourism costs and impacts. The low profit margin of most tour companies precludes much 'giving back'. Companies that do attempt to practice an ethic of reciprocity with indigenous communities are usually unsure of how to approach partnership building or structure an enduring cross-cultural business relationship.

The prevalence of 'unsustainable' products

Although 60–70 per cent of developed country residents participating in consumer surveys typically profess a willingness to pay more for 'sustainable' products, most will only selectively change their spending habits. Tourism, marketed as escapism, is an area where such pledges are highly inconsistent. So-called ecotourists will normally take a short 'ecotourism' excursion within a larger mainstream holiday. Alternatively, they will buy a costly safari that supports local parks and conservation initiatives for one holiday, and then for the next trip book a generic tour package to a hotspot such as Hawaii, where indigenous land rights and related issues are contentious. For most tourists, the desire for prestige or adventure is more of a factor in purchasing patterns than altruism. Travel companies position their products and deliver services accordingly.

The absence of effective regulation

Tourists shopping for escapism generally abide by one fundamental consumer ethic: receipt upon payment. Consumer advocates like *Conde Nast Traveler* magazine may intervene where inferior customer service is delivered. However, the actual sustainability of corporate practices is self-regulated. This conflict of interest within industry, and consumers' low awareness of tourism impacts, have led to widespread abuse of 'green' labelling on the market. 'Authentic' offerings of culture rarely involve the prior informed consent of the targeted indigenous community. Where consent is said to exist, it has normally been obtained outside the customary protocol of the indigenous people concerned and is thus misleading to visitors and 'hosts' alike. Once an industry presence is established, there is little a community can do to prevent escalating intrusion, unless it has recourse to asserting and exercising customary land rights. In very few instances do indigenous peoples have partial or full recognition of land rights, places like Vanuatu and Canada being the exception.

The misrepresentation of 'ecotourism'

Consumer demand for ecotourism is growing at 3–4 times the pace of regular tourism. Although much promise initially surrounded the ecotourism concept, most ecotourism today is merely a market brand, with the same damaging characteristics as other forms of mass tourism. In fact, ecotourism impacts can be even more acute, due to the ecologically and culturally sensitive areas targeted. Consequently, the majority of ecotourism destinations are irreversibly damaged within 15 years (Ashton, 1999). Consumers, meanwhile, become desensitized to what constitutes a viable ecosystem or community. For example, they are left with the impression that indigenous peoples perceive the availability of jobs as a beneficial or adequate trade-off for visitation. In most cases, indigenous leadership would object to both the quality of employment offered and the relegation of their people to a sideline role. They would cite the absence of royalties to communities and/or credible business partnerships as an impediment to stewardship of the land.

These types of issues can be described and categorized in different ways, using a variety of examples, but the theme of human rights is a continuum. Where a tourism economy is promoted in the midst of marked social inequity, the true story about a project's success is always more complex than what standard indicators suggest. Globalization has only intensified the hardship that the tourism industry causes for many indigenous peoples (de Chavez, 1999).

Human rights issues specific to indigenous peoples

The wilful or circumstantial involvement of indigenous peoples in tourism is bringing into focus many of the human rights issues associated with the travel industry. The general human rights problems documented tend to be most pronounced in indigenous communities of the developing world, because indigenous peoples rank as the poorest of the poor globally. Their communities also encounter severe political and social barriers to securing fair terms of trade. Illustrating this is the situation of most indigenous peoples living in areas of high biological diversity, particularly in or around parks and other protected areas, where ecotourism is concentrated. Even in the midst of government and corporate commitments of participation or an equity role, they find themselves unable to regulate the type or quantity of tourism conducted within their traditional territory. Instead, they find that so-called 'development' is passing them by. The 'jobs for the Indians' approach is convincing few at the community level otherwise.

A common dilemma is the disruption of traditional food harvesting to take up employment as porters along popular ecotourism corridors like the Inca Trail in Peru. The average porter wears unstable sandals for footwear along steep and rocky paths, is fed white bread or its nutritional equivalent for stamina, is denied access to the official trip first aid kit, and earns a sub-minimum wage. He will take home needed currency, but each day away from home breaks the transmission of cultural knowledge to the next generation. In indigenous communities, where it is believed that 'it takes a whole community to raise a child', the cost of this seasonal employment cycle for the next generation is significant. Skills vital to food security, health and cultural survival are lost. None the less, this sequence of events is not experienced by indigenous peoples alone. Variations of this trend are seen in non-indigenous host communities worldwide.

What is unique for indigenous peoples is how the different types of rights recognized within international law intertwine. For instance, over time, market forces like those described above can undermine an entire people's continuous occupancy of the land. Since occupancy is key to defending ancestral land under post-colonial property law regimes, and since indigenous rights flow from land title, the effect is to strip away any prospect of justice under international law. Therefore, what first appears as simply another case involving individual human rights, actually has another layer which involves the infringement of the collective rights of a people (discussed below).

Indigenous Rights

In international law the body of rights applicable to indigenous peoples includes both individual human rights and another set of collective rights known as indigenous rights. This distinction is not well understood within the tourism industry, or by proponents of community-based tourism. Indeed, many indigenous communities themselves are too isolated or too impoverished to have access to information on the scope and current status of their rights. One of the main challenges facing indigenous leadership today is to educate community members as to how rights are defined and the best avenues and tools for protecting them. The slow process of undertaking this type of community education, and of networking with other communities to learn more about the nature of tourism, is frequently capitalized on by tourism developers. It is a rare business speculator that approaches an indigenous community directly, as opposed to through a paid intermediary (who is to expedite the approval process or relationship building). Also rare is the developer who will work together with the targeted community to ensure equivalent readiness to negotiate. The non-indigenous way of business tends to be 'every man for himself'.

Self-determination

The central principle of indigenous rights is self-determination. A number of legal instruments adopted by the General Assembly of the UN affirm this right. The *Declaration on the Inadmissability of Intervention in the Domestic Affairs of States and the Protection of their Independence and Sovereignty*, the *Declaration on the Preparation of Societies for Life in Peace*, and the *Manila Declaration on the Peaceful Settlement of International Disputes* all stipulate that states must honour a people's right to self-determination. Indigenous peoples active in the development of the *UN Draft Declaration on the Right of Indigenous People* are thus firm on the inclusion of this principle in the text. It is clearly articulated in several articles, including:

Article 3:   Indigenous people have the right to self-determination.

Article 12:   Indigenous people have the right to the restitution of cultural, intellectual, religious and spiritual property taken without their free and informed consent or in violation of their laws, traditions and customs.

Article 29:   Indigenous people are entitled to the recognition of the full ownership, control and protection of their cultural and intellectual property (United Nations Commission on Human Rights, 1999).

Many governments, particularly those facing active land claims by indigenous peoples (e.g. Canada, Australia and New Zealand), are attempting to water down indigenous peoples' demand for 'prior informed consent' to 'consultation'. None the less, full self-determination remains the benchmark in international law.

In the context of tourism, self-determination means the right of a community to decide whether it wants to have a tourism economy, which parts of its culture will be shared and which will remain private, and what type of protocols will govern access to and use of cultural property. By implication, it entails land rights. Neither abstinence from tourism, nor regulation or entrepreneurship, are possible without title over ancestral lands. The cultural survival of indigenous peoples is dependent on land title. Within the UN Commission on Human Rights, indigenous peoples' relationship with the land is recognized as the foundation of culture (Daes, 1999).

The subject of land title, consistently raised by indigenous peoples in discussions on tourism, has proved to be a difficult point of communication. To business interests familiar with European concepts of property, 'title' means the equivalent of free simple ownership. However, in reality ancestral title is a much more onerous form of stewardship, which is spiritually defined. It carries obligations to care for the lands that are considered sacred. The land is to be held in trust for future generations and cannot be sold. Some indigenous peoples call this the 'Seventh Generation Principle'. Any potential for an indigenous community to profit from tourism would normally be assessed in this light, unless some form of duress, such as extreme poverty, interferes with decision-making.

Indigenous peoples' concepts of development stem from their relationship with the land. While these concepts are personalized within each culture, there are shared characteristics across continents. One of the shared values is to look after not just the material or physical (e.g. economic) needs of community members, but also the mental, emotional and spiritual. As such, indigenous knowledge about 'development' has spiritual dimensions, which take precedence.

Expertise is not divorced from prayer and ceremony, but rather dependent
on it. Visions and prophecies are understood as vital cues to co-existence and
survival. Elders and spiritual leaders are looked to for wisdom and sacred
places provide a reminder of the holistic relationships between Creator and
Creation.

(Johnston, 1997: 5)

Globally, the legacy of this history is high biological diversity within
indigenous territories (Reichel-Dolmatoff, 1999). Scientists have accepted
the link between cultural and biological diversity as a major theme in UN
negotiations on biodiversity (discussed below). Meanwhile, many indigenous peoples witnessing the ecological damage achieved elsewhere within
a short time through western concepts of development have been
instructed by their Elders to teach, or to help outsiders understand that all
things are connected. Some of these communities are now developing pilot
projects to share elements of their traditional knowledge through tourism.

One of the common misconceptions that arises from an indigenous
community's objection to a tourism proposal or to existing tourism
activities is that it is challenging jurisdiction or objecting simply to make
a political point. In a secular society, this interpretation might seem
logical. However, indigenous peoples' customary laws for using the land
are grounded in a long time horizon, within a different understanding
of purpose, space and time. Ecologist David Suzuki (1997), following his
work with a number of indigenous peoples around the world, described
this vision as 'The Sacred Balance'. The difference in world view that Suzuki
observed is not cause for conflict, but rather reason for dialogue. The key to
communicating about self-determination is to understand that protocol is
involved. Successful partnerships with indigenous communities occur when
both parties take a sincere interest in relationship building, placing people
and not business at the centre of discussion.

Prior informed consent

Securing a baseline of prior informed consent in negotiations with outside
business interests is one of the greatest challenges faced by indigenous
peoples. Equally difficult is the process of making an independent
community-tourism initiative airtight to industry profiteering. In both
instances, there are not only a variety of access and benefit sharing issues to
address, but also the complex question of intellectual property (Johnston,
2000). The first concern most often stated by indigenous peoples in international forums is their right not to sell, commoditize or have expropriated
certain domains of knowledge and sacred places, plants, animals and
objects (Posey, 1995: 10).

One area where indigenous communities have experienced great frustration in this regard is in relation to protected areas. To many governments, protected areas are the vehicle of choice for biodiversity conservation, as they greatly increase a country's marketability to ecotourists, as well as to an array of funding agencies, who are interested in supporting environmental initiatives. This model of conservation is seen as a win–win solution to land conflicts, showing that ecotourism can serve as a financial incentive for biodiversity conservation.

While there are notable examples internationally of co-management agreements between government and indigenous communities whose traditional territory is incorporated within a protected area, most indigenous peoples' response to the protected areas movement has been guarded. Many feel that protected areas provide a politically correct way for government to negate indigenous land title. The perception is that protected areas can essentially privatize a peoples' ancestral homeland. Government criteria are utilized in processing visitation applications. Henceforth, an indigenous community can seldom prevent unwanted tourism, or maintain a stewardship role by giving conditional approval.

Some indigenous communities have chosen to circumvent the issues of prior informed consent around protected areas by developing their own tourism enterprises on lands in danger of destructive resource extraction. There are several examples of this within the Amazon basin of Ecuador. Through tourism and the presence of tourists, peoples like the Cofan and Hoarani have scored successes against Ecuador's environmentally savage oil industry (Kane, 1998).

That said, asserting self-determination on one front does not eliminate the need for a community to cross-check all other directions for possible encroachment. In August 1999 another neighbouring tribe in this same region of Ecuador lost eight members to military gunfire at a peaceful roadblock, during their attempt to prevent oil-drilling machinery from entering their territory, by a means other than tourism. In this case, the right to prior informed consent was forcefully seized. No news of this event reached the popular media.

This oblivion is a daily threat that many indigenous communities live under. Many are therefore attempting to build information-sharing alliances outside of their own country with indigenous peoples and other supportive groups that can provide technical assistance, including legal and media intervention. Tourism is a frequent topic of discussion on this 'moccasin telegraph', as both a threat to cultural survival, and a tool to exercise rights to control, utilize and manage collective cultural property. Access to information and the ability to analyse it and freely communicate findings are the prerequisites to prior informed consent in the realm of tourism.

Like protected areas, the subject of indigenous knowledge is generating a flurry of dialogue with respect to prior informed consent. Around the world, indigenous peoples have in common complex oral and artistic systems for documenting their expertise (i.e. in ecosystem conservation and other sustainability processes) and for passing these skills to coming generations. Much of this knowledge, such as the use of medicinal plants, is considered sacred, and therefore has traditionally been subject to regulation by the Elders. However, now that indigenous knowledge is of value on the international market, owing to the interest of New Age followers, thrill seekers, and pharmacology researchers and investors, it is possible in some indigenous communities for tourists to purchase curative treatments or guided forest tours (Proctor, 2001). While this type of tourism product often tells of a break in protocol between generations or families in a community, in some cases the Elders are fully involved and believe that this knowledge can be shared on respectful terms.

Regardless of the scenario, a constant within most communities offering such tourism exchanges is a dangerous lack of knowledge about the indigenous rights issues surrounding what has become known in the Western world as intellectual property. Thus, in some Maasai communities in Kenya, it is possible to go on a guided walk, where the species and medicinal applications of each local plant are labelled in English for all to see. Such communities rarely 'catch up' with the legal and political implications of showcasing their knowledge before it is too late, and this exposure has jeopardized the very elements of culture they intended to protect.

There is no prospect in sight of a reliable mechanism for indigenous peoples to alert one another of the dangers of responding to the 'knowledge seeking' trend among tourists and potential investors posing as tourists, since it is in the financial interest of governments and industry to liberalize access to resources, and funding is directed accordingly. Under current international modes of business and standards of conduct, it can safely be said that there is no incentive for tourism companies to establish the conditions necessary for prior informed consent. The few instruments for comprehensive cultural protection that exist internationally have been formulated and championed by a handful of indigenous peoples whose circumstances allow them to plug in to the now globalized discussion of indigenous rights. No international institution of significant size is coming forward to facilitate technical support from indigenous peoples that have this type of expertise directly to those communities that badly need it.

Policy and Community-level Considerations

Policy development at the United Nations

In the last 5 years, the language of international policy debates concerning the impacts of tourism on indigenous peoples and other local communities has changed substantially. Several NGOs, both tourism specific and more broadly focused conservation and/or social justice groups, have pressed governments to take action to mitigate tourism impacts. As a result, a structured debate on tourism standards is now underway through a broad framework of UN processes. Tourism is under review within the UN Commission on Sustainable Development (CSD) and the *UN Convention on Biological Diversity* (CBD), as well as subsidiary processes like the *UN Convention on Climate Change*. These intergovernmental discussions are proceeding with an unprecedented level of detail.

Indigenous leaders working to protect their peoples' rights via international forums like the UN have been vocal about social and environmental issues specific to their communities. As a result, indigenous peoples now stand apart from NGOs as observers at multilateral negotiations on sustainable tourism. Their persistence at articulating the difference between individual rights and collective rights has brought several new issues to the agenda, especially in relation to intellectual property and the conservation of biological diversity (Johnston, 2000). Governments have met this change with considerable resistance, understanding well the distinction between different classifications of rights, and the influence this could have on future guidelines or standards adopted for the tourism industry. Nevertheless, the lens of debate is now broader than simply human rights.

Gradually, indigenous peoples are finding that they have a voice in international policy on tourism. The CBD, signed by 175 countries since 1993, has been pivotal in facilitating this breakthrough. It is legally binding and provides clear benchmarks for safeguarding the interests of indigenous peoples and other local communities. Most significant in this regard is Article 8(j), which obliges governments to protect and promote indigenous knowledge systems for the conservation and sustainable use of biodiversity, while ensuring the equitable sharing of related benefits.

Article 8(j) of the CBD has particular immediacy in relation to ecotourism. As noted earlier, most ecotourism targets indigenous homelands, where high biodiversity remains due to the sophisticated stewardship practices applied over millennia (World Wildlife Fund, 2000). There remains the ideal, however rare in actual practice, that ecotourism involves host communities on respectful terms. Article 8(j), recognizing the vital contribution of indigenous knowledge and innovation systems to conservation, revives the principle that sustainable ecotourism should entail meaningful involvement by indigenous communities in analysis and decision-making.

The dialogue on how to broaden the discussion of sustainability in the tourism sector is now in transition. Parallel to the CBD, a set of principles called the *Berlin Declaration on Sustainable Tourism* was signed in 1997 by multilateral agencies like the Secretariat of the CBD, the UN Environment Programme and the Global Environment Facility, plus 18 country signatories of the CBD. Through this declaration, international leaders agreed that tourism should be restricted and, where necessary, prevented, in ecologically and culturally sensitive areas. While this statement brought visibility to the culture loss triggered by tourism, there is still no accepted definition of what constitutes culturally sustainable tourism. Nor is there significant support within government or industry for indigenous peoples, especially those with authority and perspective from the community level, to take a lead in developing appropriate criteria. Instead, indigenous communities face an immense burden of proof in registering an area as 'sensitive'.

In the absence of industry guidelines consistent with the Berlin declaration and with the spirit of the CBD, many indigenous organizations are in the midst of developing standard legal and *sui generis* protective mechanisms, pooling results in an effort to help those communities that are too isolated or impoverished to challenge damaging modes of business independently. Instruments of prior informed consent and agreements to govern benefit sharing are considered vital, even if they exist only in draft form to serve as a reference point for internal decision-making, or for working through a cross-cultural process with prospective partners. The most effective of these regulatory tools are usually those initially drafted right in the community, away from lawyers or other outside 'experts' distanced from the day to day manifestations of the issues.

> Indigenous communities need to sort out amongst themselves – without the interference of non-members – the tribal, sub-tribal and family 'ownership' of knowledge. What is common property? Who has the right to give consent? Elders or youth? Tribal political structures or new additional specialist tribal organizations? What structures will they put in place? Should regional and national structures also be established? By whom?
>
> (Mead, 1995: 7)

These documents are sometimes drafted with facilitation assistance, so as to bring the experience of Elders and younger leadership together into a coherent vision. Examples include the Kuna People's *Statute on Tourism* (Kuna General Congress, 1996). The Kuna People of Panama stand out for their success in being able to develop a formal mechanism to combat industry trends. The opening article of the Kuna *Statute on Tourism*, ratified in 1996 by the Kuna General Congress, states:

> The only tourist activities and infrastructures possible in Kuna Yala will be, strictly and solely, those that respect, conserve, value and defend the natural resources, environment and biodiversity of the *comarca* (i.e. the Kuna territory), as well as the socio-cultural, political, and religious Kuna norms and customs.

The statute specifies how this vision will be achieved, and is now being tested by the Kuna Congress (Snow, 2001).

Although some observers have criticized the Kuna for being slow to enforce its provisions, there is in reality a multiplicity of factors, not least of which is the machinery of the tourism industry itself. It should be remembered that moving from a colonized economy to one of self-determination is a slow process of reversing centuries of economic oppression and indoctrination, and re-working business relationships from the inside out.

Meanwhile, steps have been taken by multilateral organizations to redress the lack of protection for culture and cultural property within national legal frameworks. In July 1998, the World Intellectual Property Organization (WIPO) initiated the annual *Roundtable on Indigenous Peoples and Intellectual Property* to assess the shortcomings of existing legal tools. Many indigenous peoples maintain that the very structure of such forums is an infringement of indigenous rights, because there is a predetermined process to plug into (i.e. consultation) rather than a mutual exchange of ideas for how best to undertake problem solving. But with industry pressuring governments for a more secure investment climate, these processes are being pushed forward, with or without indigenous endorsement, and with or without true indigenous participation. As well, some issues are being fast-tracked, as a means to mediate between corporate and community interests. UNESCO, for example, organized the *International Symposium on Natural Sacred Sites, Cultural Diversity and Biological Diversity* in September 1998, and now has a new work programme on indigenous knowledge.

In time, such multilateral processes will have broad application to the tourism industry. Dynamics being addressed include unauthorized activities such as the use of indigenous cultural symbols on souvenirs like T-shirts and tea towels, the sale of photos of indigenous peoples for tourism brochures and postcards, and performances or adaptations of indigenous dances and songs. That said, a weak link in these discussions is the feedback of recommendations to industry. As of yet, there is no clear directive for industry to work with indigenous peoples towards developing and implementing respectful interim measures.

Indigenous peoples, deeply concerned by what they see as tacit approval by governments for 'business as usual', consistently raise three caveats with regard to forums seeking their 'participation' or 'consultation'. First, the format, agenda and outputs of such processes addressing indigenous rights should be determined at the outset through consensus with authentic indigenous leadership. Secondly, adequate funding should be made available for indigenous peoples to conduct their own analysis in preparation for dialogue. Finally, participating government bodies and other organizations should be required to honour international law concerning indigenous and human rights (e.g. *International Labour Organization Convention 169*), as well as parallel standards (e.g. *UN Draft Declaration on the*

Rights of Indigenous People). Otherwise, indigenous peoples face a fire-fighting situation, where third party infringement of their rights is a constant threat, detracting scarce resources away from community projects for rebuilding sustainable economies.

Despite recent advances made towards defining new relationships in tourism, there are several tough questions left to tackle. How can indigenous peoples protect themselves against displacement, industry profiteering and exploitation? What policy is needed to facilitate indigenous communities in developing their own tourism business concepts? What incentives are required for industry to enter into respectful partnerships with indigenous peoples? Who will determine the accepted thresholds for cultural erosion, or what constitutes a 'culturally sensitive' area, as per the Berlin Declaration? Questions like these must be tackled if indigenous communities are ever to remove the product label attached to them by the tourism industry.

Community responses to policy level developments

One result of the recent attention accorded in policy circles to indigenous communities affected by the tourism industry is increased awareness of aspects of culture in development programming. Several NGOs and for-profit social justice organizations have taken note of the core issues and tried to work with indigenous communities to develop an income source from tourism that supports local objectives. While overtures from these groups initially brought hope among indigenous peoples that more productive partnerships would follow, many have expressed disappointment at the outcomes. Most professionals and other volunteers playing a supportive role to indigenous peoples with regard to tourism are very familiar with human rights issues, but have a limited understanding of indigenous rights, as well as indigenous values and customary practices. As a result, they often proceed in ways that compromise indigenous rights, all the while believing that they are doing good.

Another challenge encountered by indigenous peoples has been the motivation for some of these groups to enter into an alliance on a community tourism enterprise. It is now extremely fashionable for NGOs to have an indigenous component to their programming, especially in relation to biodiversity or general environment issues, as this combination represents a niche in the advocacy world. There is a tendency among these organizations to want to affiliate with an indigenous project for fundraising or public relations purposes. This has led to inappropriate behaviour on the part of both office and field staff, ranging from unauthorized accompaniment by photographers or cinematographers on project trips, to fudged statements or 'quotes' with regard to indigenous projects in NGO promotional literature. Similar mixed messages have been delivered by some tourism 'companies with a conscience'. For this reason, indigenous leaders are becoming much more systematic in the way they approach such collaboration, defining expected roles and responsibilities in advance through a memorandum of understanding or similar regulatory tool.

The almost competitive spirit of some tourism and environment NGOs in pursuing their respective project portfolios, with indigenous tourism as a component, has highlighted for many indigenous leaders, the need to reiterate their concerns around tourism, spelling out their own advocacy agenda. Existing codes of conduct for tourism developed by NGOs, while useful as an overview of human rights, do not name or delineate subjects of priority to indigenous peoples. The most serious oversight of these documents is with regard to process. At the community level as well, it is assumed that 'participation' or a 'stakeholder' role in decision-making is what indigenous peoples want or require. But by definition, a 'stakeholder' consultation process is designed to accommodate third-party interests, not human rights or indigenous rights.

The prevailing assumption among governments and industry, meanwhile, is that indigenous communities have a compensation mentality, and therefore will be satisfied if economic development is 'delivered'. While most indigenous communities are in search of a means to secure independent financial resources, many would expect that any discussion process established should also provide for the simultaneous resolution of outstanding grievances. As indigenous communities learn about successful negotiation models elsewhere, including viable interim measures to anticipate and resolve conflict, they are less likely to enter into a standard consultation process, which could prejudice or extinguish their rights.

To underline this expectation, some indigenous communities are opting to undertake peaceful direct action (such as the unarmed road blockade described above) in order to demand fair negotiations of tourism activities within their traditional territory. In the province of British Columbia, Canada, indigenous communities have gone a step further, targeting shutdowns of the tourism industry (which is replacing timber as the reliable source of government revenue) as a means to open a negotiating table with government on forest practices. These communities want consistency in policy and practice from the various government ministries and ministry offices.

The presumption that indigenous communities should 'negotiate' rights, or partake in 'interest based' negotiation, is one of the primary obstacles to problem solving in the tourism industry today. Proposals for this type of dialogue process with communities are steeped in the delivery mode of thinking – programme delivery, service delivery or a magic potion for development itself. They may imply self-government, but always within a framework of top-down development assistance. This principle is markedly different from self-determination.

Steps to Bridge the Policy–Community Divide

Traditional resource rights

One of the priorities of indigenous peoples is to secure recognition for title to their ancestral lands, which define their culture and spirituality. One way to achieve this in today's 'use or lose' world is to offer a well-conceived tourism product that supports customary practices. Some southern communities have chosen to link with northern indigenous economies to create a tourism of solidarity. Other southern indigenous peoples are considering strategic marketing possibilities like the Canadian and American bar associations, whose members might be persuaded to offer support post-holiday.

Such options do not remove the need to structure protective protocols, setting out not just what is for sale and by whom, but also the terms of exchange. At a community level, this awareness in itself has created concerns. Many indigenous peoples are anxious about the ever growing number of agreements between corporations and communities (Indigenous Peoples' Biodiversity Network, 1996). Often these arrangements are negotiated in isolation or under conditions that constitute duress, without the benefit of precedents from other indigenous territories. Furthermore, because they are entered into as a single community rather than as a people, there may be loopholes in the language that put collective rights at risk.

Much of the current networking among indigenous peoples is aimed at creating a synergy between what is needed at the community level and legal developments or other relevant happenings nationally and internationally. Communities have to learn how to design protocols which combine their own customary law with international legal and moral doctrine that would support it. In this way, protocols developed at the community level can be strengthened in order to withstand tests from outside interests who are politically and legally shrewd.

Many indigenous peoples have turned to the traditional resource rights (TRRs) concept as a means to raise awareness of the statutory obligations set in the international arena. TRRs, linking different categories of indigenous cultural and customary rights with specific international laws and directives established within the UN or its related institutions, synthesize government responsibilities towards indigenous peoples (Posey and Dutfield, 1996). This framework removes the mystery for communities as to how distant multilateral processes relate to home. Communities can extract portions of it to incorporate into their own protocol agreements, alongside what is handed down by their Elders. An important precedent of a document drafted in this way is the *Mataatua Declaration* of the Maori in New Zealand, which was submitted to the UN Working Group on Indigenous Populations in 1993.

The need for an integrating concept like TRR is especially high for indigenous peoples residing in countries where national laws offer only weak protection for their collective rights. Only a few countries have domestic legislation with provisions comparable to international law. These include Canada and the Philippines, which have the supreme court *Delgamuukw* decision and the *Ancestral Domain Law*, respectively. Even where this type of safeguard exists, national action usually lags far behind what is recognized and provided for in law (Johnston, 1997). This lack of diligence offers much temptation to a self-regulated industry like tourism.

Partnership building

For sustainable partnerships to be built in the tourism sector between indigenous peoples and outside parties, it will be on a case-by-case basis, as common interests are identified. The main ingredient in any successful cross-cultural partnership is the individual who decides to serve as a 'champion' for change. These persons go beyond their job description, their career thinking and sometimes their cultural comfort zones to establish trust and a personal connection. They are willing to put their signature on new types of agreements, and to provide the leadership necessary for trying a new way.

Principles for building a successful partnership start at the personal level. It is individuals that carry principles into an organization or company, and demonstrate how they apply to the business at hand. Principles to consider in relation to working with indigenous communities on tourism and the wide realm of interconnected issues include:

- *Preparation*: taking a sincere interest in learning about the historical and contemporary issues of priority to indigenous peoples.
- *Protocol*: showing respect for the cultural traditions that govern relationship building and decision-making. Respecting the role of ceremony and prayer in the 'workplace'.
- *Presence*: arriving in a community as a whole person, not as merely a professional or representative. Sharing your own personal values.
- *Participation*: accepting invitations to listen to the Elders and other recognized community authorities who speak for the people.
- *Process*: approaching problem solving through inclusive community means like sharing circles rather than just impersonal and linear 'expert' methodologies.

Within indigenous peoples' organizations there is increasing awareness of the need to identify and train such 'champions'. Many indigenous leaders are mindful of the bridges that can be built by welcoming to their inner circle gifted non-indigenous professionals and other individuals whose vision for sustainability is compatible. This type of partnering, combined with the politics of 'perseverence' practiced by indigenous peoples, is slowly but fundamentally changing the direction of discourses on sustainable tourism. Expert forums on tourism, such as the process established under the *UN Convention on Biological Diversity* are for the first time having to address indigenous peoples' experiences with tourism and other industrial economies, as a core issue. Indigenous peoples have sent the message that sustainable economies will not be achieved through 'business as usual'.

Conclusion

Thus far, most talks on tourism involving indigenous communities have polarized around questions of control. The tourism industry envisions continued self-regulation, while affected communities seek safeguards for their traditional resource rights. Such differences cannot be readily resolved, given that they are ultimately value based. Therefore, effective mediating tools are required. These include indicators and early warning systems which address cultural sustainability.

For indigenous peoples to articulate their part of this equation, and build successful partnerships with outside interests, the topic of indigenous rights cannot remain a taboo subject. Self-review of tourism projects, according to their own values and knowledge, is necessary to provide technical parameters for innovation. Partnerships built on this foundation, and carried forward through the personal commitment of leadership on both sides, can lead to new prospects for indigenous communities seeking to maintain their cultural identity and peoplehood while pursuing a tourism economy.

References

Anaya, S.J. and Williams, R.A. (2001) The protection of indigenous people's rights over lands and natural resources under the Inter-American Human Rights System. *Harvard Human Rights Journal* 14, 33–86.

Ashton, R.E. (1999) Working for a successful ecotourism story: the case of Punta Sal National Park. In: Singh, T.V. and Singh, S. (eds) *Tourism Development in Critical Environments*. Cognizant, New York, pp. 89–101.

Butler, R.W. and Hinch, T. (eds) (1996) *Tourism and Indigenous Peoples*. International Thomson Business Press, London.

Daes, E.I. (1999) *Indigenous People and their Relationship to the Land: Second Progress Report*. United Nations Commission on Human Rights, Geneva.

De Chavez, R. (1999) Globalization and tourism: deadly mix for indigenous peoples. *Tebtebba* January, 7–8.

Hatton, M.J. (1999) *Community-based Tourism in the Asia-Pacific*. Canadian International Development Agency, Ottawa.

Indigenous Peoples' Biodiversity Network (1996) *Proceedings from the Indigenous Peoples' Workshop on Developing a Framework for the Protection of Knowledge and Practices of Indigenous Communities*. Indigenous People's Workshop, Ottawa.

Johnston, A. (1997) *Report on the International Workshop on Indigenous Peoples and Development*. Indigenous Peoples' Development Network, Ollantaytambo, Peru.

Johnston, A. (2000) Indigenous peoples and ecotourism: bringing indigenous knowledge and rights into the sustainability equation. *Tourism Recreation Research* 25(2), 89–96.

Kane, J. (1998) The rebels of the rainforest. *Conde Nast Traveler* 33(12), 18–19.

Kuna General Congress (1996) *Statute: Tourism in Kuna Yala*. Chen Editorial, Panama City.

Mead, A.T.P (1995) Biodiversity, community integrity and the second colonialist wave. *Abya Yala News* 8(4), 6–8.

Notzke, C. (1999) Indigenous tourism development in the Arctic. *Annals of Tourism Research* 26, 55–76.

Posey, D. (1995) Safeguarding indigenous knowledge: intellectual property rights and the search for a new framework. *Abya Yala News* 8(4), 9–12.

Posey, D. and Dutfield, G. (1996) *Beyond Intellectual Property: Toward Traditional Resource Rights for Indigenous Peoples and Local Communities*. International Development Research Centre, Ottawa.

Price, M.F. (ed.) (1996) *People and Tourism in Fragile Environments*. John Wiley & Sons, Chichester.

Proctor, R. (2001) Tourism opens new doors, creates new challenges for traditional healers in Peru. *Cultural Survival Quarterly* 24(4), 14–16.

Reichel-Dolmatoff, G. (1999) A view from the headwaters. *The Ecologist* 29(4), 276–280.

Snow, S.G. (2001) The Kuna General Congress and the Statute on Tourism. *Cultural Survival Quarterly* 24(4), 17–20.

Sofield, T.H.B. (1993) Indigenous tourism development. *Annals of Tourism Research* 20, 729–750.

Strelein, L. and Behrendt, L. (2001) Old habits die hard: indigenous land rights and mining in Australia. *Cultural Survival Quarterly* 25(1), 51–53.

Suzuki, D. (1997) *The Sacred Balance: Rediscovering Our Place in Nature*. Greystone, Vancouver.

Timothy, D.J. and White, K. (1999) Community-based ecotourism development on the periphery of Belize. *Current Issues in Tourism* 2(2/3), 226–242.

United Nations Commission on Human Rights (1999) *Draft Declaration on the Rights of Indigenous People*. Working Group on Indigenous Populations, Geneva.

Whitford, M., Bell, B. and Watkins, M. (2001) Indigenous tourism policy in Australia: 25 years of rhetoric and economic rationalism. *Current Issues in Tourism* 4(2), 151–181.

World Wildlife Fund (2000) *Map of Indigenous and Traditional Peoples in Ecoregions.* World Wildlife Fund, Gland, Switzerland.

Zeppel, H. (1998) Indigenous cultural tourism: 1997 Fulbright Symposium. *Tourism Management* 19, 103–106.

Generating Goodwill in Tourism through Ethical Stakeholder Interactions

8

DAVID A. FENNELL[1] **and KRZYSZTOF PRZECLAWSKI**[2]

[1]*Department of Recreation and Leisure Studies, Brock University, St Catharines, Canada;* [2]*University of Warsaw, Wilcza, Poland*

Introduction

In their text on the social psychology of leisure, Mannell and Kleiber (1997) write that the best tourism experiences are those characterized as having special qualities. Some tourists may be in search of spirituality (Cohen, 1979), some search for authenticity (MacCannell, 1989), others for meaning (Meyersohn, 1981; Krippendorf, 1987) and still others seek to understand themselves and others better through an exploration of values and ethics (Przeclawski, 1985). This chapter relates most specifically to the latter of these, in particular, to how values and ethics may be employed in an industry that continues to grow at a phenomenal rate and which has very quickly developed into an agent of social and ecological change. This chapter examines the concepts of value and ethics in detail, and proceeds to link tourism and ethics through an analysis of past research. The focus is largely on the ethical interactions that exist between tourists, residents and brokers and makes an attempt to fit these numerous interactions into a comprehensive ethical framework.

Przeclawski (1997: 105) wrote that tourism is 'the phenomenon pertaining to spatial mobility, connected with a voluntary, temporary change of place, the rhythm of life and its environment, and involving a personal contact with the visited environment (natural, and/or cultural and/or social)'. Until recently, people and their community networks were intricately defined, and tied, by spatial proximity. The interplay between geography and culture helped define the characteristics of communities, particularly in regard to fundamental values. The associated development of community norms made it easier for individuals to establish a sense of support and identity in the social group. However, mass migrations from rural regions to cities, and the intensive development of towns brought about the disintegration of traditional local economies, community dynamics, and thus neighbourly relations. This process has accelerated in recent years through the development of computer and information technologies, which will no doubt affect the value systems of countless societies around the world.

Tourism, too, has been subject to intense transformations as a result of a number of global phenomena, including industrialization and urbanization, the rise of the tourist-oriented industry, higher standards of living in many countries, development of education and of 'mass culture', increases in discretionary time and money, and new labour legislation allowing for paid holidays. Alongside these significant socioeconomic changes, several industry-specific developments have had a direct impact on the development of contemporary mass tourism. These include, for example: (i) changes in passport regulations; (ii) liberalization of currency and customs procedures; (iii) the development of tourism-specific infrastructure; (iv) increased promotional efforts; and (v) improved access.

As the tourism industry presses on with increasing magnitude, it often does so with associated human and ecological costs. As a form of human behaviour, the act of travel may be viewed as a window into the soul of the individual and of society for, as Goethe believed, 'behaviour is a mirror in which one shows his image'. The image is thus a testimony to what is both good and bad about tourists and the tourism industry. In examining what is good and bad, and right or wrong with the industry, and its various constituent parts, a broadly based ethical perspective needs to be understood.

The Importance of Ethics

Ethics, like law or aesthetics, are phenomena strictly connected to the human condition. People have the possibility to act reasonably (to be goal-oriented) and to make choices. For thousands of years, humankind has sought to understand human virtues and the determinants of ethical and non-ethical behaviour. For example, Socrates argued that 'virtue is knowledge', and that without a good grasp of ethics people would not know how to live, Plato spoke about the intellectual communication with the 'idea of the right', Aristotle was convinced that humans self-actualize through striving for the supreme right, and Stoicism praised the righteous life. While the Western ideal of ethics and virtue is founded principally on the basis of the aforementioned scholars, so-called Eastern philosophies too have been used to examine ethical and human behaviour (e.g. through *The Book of Chuang Tzu* and *The Bhagavad Gita*) for millennia.

Over the last few hundred years, ethics has been richly sustained through the work of many scholars. Kant, for example, spoke about the moral duty – the knowledge of one's duty as being a primary motivating factor determining behaviour. This 'deontological' school of ethics suggests that right behaviour is a function of one's ability to follow pre-established doctrines or rules. This popular position was contrary to the perspective held by Hume, who suggested that reason alone was not enough to determine right or wrong, but rather passion and sentiment. Kierkegaard pushed our understanding of ethics in a different direction, away from the categorical imperative as established by Kant, to one advocating a teleological suspension of the ethical (teleos meaning 'end'). He argued that one could be considered ethical, and at the same time admired, if he or she overrode universal rules. He wrote that the integrity of the individual is secured not by associating with society's rules, but rather by being true to oneself (see Cooper, 1998). This personal authenticity manifesto had a significant influence on existentialist writers of a later time. The teleological perspective was later diversified through what has been called the principle of greatest happiness, or utility, as proclaimed by J.S. Mill. This utilitarianism posits that the principal determinant of ethical conduct is the good end which results from one's actions, instead of the means and intent, which are of secondary importance (Russell, 1979).

Nietzsche was notorious for suggesting that Kant's universalism, in the manner briefly discussed above, only served to level humanity in a way that was contrary to human behaviour and social systems. He wrote that humanity was rank ordered, and that moral values which were suitable for governing the behaviour of one group of people (e.g. the weak), serve only to diminish the lives of a higher order group (Cooper, 1998). Nietzsche further deconstructed the tenets of ethical thought, in attempting to reinvent morality (Benn, 1998), by suggesting that 'there are no moral facts', only moral 'interpretations'. His interpretations of 'good and evil' and 'good and bad' were instrumental in illustrating the importance of values in our understanding of ethics.

Finally, and more central to the thesis of Kierkegaard, was the existential perspective, which theorizes that individuals make ethically sound judgements through self-determined, authentic action. As illustrated by Fennell and Malloy (1995), the focus of existentialism rests squarely with the individual, not within the normative perspective as determined through society, and the ability to choose freely and take responsibility for personal behaviour (being authentic). Existentialism, therefore, is an ethical approach, which suggests that an act is right or wrong based upon the actor's free will, responsibility and authenticity (Guignon, 1986). Although existentialism has been criticized (see Raphael, 1989), it may be offered as, in the words of Guignon, a means by which to evaluate different ethical standpoints and applicability to specific contexts of action than the slavish rule-follower (deontologist) or the cool cost–benefit calculator (teleologist). The normative ethical approaches (deontology and teleology) are compared along with existentialism in Table 8.1.

More recently, there has been a new-found interest in the applicability of ethics to the many real world dilemmas confronting humanity. Partly in response to those who argue for ethics and responsibility from an academic perspective (Buber, 1991, 1992), but also from those who are most prominently in the public eye (e.g. Karol Wojtyla, John Paul II, speaking about the necessity and importance of ethics). In fact many disciplines (e.g. medicine, environment, law and business) are now looking to ethics to tackle many of the issues (e.g. genetic cloning, deforestation) encountered in their respective fields.

Ethics and Values

Mitchell (1983: 3) wrote that 'more than anything else, we are what we believe, what we dream, what we value'. In general, the study of values has been dominated by Rokeach (1968, 1973) and more recently by Schwartz (1994, 1996). Rokeach (1973) wrote that once learned, values are assembled hierarchically according to their perceived importance. Conflict is activated in situations where one or more conflicting values becomes activated. Citing a number of studies that link human behaviour to values, Madrigal (1995) writes that because of their centrality to one's cognitive structure, values have long been recognized as effective predictors of human behaviour.

Table 8.1. Application of ethical theory to tourism. Source: adapted from Malloy and Fennell (1998a).

Ethical approach	Basic premise	Application
Deontology	Behaviour based upon duty, principles, policies, procedures and codes	Ensuring that customs and traditions are respected and followed
Teleology	Behaviour based upon the perceived/calculated best end for the greatest number	Ensuring that most individuals have experienced some degree of pleasure
Existentialism	Behaviour based upon self-determined authentic action, freely chosen and responsible	In the absence of clearly defined codes or rules, choosing to act in a way that would benefit the local environment and people

In the 1990s the study of values resurfaced through a number of studies conducted by Schwartz (1996: 2), who defined values as 'desirable transitional goals, varying in importance, that serve as guiding principles in people's lives'. Schwartz and Bilsky (1990) wrote that human values can be traced to three principal requirements of human existence, namely: (i) needs of individuals as biological organisms; (ii) requisites of coordinated social interactions; and (iii) survival and welfare needs of groups. These universal principles formed the basis of ten value types employed in the Schwartz Value Scale, including benevolence, universalism, self-direction, stimulation, hedonism, achievement, power, security, tradition and conformity. The relationships that people so actively seek are essentially exchanges of values, which ultimately dictate relations (Kahle, 1983). Like Rokeach, Schwartz felt that the individual places importance on some values over others as a means to make decisions. This level of importance-ordered sequence, enables humans to grow, advancing in response to changing drives from the undeveloped towards the developed (Mitchell, 1983).

Ethics may be defined as 'inquiry into the nature and grounds of morality where the term morality is taken to mean moral judgements, standards, and rules of conduct' (Taylor, 1975: 1). Fraedrich (1993) suggests that ethics refer to values and conduct, and that such values are the result of the process of learning. The rules, maxims and situational variables that people follow are explained through the use of moral philosophy, which may be used to justify decisions as being ethical or not. Therefore, the key important problem of ethics is the hierarchy of values.

Ethics, as suggested earlier, have a number of applications to many of the real world issues confronting humanity. For example, a good deal of research has been conducted on corporate ethical values and behaviour, especially from the perspective of marketing. Hunt *et al.* (1989) illustrate that for society, values help define the core of people, including what they hate or love, and the sacrifices they make to attain their goals. Values within the organization include those that convey a sense of identity to its members and which guide decision-making. Hunt *et al.* (1989), however, suggest that underlying these corporate values are corporate ethical values, which help establish and maintain standards, and determine the right course of action. Consequently, there is a close tie between values/core characteristics of people and ethics, which are the moral judgements people make.

Linking Ethics and Tourism

As an interdisciplinary science, tourism is vitally linked to a number of social and natural sciences, including economics, planning, geography,

sociology, psychology, pedagogics, ecology, law and so on. While historically ethics has not been a subject area associated with tourism, a growing
number of researchers would argue that it should be (Przeclawski, 1994;
Fennell and Malloy, 1995; Hultsman 1995; Karwacki and Boyd, 1995; Payne
and Dimanche, 1996; Malloy and Fennell, 1998b; Fennell, 1999). Although
the bond between tourism and ethics is easily defended, there are two
contributing forces that have no doubt reinforced such a link. These
include: (i) the Congress of AIEST in Paris, 1992, proposing the creation
of a commission dealing with ethical problems of tourism; and (ii) the
International Academy for the Study of Tourism meeting in Cairo, 1995,
which proposed the *Declaration of Ethics in Tourism.*

   More specifically, a number of conditions make tourism an appropriate
candidate for ethical scrutiny, apart from the fact that it deals with human
behaviour, as suggested above. It involves many different actors representing many different positions, it has an applied context, it has social, economic and ecological dimensions, and it is noted for its ability to create
a mix of significant impacts. In a recent paper, Fennell (2000) developed
an ethical model of tourism interactions that applies to actors involved in
tourism, including the environment. Based on the assumptions and beliefs
these individuals/groups have towards one another (i.e. assumptions and
beliefs about tourism and tourists, local people, the environment, profit,
preservation, time and space), their interactions present a number of
ethical dilemmas. Inappropriate behaviour from these interactions often
leads to impacts, which in turn elicit responses that are then fed back into
the basic assumptions and beliefs one group holds towards another.

   Figure 8.1 attempts to expand on this model, by focusing on types
of evaluations which actors may make (e.g. deontological, teleological or
existential), in generating sound ethical judgements, with the ultimate goal
of avoiding impacts and developing positive relationships amongst actors.
This addition is based on the work of Fennell and Malloy (1995) who wrote
that actors may employ a triangulated ethical approach as a basis for their
behaviour, as well in regard to the numerous interactions which may occur
with other tourism actors. The figure illustrates that for those actors who
avoid making ethically based evaluations or actions, the chances of creating
impacts are higher (indicated by the solid black line) than those who do
(indicated by the broken line). Similarly, the act of making ethical judgements does not eliminate the possibility of creating an impact, but one's
chances of avoiding impacts are thought to be much stronger if they
employ normative and introspective evaluations in situations that demand
them. The model is driven by the perspective that tourism will emerge and
remain an agent of good will if actors are capable of making ethically sound
decisions.

   The 'roots' of many of the negative consequences of tourism
(i.e. behaviour contradictory to ethical norms, etc.), can be found in the

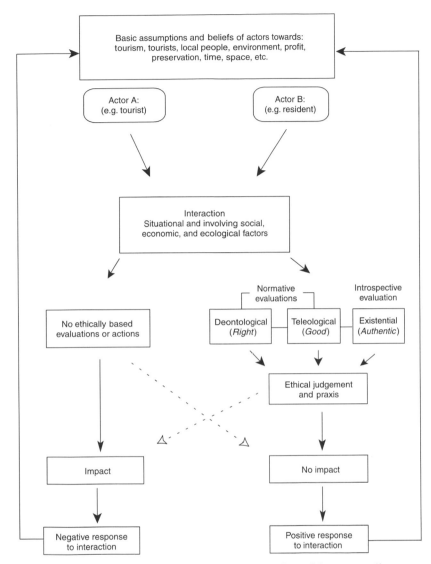

Fig. 8.1. Tourism ethics – interaction framework. Adapted from Fennell, 2000.

behaviour of three main groups: (i) tourists; (ii) inhabitants of the visited localities; and (iii) 'brokers', including tour operators, hotel staff and so on (see Fig. 8.2). At this point it would be useful to consider, from an ethical point of view, some examples of this behaviour and some ethical evaluations that may be instrumental in dictating appropriate patterns of behaviour within and between these various groups.

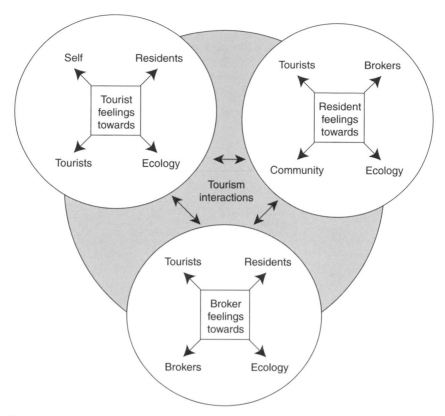

Fig. 8.2. Tourism actor interactions.

Tourism Actor Interactions

The behaviour of tourists

The behaviour of tourists can be viewed mainly from four perspectives: (i) the tourist as self; (ii) tourist–resident interactions; (iii) tourist–tourist interactions; and (iv) tourist interactions with the natural and cultural environment of the region visited.

The tourist as self

As an individual, the tourist has the opportunity to become better acquainted with him/herself, with residents and their customs, and also with the natural world of the region/area visited. While tourists travel for a number of different reasons (see Iso Ahola, 1982), travel, especially for extended periods of time, allows the tourist to better understand his/her role within family, work, and within a broader community. The tourist also has the opportunity to enjoy a sense of freedom from his/her duties in everyday life. The tourist must take responsibility for the use of this freedom, in ensuring that behaviour is consistent with the authentic self, but also the culture in which one is interacting (normative rules). This will require attaining knowledge about the people the tourist will visit, their culture and habits. The tourist must also be conscious of the fact that he/she can learn much from the local people of the destination.

Behaviour of tourists towards residents

de Kadt (1979) identified three tourist–resident contact situations which influence local values and attitudes: (i) when tourists purchase a good or service from a resident; (ii) when tourists and residents find themselves side by side at an attraction; and (iii) when the two parties come face to face with the object of exchanging information and ideas. de Kadt suggests that transitory and commercial exchanges (i and ii) far outweigh the latter case. The implications of such a relationship strongly support the contentions of many researchers who have documented the sociocultural dislocation that has occurred within many destinations over time. As outlined by Ryan (1991), tourism often puts a way of life, culture and values at tremendous risk. Ethically speaking, tourists must be conscious of the fact that residents will formulate opinions about the country which he/she is coming from. The tourist should respect the basic values of the inhabitants as well as the social order of the destination community. This includes a sense of responsibility for the formation of values of the visited population, especially in regard to the young. Consequently, local inhabitants should be viewed on equal terms, and not as objects, for it is forbidden to manipulate, humiliate or take unfair advantage of them, regardless of their level of education, colour of skin or customs. While on holiday, tourists need to consider that the local people with whom they interact are often working, and to consider this fact in their interactions.

Tourist–tourist interactions

In his sociological account of the tourist, MacCannell (1989) contends that tourists basically dislike other tourists, and naturally feel the impulse to appear holier than their fellow beings. When travelling, tourists are forced into spaces and situations that require interactions with other travellers. Tolerance and respect must be shown to the fellow traveller. Tourists should avoid inducing other travellers into behaviours that go against their ethical beliefs, but they should also choose not to follow behaviour when it does not correspond to their beliefs. During the trip it is important to share information about the destination with other travellers, and not waste the time of other travellers by arriving late for departures.

Tourist interactions with nature/culture

Finally, tourists are also responsible for respecting and caring for the environment they are visiting. It is important for tourists to realize that different environments have different capacities to absorb the pressures brought about by the industry (Getz, 1983). It is not only the actions of the individual tourist which should be viewed, but also the choices tourists make as regards the actions of others, including forms of transportation, hoteliers, operators and so on. The tourist, as a representative of the market, then becomes empowered to influence the decisions of others by virtue of the choices he or she makes. The actions of providers which contribute to pollution, crowding, destruction of resources, and other ecological disturbances (see Travis, 1982), should be tempered through a range of tourist, industry and governmental strategies designed to protect the environment. In the Himalayas, for example, Tourism Concern, in association with Nepalese tour operators and NGOs, developed a code designed to protect high-altitude environments. It requests that tourists do the following: (i) limit deforestation; (ii) remove litter; (iii) keep local water clean; (iv) leave plants to flourish; and (v) help guides follow appropriate conservation measures.

The behaviour of residents

Towards tourists

Maintaining an amicable tourism atmosphere, over time, has been one of the most formidable challenges confronting the tourism industry (Doxey, 1975). Yet it seems paramount that this must be one of the most important themes to ensure the overriding success of the local industry. Too often the economic significance of tourism (e.g. employment and economic impact) overwhelms other more intrinsic reasons for the development of the industry. Tourists, therefore, must be valued beyond their financial contributions to the region, and these values need to be consistently communicated and reinforced through culture, mission and vision statements of public and private organizations. Consequently, tourism must be viewed as a vehicle to broaden the horizons of residents. In doing so, tourism becomes an open window to the world, and promotes education, tolerance and positive attitudes towards others. At the same time, however, residents should protect their cultural identities, especially those that apply to youth, and personal and group values, especially in light of the intense pressure brought on by the tourism industry. If the main motive for local people is to gain money from tourists, very often the authentic cultural values that at one time were valued, may become over commercialized and replaced by forgeries. Finally, tourists should not be discriminated against in regard to race, nationality, beliefs or gender, and should be offered good medical aid and high quality services.

Towards own community

The tourism industry has been severely criticized in the way in which it has penetrated to practically every corner of the planet, and for many associated irreversible changes introduced along the way (Zurick, 1995). It is because of this change, and the loss of control that often accompanies development, that communities must be made aware of how the industry is planned, developed and managed. Residents will no doubt need to seek spaces and places within the community away from the industry, if this is possible, where natural and cultural processes are allowed to function without interruption. The community must therefore protect itself and its citizens, and allow many of the benefits of tourism to be felt across the community in either a direct or indirect fashion. Other like-minded guidelines have been suggested by the Pro Erschmatt Society (Mason and Mowforth, 1995: 49), which supports a tourism industry, and is specifically adapted to the needs of local people, based on the following criteria:

1. It must benefit the population as a whole and not the individual speculators.
2. It must not abuse the environment – our capital – through speculation and thereby rob it of its recreational quality, but respect both the landscape and village architecture.
3. It must take into account future generations and be based on medium and long-term solutions, rather than on short-term ones.
4. It should allow the community to develop and should not impose a prohibitive infrastructural burden on it.
5. It should not involve speculation leading to rocketing land prices, which make property too expensive for the local population.
6. It should not lead to a sell-out of the host country.
7. It must not generate dead holiday villages, inhabited for only a few weeks in the year.
8. It must be based on autonomous local decision-making, i.e. on equal participation of the local population in the planning and realization of tourist projects.
9. It must create attractive jobs, take into account the local business and not waste building land.

One of the responsibilities of the host population is to recognize the desire of many tourists to meet and interact with local people and to be prepared to foster the host–guest relationship in tourism. The host population should have an active say in the kind of tourism appropriate to their own lifestyles, cultures and natural resources, and be free to reject tourism as an economic option if other options are available (Mason and Mowforth, 1995: 51).

Towards own environment

The local population should take care to protect the natural and cultural heritage in which they must live and work. Residents must therefore engender a culture of valuing and protecting their local resources. The philosophy of the land ethic must be adopted by local people, and the sense that through appropriate planning, resources may be used, conserved and preserved in an appropriate manner. As Leopold (1966: 238) suggested, an ethic, ecologically, is a limitation on freedom of action in the struggle for existence. To Leopold, the land ethic simply enlarged the boundaries of the community to include elements such as soil, water, plants and animals. Conscience is very important to the concept of ethics. People must extend the social conscience from humans alone to land. The 'Communities in Bloom' concept in Canada is a programme designed to foster community pride through a conscious effort by citizens to improve and beautify local environmental conditions. In doing so, residents provide a better home for themselves and tourists alike.

Towards brokers

Tourism, as suggested earlier, is considered to be a viable mechanism that has great potential to bring social and economic prosperity to a region, although the reverse is also possible. Although this interaction is less apparent, there still need to be clearly defined lines of communication between providers and residents. These may come in the form of public meetings, or other forums allowing residents a chance to voice concerns over developments that affect their lives (see Timothy and Tosun, Chapter 10 this volume; Sheyvens, Chapter 12 this volume). Also, residents will be interested in employment opportunities within the industry, and to benefit directly or indirectly from other developments or endeavours that may benefit the community. Some regions have established trust funds from the economic impact of the tourism industry. Through community interaction and exchange, the monies from these trusts may be used to build facilities for recreation or education that may benefit the whole community.

The behaviour of brokers

In general, tourism brokers include those who are involved in administration, marketing, tour operation/guiding, and hotel and tourist information staff. An effort is made to distinguish their behaviour relating to tourists, residents, other brokers and the environment.

Broker behaviour towards tourists

The tourism administration, as well as local, regional and national governments, are responsible for tourism policy and for creating the necessary conditions for the development of tourism. From an ethical standpoint, it is especially important that they critically examine the economic, social, cultural and educational consequences of their policies.

Tour operators and guides must strive to secure appropriate levels of certification and accreditation which will enable them to structure the best and safest programmes, convenient and safe transportation, hygienic conditions, and to protect the rights of their clients. In addition, operator programmes must be sensitive to the ecological and social conditions of the attractions that are central to their itineraries. Operators must also be sensitive to the fact that different categories of tourists have different needs and desires (e.g. education, age, abilities), and that programmes must be adjusted accordingly. Disabled people have the same right to travel and, increasingly, tour operators will be called upon to facilitate their needs, particularly in the areas of transportation and accommodation.

The basic task of hotel and information staff is to ensure the safety of the tourists, the appropriate comfort, hygiene, peace and quiet, and a range of other high quality services. Hotel staff must also facilitate the tourist's experience through the provision of information that is objective and not dependent on either politics or economic profit. The information on the locality and on tourist attractions must be honest and not create a false image of places and objects. It is also very important to give information about the local culture, customs of the inhabitants and their religion and ethics, in order to facilitate the possibility of mutual understanding and dialogue.

Broker behaviour related to residents

Tourism administrators and governments should strive to promote what may be termed 'humanistic tourism', a kind of tourism based on social, cultural, ecological and educational well-being. The rights of the inhabitants, and their interests, must therefore be taken into account in planning and developing the industry (see Johnston, Chapter 7 this volume). Residents must be allowed to get a sense of how they are benefiting economically and socially, either directly or indirectly, from the development of tourism in their region. It is also very important that local people are prepared for contact with tourists. Accordingly, it seems necessary to inform the inhabitants about the culture, customs and behaviour of tourists coming from various countries. On the other hand, one has to help inhabitants in developing an attitude of hospitality and tolerance. It is also important to attempt to structure mechanisms that promote the authentic local traditions and values of resident and indigenous populations, which will act both to preserve culture and secure a more realistic tourism product.

The investors and tour operators organizing the physical planning of tourism development as well as organizing the trips, must take into account the rights and interests of the local population in a way that does not destroy their cultural heritage and the natural environment through commercialization. They must have respect for local values, ethical norms and religious beliefs. If possible the everyday life of the inhabitants and their customs should not be disturbed by the presence of tourists. The rights and interests of the local population should also be respected as regards the construction of new hotels, and such developments should not aggravate the living conditions of the local population (Fennell and Malloy, 1999; Timothy and Ioannides, 2002).

Towards other brokers

Tourism, like other economic activities, is competitive. While economic success is often the most important criterion in gauging the success of one's venture, all efforts should be made to foster an atmosphere of respect and cooperation among those working in the industry. Success is often contingent upon a host of externalities outside the grasp of the operator. Accordingly, the industry, through organizations and associations, should share information, technologies and expertise in generating success, which may be shared among all of the various businesses which are tied into the industry. Governments must therefore provide leadership in the areas of marketing and promotion, and must be equitable in their dispensation of information and aid in the development of the industry. Literature on business ethics points to the fact that those with clearly defined ethical strategies, which echo throughout the organization, stand a better chance of succeeding than those who do not (Reidenbach and Robin, 1988). Thus, tourism associations must take it upon themselves to include corporate ethical values in marketing, promotion and programming.

Towards the environment

Malloy and Fennell (1998b) argued that as the ecotourism industry matures, the need to address ethical conduct from an organizational perspective becomes increasingly important for the sector to survive and prosper in the 21st century. The approaches to planning and development in ecotourism, are transferable to the industry as a whole (Ayala, 1996). In fact it has been stated that those who are most environmentally competent are those who stand the greatest chance of being successful in the future. With this in mind, all of the various brokers involved in the planning, development, management and delivery of tourism, in association with other industries, must share the task of creating the cleanest and most efficient product possible through the newest and best technologies available.

Conclusions

It is a rather difficult task to examine all of the aforementioned ethical interactions from a theoretical perspective (i.e. viewing all from deonto-logical, teleological and existential positions), although it is useful to provide a stronger link between certain interactions and the proposed theories. From the deontological perspective, tourists, residents and brokers would act according to duty and principle established by community, country or those of a more universal nature. The finest example of such 'right' behaviour would involve following codes of ethics, which currently exist for operators, tourists and governments. Using the Pro Erschmatt Society code of ethics outlined earlier, principled community-tourism brokers would, for example, not develop the industry if it leads to a sell-out of a country. Teleologically, actors may achieve the desired level of utility or happiness by benefiting through an experience (e.g. having attained a certain level of education through an experience). This may also relate to the positive feelings that tourists have in receiving the most value for their money, or that operators have when they prosper economically and at the same time offer tourists experiences that exceed their expectations. Finally, authentic behaviour (the existential perspective) is realized when brokers have, through their own sense of freedom, accepted the responsibility to commit genuinely to the values, goals and mission of their organization and, in doing so, fulfil their own expectations of appropriate conduct and perhaps the expectations of others.

Earlier it was suggested that if actors could make ethically sound decisions, then the industry would have more of a chance of being a vehicle of good will. The task that we have at hand is to develop mechanisms to aid in making this a reality. This will involve a better understanding of ethics, from a theoretical perspective, but also how these theories may be applied to real world community-tourism dilemmas. At present there is a series of normative codes of ethics and conduct for operators, hosts, tourists and governments. Although these are a function of what a society, or a region, views as being important; to a large degree, we must rely on the free will of actors to ensure appropriate ends. Thus, the education of all the various actor groups is vitally important to ensure that each is cognisant of the potential it has to create negative impacts. Consequently, further research is needed, particularly in the form of case studies, to examine situations involving the aforementioned actors and the various ethical situations developed from their interactions. From this, researchers may begin the task of using theory to aid in the amelioration of these situations. It should be further noted that philosophers alone will not be able to accomplish this task. Input is required from the actors themselves, including operators and hoteliers, and those in tourism policy, economic development, resource management, and other areas.

References

Ayala, H. (1996) Resort ecotourism: a paradigm for the 21st century. *Cornell Hotel and Restaurant Administration Quarterly* 37, 46–53.

Benn, P. (1998) *Ethics*. McGill-Queen's University Press, Montreal.

Buber, M. (1991) The true barbarians. *Contours* 5(4), 8–9.

Buber, M. (1992) *Ja i Ty (Me and You)*. Pax, Warszawa.

Cohen, E. (1979) A phenomenology of tourist experiences. *Sociology* 13, 179–201.

Cooper, D.E. (1998) *Ethics: the Classic Readings*. Blackwell, Malden, Massachusetts.

de Kadt, E. (ed.) (1979) *Tourism: Passport to Development?* Oxford University Press, Oxford.

Doxey, G.V. (1975) A causation theory of visitor–resident irritants; methodology and research inference. Paper presented at the annual Travel and Tourism Research Association Conference, San Diego, California.

Fennell, D.A. (1999) *Ecotourism: an Introduction*. Routledge, London.

Fennell, D.A. (2000) Tourism and applied ethics. *Tourism Recreation Research* 25, 59–69.

Fennell, D.A. and Malloy, D.C. (1995) Ethics and ecotourism: a comprehensive ethical code. *Journal of Applied Recreation Research* 20, 163–183.

Fennell, D.A. and Malloy, D.C. (1999) Measuring the ethical nature of tourism operators. *Annals of Tourism Research* 26, 928–943.

Fraedrich, J. (1993) The ethical behavior of retail managers. *Journal of Business Ethics* 12, 207–218.

Getz, D. (1983) Capacity to absorb tourism: concepts and implications for strategic planning. *Annals of Tourism Research* 10, 239–263.

Guignon, C. (1986) Existential ethics. In: Demarco, J. and Fox, R. (eds) *New Directions in Ethics: the Challenge of Applied Ethics*. Routledge and Kegan Paul, New York, pp. 73–91.

Hultsman J. (1995) Just tourism: an ethical framework. *Annals of Tourism Research* 22, 553–567.

Hunt, S., Wood, V. and Chonko, L. (1989) Corporate ethical values and organizational commitment in marketing. *Journal of Marketing* 53, 79–90.

Iso Ahola, S. (1982) Toward a social psychological theory of tourism motivation: a rejoinder. *Annals of Tourism Research* 12, 256–262.

Kahle, L. (1983) Dialectical tensions in the theory of social values. In: Kahle, L. (ed.) *Social Values and Social Change*. Praeger, New York, pp. 275–283.

Karwacki, J. and Boyd, C. (1995) Ethics and ecotourism. *Business Ethics* 4, 225–232.

Krippendorf, J. (1987) *The Holiday Makers: Understanding the Impact of Leisure and Travel*. Heinemann Publishing, Oxford.

Leopold, A. (1966) *A Sand County Almanac*. Ballantine Books, New York.

MacCannell, D. (1989) *The Tourist: a New Theory of the Leisure Class.* Schocken Books, New York.

Madrigal, R. (1995) Personal values, traveler personality type, and leisure travel style. *Journal of Leisure Research* 27, 125–142.

Malloy, D.C. and Fennell, D.A. (1998a) Codes of ethics and tourism: an exploratory content analysis. *Tourism Management* 19, 453–461.

Malloy, D.C. and Fennell, D.A. (1998b) Ecotourism and ethics: moral development and organizational cultures. *Journal of Travel Research* 36, 47–56.

Mannell, R. and Kleiber, D. (1997) *A Social Psychology of Leisure.* Venture, State College, Pennsylvania.

Mason, P. and Mowforth, M. (1995) *Codes of Conduct in Tourism.* University of Plymouth, Department of Geographical Sciences, Plymouth.

Meyersohn, R. (1981) *Tourism as a Socio-cultural Phenomenon: Research Perspectives.* Otium Publications, Waterloo, Ontario.

Mitchell, A. (1983) *The Nine American Lifestyles.* MacMillan, New York.

Payne, D. and Dimanche, F. (1996) Towards a code of conduct for the tourism industry: an ethics model. *Journal of Business Ethics* 15, 997–1007.

Przeclawski, K. (1985) The role of tourism in contemporary culture. *The Tourist Review* 40, 2–6.

Przeclawski, K. (1994) *Tourism and the Contemporary World.* University of Warsaw, Warsaw.

Przeclawski, K. (1997) Deontology of tourism. In: Cooper, C. and Wanhill, S. (eds) *Tourism Development: Environmental and Community Issues.* John Wiley & Sons, Chichester, pp. 105–111.

Raphael, D. (1989) *Moral Philosophy.* Oxford University Press, Oxford.

Reidenbach, R.E. and Robin, D.P. (1988) Some initial steps toward improving the measurement of ethical evaluation of marketing activities. *Journal of Business Ethics* 7, 871–879.

Rokeach, M. (1968) *Beliefs, Attitudes and Values.* Jossey-Bass, San Francisco.

Rokeach, M. (1973) *The Nature of Human Values.* Free Press, New York.

Russell, B. (1979) *History of Western Philosophy.* Unwin, London.

Ryan, C. (1991) *Recreational Tourism: a Social Science Perspective.* Routledge, London.

Schwartz, S.H. (1994) Are there universal aspects in the structure and contents of human values? *Journal of Social Issues* 50, 19–45.

Schwartz, S.H. (1996) Value priorities and behavior: applying a theory of integrated value systems. In: Seligman, C., Olson, J. and Zanna, M. (eds) *The Psychology of Values: the Ontario Symposium.* Lawrence Erlbaum, Mahway, New Jersey, pp. 1–24.

Schwartz, S.H. and Bilsky, W. (1990) Toward a theory of the universal content and structure of values: extensions and cross-cultural replications. *Journal of Personality and Social Psychology* 58, 878–891.

Taylor, P. (1975) *Principles of Ethics: an Introduction.* Dickenson, Encino, California.

Timothy, D.J. and Ioannides, D. (2002) Tour operator hegemony: dependency, oligopoly and sustainability in insular destinations. In: Apostolopoulos, Y. and Gayle, D.J. (eds) *Island Tourism and Sustainable Development: Caribbean, Pacific, and Mediterranean Experiences.* Praeger, Westport, Connecticut, pp. 181–198.

Travis, A.S. (1982) Physical impacts: trends affecting tourism. *Tourism Management* 3, 256–262.

Zurick, D. (1995) *Errant Journeys*. University of Texas Press, Austin.

CHALLENGES AND OPPORTUNITIES FOR DESTINATION COMMUNITIES

Development Issues in Destination Communities

9

DAVID J. TELFER

Department of Recreation and Leisure Studies, Brock University, St Catharines, Canada

Introduction

Countries around the world continue to use tourism as an agent of development yet there has been little acknowledgement of the overriding development paradigms within the tourism literature (Telfer, 1996, 2002a). The evolution of development thought has become increasingly complex over time with much current thinking putting people and communities at the centre of development. This chapter examines the evolution of development thought to its present-day focus on community development. Within this context, tourism is examined against four main development paradigms that have evolved since the Second World War: modernization, dependency, economic neo-liberalism and alternative development (Telfer, 1996, 2002a). The relationships between tourism and development are explored, highlighting the changing nature of the two fields and the emerging nature of the linkages with community development. It is argued that the potential for community development associated with tourism will be determined in part by the overriding paradigm guiding the development process.

The main part of the chapter then focuses in on community development as part of the alternative development paradigm drawing heavily on the community development literature. As tourism continues to be a preferred agent of development, it is important to understand the nature of community development and who ultimately controls and benefits from tourism. The concept of community development is explored in terms of empowerment, participation, partnership, community capacity and community change. Returning more specifically to tourism, the chapter then highlights examples of the challenges and issues that tourism faces in promoting community development under these five concepts.

If tourism is to be used successfully as an agent of development at the community level it is important to understand the extent to which community capacity is enhanced. In examining community development across international borders, Campfens (1997a: 142) argues that there are several factors having considerable influence on the level at which community development is supported and can be practised. Community development needs to be placed in a framework that acknowledges new forces at work at the global level. There are also vast differences in political systems and policy practices of governments, as well as differing economic conditions and social inequalities. The social and ethno-cultural composition of different populations, and differences in relations between the state and civil society all need to be considered (Campfens, 1997b). Tourism also needs to be considered within this global framework. If tourism is to act as an agent of development at the community level, an understanding of the fundamentals of development and the context in which it is pursued is required. The chapter concludes by linking together tourism and community development in an adapted framework under the three approaches of locality development, social planning/policy and social action.

Tourism as an Agent of Development

Social theorists have long debated the concept of what development means and how it is achieved. As Harrison (1988: 154–155) suggested, development has had several meanings including 'economic growth, structural change, autonomous industrialisation, capitalism or socialism, self-actualisation and individual, national, regional, and cultural self reliance'. In examining questions of uneven development and socioeconomic and spatial inequalities in developing countries, especially in Africa, Konadu-Agyemang (2000: 470) outlines wide disparities in 'incomes, access to health care, education, and other services not only between rural and urban areas but also between regions and genders'. The problems of underdevelopment have continued to perplex agencies and researchers, leading some to question the validity of development theorizing and others to search for new ground to break through the impasse in development theory (Schuurman, 1993). Analysing social change and social theorizing is an attempt to make sense of the social world (Preston, 1996). It is based on complex, interlinked claims on the nature of the social world (ontology), the nature of the knowledge in respect of the social world (epistemology), the manner in which the knowledge is secured (methodology), and the manner in which the knowledge is put to use (practice) (Preston, 1996). The various influences on theory and their links to practice have long been at the centre of the debate surrounding development. Hettne (1990) argues that development theory can be divided into development ideology (the means) and development strategy (ends). He also suggests that there can be no final definition of development, only suggestions of what development should imply in particular contexts. Thus, development involves structural transformation that implies political, cultural, social and economic changes (Hettne, 1990).

With the end of the Second World War and the formation of new nation states, there have been various distinct approaches to the issue of development, which have found practical expression through a variety of agencies responsible for social intervention and reform (Preston, 1996). Tourism is one such method used by a variety of agencies (public, private and non-profit) to generate development. The pertinent question for this chapter then is what is the role of tourism in development and correspondingly who benefits from that development. Can community capacity be built through tourism development?

Preston (1996) suggests three approaches to characterize and secure development. The first approach presents arguments for state actions to secure order. This is advocated by agencies, including international ones linked to the United Nations (UN), which are committed to the development goal of effective statehood. The second approach is guided by a set of ideas, which argue for the spontaneous order of the marketplace. A self-regulating market and minimum state interference are at the heart of this approach. The institutional vehicles of development under this are monetary organizations such at the International Monetary Fund and the World Bank. Finally, the third approach argues for the polity in achieving order and development. The ideas here relate to the power of the political community to secure rational goals for development. A central role is allocated to the public sphere with rational dialogue. The approach is oriented to securing formal and substantive democracy, and the institutional vehicles are non-governmental organizations (NGOs), charities and dissenting groups.

Changes in development theory since the end of the Second World War and the corresponding trends in the tourism industry have been examined by Telfer (1996, 2002a). Telfer (1996) used the following four categories for analysis of development and tourism: modernization, dependency, economic neo-liberalism and alternative development. Each paradigm can in part be seen as a reaction against the previous paradigm and certain paradigms have taken a position of hegemony over other development theories. The paradigms are also influenced to a certain degree by views from across the political spectrum. The following sections briefly trace the evolution of development thought since the Second World War making reference to tourism and community development under these four paradigms, although this is only one way of classifying development thought. As indicated in the introduction, the potential for community development associated with tourism will be determined in part by the overriding paradigm guiding the development process.

Modernization

Modernization has been defined as a process of socioeconomic development that follows an evolutionary path from a traditional society to a modern society such as North America (Schmidt, 1989). Sklair (1991) suggests that modernization theories of the global system are largely based on the distinction between the traditional and the modern. Within the modernization paradigm is the work of Rostow (1967) and his *Stages of Economic Growth*. He argued that for development to occur, a country had to pass through the stages of traditional society, preconditions for take off, the drive to maturity, and the age of high-mass consumption. Tourism has been offered as a solution to move a country from a state of underdevelopment to one of development. It has been promoted as a strategy to transfer technology, increase employment, generate foreign exchange, increase the gross domestic product, and to attract development capital as well as a way to promote a modern way of life (Britton, 1982; Mathieson and Wall, 1982; Cater, 1987). Large-scale mass tourism has been seen as a way to infuse foreign capital and generate foreign exchange quickly. The notion of moving to a state of being developed can also be seen in the strategies of regional economic development theorists such as Perroux's (1988) growth poles and Myrdal's (1963) spread effects. Countries such as Mexico and Indonesia, for example, have also used tourism as a regional economic development tool, setting up tourism growth poles in the hope that the multiplier effect of tourism would spread throughout the region (Telfer, 2002b). Concepts on the evolutionary growth of tourism, in a format with parallels to the work of Rostow, have also been proposed by Butler (1980) and adapted widely in the tourism literature. As tourism grows over time, development proceeds; however, local control can be lost to outside forces and hence the community ends up playing a minor role. Depending on conditions in the destination, there may be limited potential for community development in the drive to modernize through large-scale mass tourism. Economic growth is often associated with modernization and in terms of tourism development it is important to understand whether the economic benefits reach the local community and help build community capacity. The difficulty with tourism as a development tool is further highlighted in Butler's model when a destination stagnates and falls out of favour.

Dependency

The dependency paradigm gained prominence in the 1960s as a critique to modernization. North American Marxists or neo-Marxists and Latin American intellectuals concluded that the international system 'far from guaranteeing the South's prosperity, brought domination effects to bear upon it and locked it in dependence' (Rist, 1997: 109). It is argued that there are internal political, institutional and economic structures in developing countries that keep them in a dependent position in the global economic system controlled by developed countries. The resulting international capitalistic system of rich and poor countries leaves an unequal power relationship between the developed (centre) and the developing (periphery) (Cardoso, 1979; Frank, 1988; Todaro, 1994). The dependency paradigm has been raised in tourism in terms of the centre–periphery relationships that have evolved within the industry. It has been argued that tourism generates a form of neocolonialism whereby large multinational corporations, such as airlines, tour operators and hotel chains, control the industry from the developed countries leaving the developing countries at the mercy of these global giants (Britton, 1982). Power structures emerge in the tourism industry reinforcing the dependency and vulnerability of developing country destinations (Telfer, 1996). Within the framework of neocolonialism, the power and control of the tourism industry is external, leaving limited potential for community development through tourism as destinations are exploited by the tourism industry. To counteract these forces, advocates of the dependency perspective argue for state intervention and protectionist policies. There have been attempts by some countries to develop their own state-sponsored tourism (e.g. state-run hotel chains) in an attempt to promote self-reliance (Curry, 1990), a concept that will be discussed below in the context of community development.

Economic neo-liberalism

The rise of economic neo-liberalism was developed in reaction to strong state intervention including that promoted by structural dependency theorists (Telfer, 1996). The movement favours supply-side macroeconomics, free competitive markets and the privatization of state enterprises as seen in the conservative government policies in the 1980s in the USA, Canada, UK and West Germany (Todaro, 1994). Agencies such as the International Monetary Fund and the World Bank have promoted the use of Structural Adjustment Lending Programmes directed at specific policy changes in the receiving countries. The impacts of structural adjustment have been explored by Mohan *et al.* (2000) and Konadu-Agyemang (2000). Campfens (1997b) noted the move to a global society in the context of community development. While it is useful to examine community development at a national level, it also needs to be understood in an international context. Mega-level changes are at work moving from an era of nation states towards a global society dominated by regional market economies and growing interdependence. Along with the trend of internationalized capital, 'many governments are turning to neoliberal monetarist policies, and this has undermined the politics of social democracy that legitimated the rise of the welfare state in many countries throughout much of this century' (Campfens, 1997b: 13). These neo-liberal strategies have been picked up within the tourism industry in the push for freer movement of people and capital between states. International agencies such as the World Bank and the European Union (EU) have provided funding for tourism develop- ment projects and some developing countries have passed laws allowing increased foreign investment to help foster the tourism industry (Inskeep and Kallenberger, 1992). Poirer (1995), for example, stated that the future of tourism in Tunisia centred on comparative advantage, economic think- ing and external pressures towards structural adjustment measures. Issues related to tourism and community development here again relate to issues of control outlined above. By attracting private multinational tourism corporations and borrowing funds for tourism infrastructure from inter- national agencies, control of the industry in the destination may be external. It is argued that it is only the local elite that benefit under the economic neo-liberal approach and the structural adjustment lending programmes have been criticized for the dire social consequences on the local population (Brohman, 1996). Unless funds are targeted to assist in community tourism development projects then the potential for commu- nity development may be lost in the pressures of the global economy. One such international funding programme which focuses on local support and involvement is the LEADER programme (Liaisons Entre Actions pour la Développement des Économies Rurales) of the EU which is intended to promote an integrated approach to rural development. Tourism has become one of the main concepts of business plans submitted for funding through this programme. In a successful case, Sharpley and Sharpley (1997) described the South Pembrokeshire Partnership for Action with Rural Communities (SPARC) in the UK, which covers some 35 rural communities and was able to provide help to over 100 different projects with many of them related to rural tourism.

Alternative development

Finally, the alternative development paradigm evolved out of criticisms of the Eurocentric, meta-narrative, economic models that preceded it and tends to be focused on basic needs, people and the environment (Schmidt,

1989). The approach is centred on a grass-roots, participatory approach, which empowers local people. Also included in this paradigm is the concept of sustainable development, which has come to mean meeting the needs of the present generation without compromising the needs of future generations, a definition that gained prominence out of the 1987 World Commission on the Environment and Development. As Redclift (1987) suggested, the dominant modernization, dependency and neo-liberal paradigms did not incorporate the environment into development. Mitchell (1997) also points out that key aspects of sustainable development include empowerment of local people, self-reliance and social justice. Alternative tourism development strategies have tended to stress small-scale, locally owned developments, community participation, and environmental and cultural sustainability; however, the strategies need to be developed within the contexts of the individual countries (Brohman, 1996). The highly contested notion of sustainable development and the need for environmental protection and community involvement have quickly been brought into tourism research. Mowforth and Munt (1998) examined the evolution of sustainability and note the fact that the meaning of sustainability is disputed by international agencies, national governments, new social and environmental movements, tour operators and tourists. The rise of environmentalism has led to investigations into the highly debated term 'ecotourism' and the development of NGOs concerned over the impact of tourism, such as Tourism Concern. Other studies have focused on the role of indigenous tourism developments (Telfer, 2000a) and the implications of tourism development on gender (Sinclair, 1997; Apostolopoulos *et al.*, 2001). Within the alternative development framework, the potential to generate community development through tourism remains high. At the heart of the approach is local control and empowerment as indicated by Mitchell (1997) above. In the case of the village of Bangunkerto, Indonesia, the introduction of agritourism was found to generate community development as the villagers cooperated on the initiative and control was maintained at the local level (Telfer, 2000a). Some of the difficulties in trying to achieve community development through tourism under this paradigm are raised later in this chapter.

As highlighted briefly above, the concept of development is a contested notion that has long been debated. The debate has given rise to the following critique from those in the post-developmental camp:

> Delusion and disappointment, failures and crimes have been the steady companions of development and they tell a common story: it did not work. Moreover, the historical conditions which catapulted the idea into prominence have vanished: development has become outdated. But above all, the hopes and desires which made the idea fly, are now exhausted: development has grown obsolete.
>
> (Sachs, 1992: 1)

Peet (1999) generalized the positions of those in the post-development camp into three categories that rejected the way of thinking and the mode of living produced by modern development. These categories include radical pluralism, simple living and reappraising non-capitalist societies. Peet (1999) suggests that support for local initiatives and the importance of community involvement in the development process are among the recurring themes from those in the post-development camp.

Having briefly traced the evolution of development thought and its relationship to tourism and community development, it is important to address the meaning of community development in more detail from the perspective of empowerment, participation, partnership, community capacity and community change.

Community Development

Within development paradigms, the importance of community has come to the forefront, placing local people at the centre of development. With tourism becoming the preferred agent of development in many communities, it is important to understand the nature of community development and who ultimately benefits from the processes of tourism. As tourism continues to expand throughout the world in a wide variety of contexts, community change occurs and recent arguments noted above suggest local people should have a greater say in that development. Tourism proceeds both as a planned intervention, as a local, regional or national development strategy, and as an unplanned free market process. In general community development terms, Arai (1996: 27) suggests, 'international strategies of community change can vary widely from programs that target a specific problem (e.g. irrigation projects, nutrition for children) to macro strategies for changing ideologies and political social structures (e.g. the human rights movement, women's movement)'. Adapting this statement to tourism, strategies of community change at the micro level could include the introduction of community- or village-based tourism to generate additional income (Telfer, 2000a). At the macro level there are the strategies adopted by tourism-related NGOs, such as Tourism Concern, which highlight the role of tourism in raising awareness of environmental and human rights issues. However, what is important in community development is the process involved rather than the product (Reid and van Dreunen, 1996).

Early contributions to the concept of community have come from sociology, such as Tonnies' characterization of communities as *Gemeinshaft* (folk) and *Gesellschaft* (urban), or Durkheim's distinction between mechanical and organic social solidarity (Pedlar, 1996). Rothman *et al.* (1995) conceive community as the territorial organization of people, goods, services and commitments, which are important subsystems of society where many locality-relevant functions are carried on. An often cited, early definition of community development comes from the UN which defined it tentatively as 'a process designated to create conditions of economic and social progress for the whole community with its active participation and the fullest possible reliance on the community's initiative' (United Nations, 1955: 6).

Walter (1997) argues however that there needs to be a shift in looking at community as a social/demographic entity or unit to a community as a multidimensional/dynamic whole or system. This expanded notion of community describes the way in which various dimensions of community such as people and organizations, actions, consciousness and context are integrally related to each other to form the community. The definition draws in multiple stakeholders with diverse interests crossing both horizontal and vertical dimensions, therefore including those who formerly would have been considered to be outside the community. As the community is viewed as multidimensional, consciousness becomes an integral part as it draws in the full spectrum of perceptions, cultural constructs and frameworks through which interaction occurs (Walter, 1997). Finally, community interaction occurs within the context of larger society and cultures, a place in history and in a physical environment. This notion of understanding the value and belief systems is also highlighted by Pedlar (1996) in her exploration of individual interest and collective interests in terms of community.

Campfens (1997b) argues that community development is a demonstration of the ideas, values and ideals of the society where it is taking place.

> In an humanitarian perspective it can be a search for community, mutual aid, social support and human liberation in an alienating, oppressive, competitive and individualistic society. In its more pragmatic institutional sense, it may be viewed as a means for mobilising communities to join state or institutional initiatives that are aimed at alleviating poverty, solving social problems, strengthening families, fostering democracy and achieving modernisation and socio-economic development.
>
> (Campfens, 1997b: 35)

Nozick's (1993) list of principles of sustainable community development also focus on building community capacity and include: (i) economic self-reliance; (ii) ecological sustainability; (iii) community control; (iv) meeting individual needs; and (v) building a community culture. Martí-Costa and Serrano-García (1995) suggest that community development is a process through which consciousness-raising promotes the utilization of human resources leading to the empowerment of individuals.

Empowerment

In a review of the literature, Arai (1996) outlined five main concepts connected to empowerment. Empowerment involves a change in capacity or control, or correspondingly an increase in power and the ability to use power. Secondly, empowerment is multidimensional in terms of psychological, economic, social and political change. The third condition is that empowerment is a multilevel construct and the previously mentioned changes occur within an individual, group or community. The fourth concept is that it is important to understand empowerment within a holistic framework, which acknowledges the interactions of the process of empowerment between various levels (individual and community) and dimensions (psychological, economic, social and political). Finally, the fifth component is that empowerment is a process or framework that describes changes which occur in an individual, group or community as they mobilize themselves towards increased citizen power (Arai, 1996) (see Johnston, Chapter 7 this volume; Scheyvens, Chapter 12 this volume).

Participation

Various authors have developed typologies or scales of public involvement in the planning process. These typologies address the notion that not all participation is actual participation and that those in power may speak to the citizens but they may not listen and implement what they have been told. In a classic, often-cited article, Arnstein (1969) developed a ladder of citizen participation with eight levels. The bottom two rungs of the ladder (*manipulation* and *therapy*) are outlined as non-participation levels, which have been contrived by some to substitute for genuine participation. The objective here is not to enable people to participate in the planning process but to enable those in power to educate or cure the participants. The third and fourth levels (*informing* and *consultation*) move into the area of tokenism where participants have the opportunity to speak but they have the lack of power to ensure that their message will be heeded. Arnsteins' fifth level is *placation*, which is a higher level to tokenism but the power still belongs in the hands of the elite. The final three levels of the ladder have increasing levels of citizen control. The sixth level of *partnership* allows citizens to negotiate and engage in trade-offs with those in power. In the seventh level of *delegated power* and the eighth level of *citizen control*, citizens have the majority of the decision-making seats or they have full managerial control.

In another context, Pretty (1994) developed a typology of how people participate in development programmes. Participation ranges from passive participation where people are told what development project is proceeding to self-mobilization where people take initiatives that are independent of external institutions. Pretty (1994) argues that if development is to be sustainable, then his fifth level of functional participation has to be achieved to involve local people forming their own groups to meet predetermined objectives related to the development project. A framework of the process of personal empowerment proposed by Arai (1996) suggests that people move from a state of powerlessness to increasing levels of empowerment though awareness, connecting and learning, mobilization and contribution. The movement through these stages in the framework is not necessarily linear and there is no end point where one is said to be empowered. The process is cyclical or helical.

Partnership

Within the concept of community development is the building of partnerships, which has collaboration at the heart of most definitions (Lord, 1998). One of the key questions in building partnerships is whether or not those who presently hold the power will willingly agree to share this power (Lord, 1998). In considering the power relations in partnerships, Lord (1998) raises several questions. Who will benefit? Who will be harmed? Is there a common purpose and value? What beliefs about people and change are inherent in the project? How will those differences be addressed? Who will control the process? How will partners work together so that each partner's experience is honoured? How will participation be maximized? How will valued resources be shared? Shaffer and Anundsen (1993) state that the way in which decisions are made and power is shared, either builds or undermines relationships, strengthens or sabotages success or renews or deadens vitality. However, in what was identified as 'partnership shock' (Lord, 1998: 7), the authors have found that 'the formal, procedural nature of most partnerships maintains rationality and existing power relations'.

Community capacity

In looking at low-income urban areas, McKnight and Kretzmann (1997) argue that for community development to occur, policies must be made on the capacities, skills and assets of the residents. Reid and van Dreunen (1996) also suggest that capacity building is one of the keys to social transformation. McKnight and Kretzmann (1997) established a framework for mapping community capacity, which can be used to generate capacity inventories. The primary building blocks in the map are the assets and capacities located inside the neighbourhood, which are largely under neighbourhood control. These can be divided into those that belong to individuals and those that belong to associations. The secondary building blocks are located within the community but largely controlled by outsiders. These assets can be grouped into three categories including private and not-for-profit organizations, public institutions and services, and other physical resources. In the final cluster of assets are the resources, which originate outside the neighbourhood and are controlled by outsiders. The community, whether it is led by existing community organizations, community development corporations, or a new asset development organization, needs to build bridges to persons and organizations outside the neighbourhood. These outside organizations include government, banks, corporations, churches and other neighbourhood advocacy groups. Table 9.1 displays a partial list of the building blocks.

Community change

The above discussion has looked at some of the key concepts associated with community development and interventions. As outlined in the first section of this chapter on development, it is also important to incorporate the various theoretical underpinnings as they apply to development and community development. Checkoway (1995) suggested six strategies for

Table 9.1. Building blocks for mapping community capacity. Source: McKnight and Kretzmann (1997).

Primary building blocks
Asset and capacities located inside the neighbourhood largely under neighbourhood control

Individual assets	**Organizational assets**
Skills, talents and experience of residents	Associations of businesses
Individual businesses	Citizen's organizations
Home-based enterprises	Cultural organizations
Personal income	Religious organizations
Gifts of labelled people	

Secondary building blocks
Assets located within the community but largely controlled by outsiders

Private and non-profit	**Public institutions and services**	**Physical resources**
Higher education institution	Public schools	Vacant land
Hospitals	Police	Commercial and industrial Structures
Social service agencies	Libraries	Housing
	Fire departments	Energy and waste resources
	Parks	

Potential building blocks
Resources originating outside the neighbourhood controlled by outsiders

Welfare expenditures
Public capital information expenditures
Public information

community change including: mass mobilization, social action, citizen participation, public advocacy, popular education and local services development. The strategy that should be selected is the one that has the greatest potential to empower the community. Rothman (1995) identifies three differing approaches to community intervention, which are: (i) locality development; (ii) social planning/policy; and (iii) social action. The locality development approach argues that community change should occur through broad participation of a wide spectrum of people at the local community level in determining goals and taking civic action. Locality development is closely linked to the definition of community development presented by the UN in 1955. This approach focuses on promoting process goals such as community competency and social integration. Leadership, direction and control are found from within the local group. Rothman (1995) raises concerns with such an approach that emphasizes consensus. With such a heavy reliance on the local community it may become inappropriate especially if the locality has lost its hold and patterns of life are significantly influenced by powerful national or regional forces.

The social planning/policy emphasizes a technical process of problem solving based on data and driven by social science thinking and empirical objectivity. Community participation is not at the core of this approach; rather, change in a complex modern environment requires expert planners to improve social conditions with the ability to gather and analyse quantitative data and manoeuvre large bureaucratic organizations. There is a reliance on needs assessments, decision analysis and the use of statistical tools. At the centre of this approach is to develop and implement plans and policy frameworks in effective and cost-efficient ways (Rothman, 1995). This rational approach has been criticized for its assumption that problems can be clearly defined when in fact they are connected to a myriad of issues in society. Others argue that interest groups should have more say in planning. In addition, in an age of fiscal restraint, many plans aim at getting by without the ability due to finances of developing elaborate schemes based on the analysis of data (Rothman, 1995).

The final approach is social action, which is based on a disadvantaged segment of the population organizing to make demands on the larger community for more resources or better treatment. The approach can be militant it its orientation towards advocacy. The approach tries to make fundamental changes in the community in terms of redistribution of power and gaining access to decision-making. Practitioners in this realm try to empower and benefit the poor, oppressed or disenfranchised. The approach is influenced by the writings of Marx, Fourier, Bakunin and Habermass (Rothman, 1995). This approach has been known for fragmentation among the groups that practise social action. Fisher (1995) has developed a further expansion of the social action approach for the 1990s, updating one of Rothman's three approaches originally developed in 1968. These three approaches are similar to the concepts of social learning, policy analysis and social mobilization as identified by Friedmann (1987).

Before linking the concepts of community development to tourism, the chapter focuses on the work of Campfens (1997a), who prepared a useful framework for comparing community development across six countries. He described his three-part 'framework theory', as an outline for policy development, programme planning and community development practice. The first part of the framework focused on contextual factors broken down into the global environment, which is becoming increasingly interconnected. At the global level, there has been a shift from East–West ideological rivalries to a new reality of North–South and domestic inequalities. There has been a rise in international capitalism, multinational corporations, speculative money markets, communications technology and heightened competition for export markets. There have been increases in social turbulence, human rights abuses and mass movements of refugees, immigrants and migrant workers, and population growth primarily in the Third World. The contextual factors at the national and regional level include urban and rural issues, and urban to rural migrations. It is important to understand the level of ethno-cultural/religious homogeneity or heterogeneity, state of the economy (developed or underdeveloped) and the relations between state and civil society. Finally, there needs to be an understanding of the democratic environment and whether there is a high degree of centralization or if the society is decentralized with a high level of local control.

The second part of Campfens' (1997a: 468) framework focuses on emerging themes in community development practice. These themes include nurturing associative communities and mobilizing circles of solidarity, self-reliance and the role of NGOs, people-development focus, group and organizational expressions of popular and community participation, social justice agenda and human rights, and finally, global networking and a worldwide civil society.

The third and final part of Campfens' (1997a: 468) framework focuses on approaches to community development, some of which are presented here. The continuum approach to practice extends from the micro level to the global level. There is a focus on group or cooperative development for mutual aid and social action. Locality development is concerned with community economic development and the liveability of the local environment. The third approach, structural functional community work is also an important approach to community development as it works towards the development of relevant policy frameworks and focuses on organizational structure and partnerships. Categorical focused community development is aimed at self-reliance and the alleviation of social problems. In particular this approach focuses on economically, politically, and socially excluded groups. The final approaches include the formulation of self-empowering organizations, 'social learning' training workshops for experts and local activists, and an 'intergroup' social interaction approach relying on mutual understanding and conflict resolution.

The above discussion has set out in some detail the nature of community development along with a series of frameworks that have been proposed regarding what needs to be considered to promote community development. The final section of the chapter builds on the previous section by linking tourism and community development together.

Tourism and Community Development

Changes in development theory since the end of the Second World War have brought the concepts of sustainability and community involvement in the development process to the forefront as part of the alternative development paradigm. McIntosh *et al.* (1995) indicate that tourism development should contain elements of community involvement including raising the living standards of local people, developing facilities for visitors and residents, and ensuring the types of development are consistent with the cultural, social and economic philosophy of the government and the people of the host area.

Empowerment, participation and tourism

The concepts of empowerment and participation are key to community development and have gained increased attention in the tourism literature. Authors in the field of tourism planning have begun to stress the need for local community involvement and cooperation in the planning process (Murphy, 1985, 1988; Haywood, 1988; Inskeep, 1991; Gunn, 1994; Simmons, 1994; Scheyvens, 1999; Timothy, 1999; Tosun, 2000). Murphy (1985) advocated a community approach to tourism planning arguing that each community should identify tourism goals to the extent that they satisfy local needs. In his ecological model of tourism planning, Murphy (1985) places resident participation in the centre of the model and identifies a number of examples for facilitating public involvement. In reviewing more recent studies of community-based tourism, Richards and Hall (2000a) suggest that the scope of the term has broadened to encompass a wide range of issues including ecological factors and local participation and democracy. Concepts of Arnstein's (1969) ladder of citizen participation and Arai's (1996) key concepts of empowerment raised earlier, for example, can be seen underlying the investigation of issues affecting approaches to sustainable tourism planning and community participation in the case of the Hope Valley described by Bramwell and Sharman (2000). These issues include the scope of the participation by the community, the intensity of the participation by the community and the degree to which consensus emerges among participants. Reflecting back on the comments by Campfens (1997a), it is important to recognize that community participation in tourism may be limited in some country contexts (Timothy, 1999; Tosun, 2000). Other forms of tourism development within the alternative development paradigm, such as indigenous tourism and ecotourism, emphasize empowerment and participation (Scheyvens, 1999) (see Johnston, Chapter 7 this volume). In the case of Nunavut in the Canadian north, the Inuit have the opportunity to develop their own businesses as hotel-keepers, chefs, pilots, outfitters and others (Smith, 1996). In another example of ecotourism in the Monteverde Cloud Forest in Costa Rica, it must be noted that while some 80 new (mostly locally owned) tourism businesses have developed, many of the businesses are small and face limiting factors in terms of costs and marketing. There is also recognition that while ecotourism has led the rejuvenation of local arts and crafts in the Monteverde Cloud Forest, social impacts have occurred which have changed the community (Baez, 1996).

Partnerships and tourism

The importance of building partnerships not only between tourism businesses but also within communities to build on the benefits of tourism has received a great deal of attention in the tourism literature. Jamal and Getz (1995) advocated incorporating collaboration theory to community tourism planning and Reed (1997) furthered their work by suggesting that the power relations in a community need to be addressed to advance the explanations of community-based tourism planning. Based on research on community-based tourism planning in Squamish, Canada, Reed (1997) found that power relations may alter the outcome of collaborative tourism planning and may even preclude collaborative action, a finding echoed by Timothy (1998) in Indonesia. Two recently edited books have focused specifically on partnerships and collaboration in tourism (i.e. Bramwell and Lane, 2000; Crotts et al., 2000). Issues highlighted in the case studies by Bramwell and Lane (2000) on tourism collaboration and partnerships raise various questions that need to be explored, similar to those posed earlier in this chapter by Lord (1998) in terms of partnerships. Are there participants from government, business and non-profit sectors, and from national, regional and local policy arenas? To what extent is the collaboration process inclusive? Are all of the participants fully involved in the discussions and are all participants equally influential in the negotiations and decision-making process? To what extent is agreement reached and what are the achievements or outputs of collaborative approaches? Hall (2000a) raises similar issues in discussing tourism collaboration and partnerships, stating that unless there are attempts to provide equity of access to all stakeholders then collaboration will become another tourism planning cliché. He also argues for a broader notion of collaboration, without which, there may be an undermining of the social capital required for sustainable development. In trying to better identify the diversity of forms of partnerships, Selin (2000) proposes a preliminary typology of sustainable tourism partnerships covering issues such as the legal basis for partnerships, locus of control, organizational diversity and size, and time frame, all accessed by geographical scale. Finally, the importance of strategic alliances in the tourism industry has begun to be recognized and that while firms or communities may need to compete against each other, it has also become important for collaboration to occur to benefit entire regions (Telfer, 2000b).

Community capacity and tourism

The components for building community capacity were highlighted from the perspective of community development literature in Table 9.1 and included primary building blocks, secondary building blocks and potential building blocks. As Reid and van Dreunen (1996) suggest, building community capacity is one of the keys to social transformation. In investigating the process of community-based round-tables used to address conflict over tourism-related development in Canmore, a town adjacent to Banff National Park, Jamal and Getz (2000) found that some aspects of community capacity were enhanced. Developing capacity is also behind the Canadian Tourism Commission's Product Club Programme, which provides funding for small tourism business in a community to work collaboratively and further develop their products for the tourism market (Telfer, 2003). The sense of building community capacity and community change through tourism can be seen in Bramwell and Lane's (2000) examination of how collaborative approaches in tourism could help further the core principles of sustainable development. Collaboration among a broad range of stakeholders, including non-economic collaboration, may promote consideration of the varied natural, built and human resources that need to be protected for present and future generations. Secondly, by involving stakeholders from a variety of fields with different interests, there may be greater potential for integrative approaches to policy making that can help promote sustainability. Thirdly, if multiple stakeholders affected by tourism development were involved in the policy-making process it could lead to a more equitable distribution of the benefits and costs associated with tourism. Increased participation should lead to increased awareness of the impacts of tourism on all stakeholders and this awareness should lead to policies which are fairer in their outcomes. Finally, broad participation in policy making could help to democratize decision-making, empower participants and lead to capacity building and skill acquisition among participants (Bramwell and Lane, 2000).

Community change and tourism

The concepts of development and community have changed over time.Definitions of the two terms have broadened in scope as they continue to receive increased attention. Similarly, how a community responds to tourism development has also changed. Communities not only act as a resource for tourism, they also receive and generate tourists. Communities can be a potential motivator for tourists wanting to experience the way of life and the material products of different communities either around the world or around the corner (Richards and Hall, 2000a). As Richards and Hall (2000a) suggest, as communities become tourism attractions, both backstage and front stage areas are established with thetourist gaze being restricted to the staged authenticity of the front stage region. Brohman (1996) argues that community-based tourism development should strengthen institutions that enhance local participation and promote the economic, social and cultural well-being of the popular majority. Not all residents, however, wish to be on the receiving end of tourism, as studies on resident attitudes towards tourism development have revealed (Doxey, 1976). Other studies such as the work by Waldren (1996) on Majorca (Mallorca) and the concepts of insiders and outsiders illustrate that a community with its own symbolic boundaries and identities can continue as a community not in spite of the presence of outsiders but because of their presence. It is important to note that communities are complex entities and vary according to different country contexts and that they will change in different ways. Communities respond to tourism development, and various groups will be more welcoming to the introduction of tourism and the changes that result in their communities than other groups (Sharpley and Telfer, 2002). In developing a list of issues related to the planning of 'new tourism', Ryan (2002) suggests that communities need to be proactive and identify their visions before proposals for development occur.

While the above discussion of tourism in the context of empowerment, partnership, participation, community capacity, and community change fits within the alternative development paradigm, there are additional barriers to successful community development that must be noted. As suggested by Campfens (1997b) earlier in this chapter, in his framework for policy development, programme planning and community development practice, there are many contextual factors from the global to the local environment that might have an impact on the implementation of community development. Various countries around the world allow citizen involvement at various levels, which can be traced through Arnstein's (1969) ladder of citizen participation. Critics of development theory state that it is often rooted in Western thought and note that other societies where there is no local voice or where it is lost in the power game of international politics and monetary movements have little ability to have an impact on any form of development including tourism. Other criticisms surrounding indigenous or community development such as problems of consensus building, barriers to participation, lack of accountability, weak institutions, and lack of integration with international funding sources (Wiarda, 1988; Brinkerhoff and Ingle, 1989) can also be raised in terms of tourism and community development. In other regions, NGOs have taken on an important role in monitoring tourism development. Richards and Hall (2000b: 298) point out in terms of tourism development,

> participation is often a problem of power relationships within the community, and empowerment practices, such as bottom-up planning strategies, are not matched by empowering philosophies. Unequal distribution of power and uneven flows of information can disenfranchise members of the community when decisions are taken about tourism development.

Joppe (1996) suggests that tourism continues to be driven by levels of government rather than community interests and there is a great deal of rhetoric surrounding community involvement. Jenkins (1993) identified the following impediments to public participation in tourism planning.

- The public generally has difficulty in comprehending complex and technical planning issues.
- The public is not always aware of, or understands, the decision-making process.
- The difficulty in attaining and maintaining representativeness in the decision-making process.
- The apathy of citizens.
- The increased cost in terms of staff and money.
- The prolonging of the decision-making process.
- Adverse effects on the efficiency of the decision-making process.

Hall (2000a,b) adds to the list above by pointing out a further problem of using a community approach to tourism planning. The structure of governance can lead to difficulties if tourism policies are not coordinated between different levels of government. For example, if a local community-based decision to reject tourism is at odds with a regional or national level plan to implement tourism, then conflicts can result. What is important in the discussion of community is that differences between communities need to be recognized.

A central question remains as to how community development should proceed in the context of tourism development. As described earlier in this chapter, Rothman (1995) identified three differing approaches to community intervention, which can result in community change. The three approaches are: (i) locality development; (ii) social planning/policy; and (iii) social action. Based on Rothman's (1995) work, Table 9.2 illustrates

Table 9.2. Community development intervention approaches and tourism. Source: after Rothman (1995: 44).

Characteristics	Locality development	Social planning policy	Social action
Direction	Community change due to tourism should be pursued through broad participation of a wide spectrum of people	Technical process of problem solving regarding substantive tourism development issues through expert planners	Presupposes an aggrieved or disadvantaged group that needs to organize to make demands surrounding tourism development
Goal	Process goals of working together to increase community's capacity with regard to tourism development	Focus on task goals to solve problems related to tourism development	Shifting of power relationships and resources in tourism development
Strategy for change	Involve a broad cross section of people in determining and solving problems related to tourism	Gathering data about potential tourism developments and making decisions on the most logical course of action	Crystallizing tourism development issues and mobilize people to take action
Characteristic change tactic	Consensus: communications among groups	Consensus or conflict	Conflict confrontation, direct action, negotiation
Medium for change	Guiding small, task oriented groups	Guiding formal organizations and treating data	Guiding mass organizations and political process
Control	Broad community involvement in tourism development issues	Tourism planners as experts	Mobilize people to take action over tourism development
Approach	Bottom up	Top down	Militant
Advantages	Build community capacity with respect to tourism development	Draw on outside expert opinions for tourism development	Raise community awareness and challenge status quo over tourism developments
Disadvantages	Difficult to build consensus around tourism development	Limited local involvement or control	Can lead to a fragmented approach

a framework for understanding these approaches to community change through tourism. Ultimately, the approach taken that best builds community capacity for a given community and spreads the benefits of tourism would have the best chance of promoting community development.

Conclusion

This chapter has documented the changes in development paradigms over time (modernization, dependency, economic neo-liberalism and alternative development), and it was noted that the potential for community development associated with tourism will be determined in part by the overriding development paradigm guiding the development process. In an era when the process of development is being questioned, the concepts of sustainable development as part of the alternative paradigm have come to the forefront. Within sustainable development are the calls for increased community participation and recognition of local conditions. As Campfens (1997b) suggests, several factors have considerable influence on the level at which community development is supported and can be practised. This chapter has outlined the main elements of community development, which have changed and become more holistic over time. Reflecting heavily on the community development literature, concepts such as empowerment, participation, partnership, community capacity and community change were explored as they relate to tourism development. An adapted framework was presented based on the main concepts of community intervention, (locality development, social planning/policy and social action), which can help in the understanding of the process at work in community tourism development. It is argued that tourism developments around the world are very situational and the potential for local involvement varies a great deal from place to place. By bringing in literature from outside tourism from two different fields (i.e. development theory and community development), this chapter has attempted to add to the knowledge base on issues related to tourism and community development. It is argued that it is important to recognize overriding development paradigms and their relationship to community development in understanding the process at work in community tourism development.

References

Apostolopoulos, Y., Sönmez, S. and Timothy, D.J. (eds) (2001) *Women as Producers and Consumers of Tourism in Developing Regions.* Praeger, Westport, Connecticut.

Arai, S. (1996) Benefits of citizen participation in a healthy community initiative: linking community development and empowerment. *Journal of Applied Recreation Research* 21, 25–44.

Arnstein, S. (1969) A ladder of citizen participation. _American Institute of Planners Journal_ July, 216–224.

Baez, A. (1996) Learning from experience in the Monteverde Cloud Forest, Costa Rica. In: Price, M. (ed.) _People and Tourism in Fragile Environments._ John Wiley & Sons, Chichester, pp. 109–122.

Britton, S. (1982) The political economy of tourism in the Third World. _Annals of Tourism Research_ 9, 331–358.

Bramwell, B. and Lane, B. (eds) (2000) _Tourism Collaboration and Partnerships: Politics, Practice and Sustainability._ Channel View, Clevedon.

Bramwell, B. and Sharman, A. (2000) Approaches to sustainable tourism planning and community participation, the case of the Hope Valley. In: Richards, G. and Hall, D. (eds) _Tourism and Sustainable Community Development._ Routledge, London, pp. 17–35.

Brinkerhoff, D.W. and Ingle, M.D. (1989) Integrating blueprint and process: a structured flexibility approach to development management. _Public Administration and Development_ 9, 487–503.

Brohman, J. (1996) New directions in tourism for third world development. _Annals of Tourism Research_ 23, 48–70.

Butler, R.W. (1980) The concept of a tourist area cycle of evolution: implications for management of resources. _Canadian Geographer_ 24, 5–12.

Campfens, H. (1997a) Comparisons and conclusions: an international framework for practice in the twenty-first century. In: Campfens, H. (ed.) _Community Development Around the World._ University of Toronto Press, Toronto, pp. 437–469.

Campfens, H. (1997b) International review of community development: theory and practice. In: Campfens, H. (ed.) _Community Development Around the World._ University of Toronto Press, Toronto, pp. 11–46.

Cardoso, F.H. (1979) The originality of the copy: the economic commission for Latin America and the idea of development. In: Hill, K.Q. (ed.) _Toward a New Strategy for Development._ Pergamon, Toronto, pp. 53–72.

Cater, E.A. (1987) Tourism in the least developed countries. _Annals of Tourism Research_ 14, 202–226.

Checkoway, B. (1995) Six strategies of community change. _Community Development Journal_ 30, 2–20.

Crotts, J., Buhalis, D. and March, R. (eds) (2000) _Global Alliances in Tourism and Hospitality Management._ The Haworth Hospitality Press, New York.

Curry, S. (1990) Tourism development in Tanzania. _Annals of Tourism Research_ 17, 133–149.

Doxey, G.V. (1976) When enough's enough: the natives are restless in Old Niagara. _Heritage Canada_ 2(2), 26–29.

Fisher, R. (1995) Social action community organization: proliferation, persistence, roots and prospects. In: Rothman, J., Erlich, M. and Tropman, J.E. (eds) _Strategies of Community Intervention_, 5th edn. F.E. Peacock, Itasca, Illinois, pp. 327–340.

Frank, A.G. (1988) The development of underdevelopment. In: Wilber, C.K. (ed.) _The Political Economy of Development and Underdevelopment_, 4th edn. McGraw-Hill, Toronto, pp. 109–120.

Friedmann, J. (1987) *Planning in the Public Domain: From Knowledge to Action.* Princeton University Press, Princeton, New Jersey.

Gunn, C.A. (1994) *Tourism Planning: Basics, Concepts, Cases.* Taylor and Francis, Washington, DC.

Hall, C.M. (2000a) Rethinking collaboration and partnership: a public policy perspective. In: Bramwell, B. and Lane, B. (eds) *Tourism Collaboration and Partnerships: Politics, Practice and Sustainability.* Channel View, Clevedon, pp. 143–158.

Hall, C.M. (2000b) *Tourism Planning: Policies, Processes and Relationships.* Prentice Hall, Harlow.

Harrison, D. (1988) *The Sociology of Modernization and Development.* Unwin Hyman, London.

Haywood, K.M. (1988) Responsible and responsive tourism planning in the community. *Tourism Management* 19, 105–118.

Hettne, B. (1990) *Development Theory and the Three Worlds.* Longman, New York.

Inskeep, E. (1991) *Tourism Planning: an Integrated and Sustainable Development Approach.* Van Nostrand Reinhold, New York.

Inskeep, E. and Kallenberger, M. (1992) *An Integrated Approach to Resort Development: Six Case Studies.* World Tourism Organisation, Madrid.

Jamal, T. and Getz, D. (1995) Collaboration theory and community tourism planning. *Annals of Tourism Research* 22, 186–204.

Jamal, T. and Getz, D. (2000) Community roundtables for tourism-related conflicts: the dialectics of consensus and process structures. In: Bramwell, B. and Lane, B. (eds) *Tourism Collaboration and Partnerships: Politics, Practice and Sustainability.* Channel View, Clevedon, pp. 159–182.

Jenkins, J. (1993) Tourism policy in rural New South Wales: policy and research priorities. *GeoJournal* 29, 281–290.

Joppe, M. (1996) Sustainable community tourism development revisited. *Tourism Management* 17, 475–479.

Konadu-Agyemang, K. (2000) The best of times and the worst of times – structural adjustment programmes and uneven development in Africa: the case of Ghana. *Professional Geographer* 52, 469–483.

Lord, J. (1998) Building genuine partnerships: potential, principles and problems. *Journal of Leisureability* 25, 3–10.

Marti-Costí, S. and Serrano-García, I. (1995) Needs assessment and community development: an ideological perspective. In: Rothman, J., Erlich, M. and Tropman, J.E. (eds) *Strategies of Community Intervention*, 5th edn. F.E. Peacock, Itasca, Illinois, pp. 257–267.

Mathieson, A. and Wall, G. (1982) *Tourism: Economic, Physical, and Social Impacts.* Longman, London.

McIntosh, R.W., Goeldner, C.R. and Ritchie, J.R.B. (1995) *Tourism: Principles, Practices and Philosophies*, 7th edn. John Wiley & Sons, New York.

McKnight, J. and Kretzmann, J. (1997) Mapping community capacity. In: Minkler, M. (ed.) *Community Organizing and Community Building for Health.* Rutgers University Press, New Jersey, pp. 157–172.

Mitchell, B. (1997) *Resource and Environmental Management.* Longman, Harlow.

Mohan, G.E., Brown, B., Milward, H. and Zack-Williams, A. (2000) *Structural Adjustment Theory, Practice and Impacts.* Routledge, London.

Mowforth, M. and Munt, I. (1998) _Tourism and Sustainability: New Tourism in the Third World._ Routledge, London.

Murphy, P.E. (1985) _Tourism: a Community Approach._ Methuen, New York.

Murphy, P.E. (1988) Community driven tourism planning. _Tourism Management_ 9, 96–104.

Myrdal, G. (1963) _Economic Theory and Under-Developed Regions._ University Paperbacks, London.

Nozick, M. (1993) Five principles of sustainable community development. In: Shragge, E. (ed.) _Community Economic Development: In Search of Empowerment and Alteration._ Black Rose Books, Montreal, pp. 18–43.

Pedlar, A. (1996) Community development: what does it mean for recreation and leisure? _Journal of Leisure Research_ 20, 5–23.

Peet, R. (1999) _Theories of Development._ Guilford Press, London.

Perroux, F. (1988) The pole of development's new place in a general theory of economic activity. In: Higgins, B. and Savoie, D. (eds) _Regional Economic Development: Essays in Honour of Francois Perroux._ Hyman, Boston, pp. 48–76.

Poirier, R.A. (1995) Tourism and development in Tunisia. _Annals of Tourism Research_ 22, 157–171.

Preston, P.W. (1996) _Development Theory: an Introduction._ Blackwell, Oxford.

Pretty, J. (1994) Alternative systems of inquiry for a sustainable agriculture. _The Institute of Development Studies Bulletin_ 25, 37–48.

Redclift, M. (1987) _Sustainable Development Exploring the Contradictions._ Routledge, London.

Reed, M. (1997) Power relations and community based tourism planning. _Annals of Tourism Research_ 24, 566–591.

Reid, D. and van Dreunen, E. (1996) Leisure as a social transformation mechanism in community development practice. _Journal of Applied Recreation Research_ 2, 45–65.

Richards, G. and Hall, D. (2000a) The community: a sustainable concept in tourism development. In: Richards, G. and Hall, D. (eds) _Tourism and Sustainable Community Development._ Routledge, London, pp. 1–13.

Richards, G. and Hall, D. (2000b) Conclusions. In: Richards, G. and Hall, D. (eds) _Tourism and Sustainable Community Development._ Routledge, London, pp. 297–306.

Rist, G. (1997) _The History of Development: From Western Origins to Global Faith._ Zed Books, London.

Rostow, W.W. (1967) _The Stages of Economic Growth: a Non-Communist Manifesto,_ 2nd edn. Cambridge University Press, Cambridge.

Rothman, J. (1995) Approaches to community intervention. In: Rothman, J., Erlich, M. and Tropman, J.E. (eds) _Strategies of Community Intervention,_ 5th edn. F.E. Peacock, Itasca, Illinois, pp. 26–63.

Rothman, J., Erlich, M. and Tropman, J.E. (eds) (1995) _Strategies of Community Intervention,_ 5th edn. F.E. Peacock, Itasca, Illinois.

Ryan, C. (2002) Equity, management, power sharing and sustainability – issues of the 'new tourism'. _Tourism Management_ 23, 17–26.

Sachs, W. (1992) _The Development Dictionary: a Guide to Knowledge as Power._ Zed Books, London.

Scheyvens, R. (1999) Ecotourism and the empowerment of local communities. *Tourism Management* 20, 245–249.

Schmidt, H. (1989) What makes development? *Development and Cooperation* 6, 19–26.

Schuurman, F.J. (ed.) (1993) *Beyond the Impasse: New Directions in Development Theory.* Zed Books, London.

Selin, S. (2000) Developing a typology of sustainable tourism partnerships. In: Bramwell, B. and Lane, B. (eds) *Tourism Collaboration and Partnerships: Politics, Practice and Sustainability.* Channel View, Clevedon, pp. 129–142.

Shaffer, C. and Anundsen, K. (1993) *Creating Community Anywhere: Finding Support and Connections in a Fragmented World.* Putnam Sons, New York, pp. 271–287.

Sharpley, R. and Sharpley, J. (1997) *Rural Tourism: an Introduction.* International Thomson Business Press, London.

Sharpley, R. and Telfer, D.J. (eds) (2002) *Tourism and Development: Concepts and Issues.* Channel View, Clevedon.

Simmons, D.G. (1994) Community participation in tourism planning. *Tourism Management* 15, 98–108.

Sinclair, M.T. (ed.) (1997) *Gender, Work and Tourism.* Routledge, London.

Sklair, L. (1991) *Sociology of the Global System.* Johns Hopkins University Press, Baltimore.

Smith, V. (1996) The Inuit as hosts: heritage and wilderness tourism in Nunavut. In: Price, M. (ed.) *People and Tourism in Fragile Environments.* John Wiley & Sons, Chichester, pp. 33–50.

Telfer, D.J. (1996) Development through economic linkages: tourism and agriculture in Indonesia. PhD thesis, University of Waterloo, Waterloo, Ontario, Canada.

Telfer, D.J. (2000a) Agritourism: a path to community development? The case of Bangunkerto, Indonesia. In: Richards, G. and Hall, D. (eds) *Tourism and Sustainable Community Development.* London, Routledge, pp. 242–257.

Telfer, D.J. (2000b) Tastes of Niagara: building strategic alliances between tourism and agriculture. *International Journal of Hospitality and Tourism Administration* 1(1), 71–88.

Telfer, D.J. (2002a) Tourism and development theory. In: Sharpley, R. and Telfer, D.J. (eds) *Tourism and Development: Concepts and Issues.* Channel View, Clevedon, pp. 35–78.

Telfer, D.J. (2002b) Tourism and regional development issues. In: Sharpley, R. and Telfer, D.J. (eds) *Tourism and Development: Concepts and Issues.* Channel View, Clevedon, pp. 112–148.

Telfer, D.J. (2003) Canadian tourism commission's product clubs. In: Laws, E. (ed.) *Tourism Marketing.* Continuum, London (in press).

Timothy, D.J. (1998) Cooperative tourism planning in a developing destination. *Journal of Sustainable Tourism* 6(1), 52–68.

Timothy, D.J. (1999) Participatory planning: a view of tourism in Indonesia. *Annals of Tourism Research* 26, 371–391.

Todaro, M.P. (1994) *Economic Development,* 5th edn. Longman, New York.

Tosun, C. (2000) Limits to community participation in the tourism development process in developing countries. *Tourism Management* 21, 613–633.

United Nations (1955) *Social Progress Through Community Development.* United Nations, New York.

Waldren, J. (1996) *Insiders and Outsiders, Paradise and Reality in Mallorca.* Berghahn Books, London.

Walter, C. (1997) Community building practice: a conceptual framework. In: Enkler, M.N. (ed.) *Community Organising and Community Building for Health.* Rutgers University Press, London, pp. 68–83.

Wiarda, H.J. (1988) Toward a nonethnocentric theory of development: alternative conceptions from the third world. In: Wilber, C.K. (ed.) *The Political Economy of Development and Underdevelopment,* 4th edn. McGraw-Hill, Toronto, pp. 59–82.

Appropriate Planning for Tourism in Destination Communities: Participation, Incremental Growth and Collaboration

10

DALLEN J. TIMOTHY[1] and CEVAT TOSUN[2]

[1]*Department of Recreation Management and Tourism, Arizona State University, Tempe, USA;* [2]*School of Tourism and Hotel Management, Mustafa Kemal University, Hatay, Turkey*

Introduction

Unregulated tourism development is a completely market-led view of tourism that simply provides attractions, facilities and services that the tourist market demands. Because of its *ad hoc* nature, it is lacking in long-term vision (Smith, 2000) and thus usually results in environmental degradation and loss of sociocultural integrity of destination areas, even though it brings short-term economic benefits (Inskeep, 1991: 30). Until quite recently this has been the form that tourism development has taken in most parts of the world. Getz (1987) applied the term 'boosterism' to this *laissez-faire* tradition. Its basic premise is that tourism is good, so it should be promoted. All natural, built and living cultural resources are usually exploited for the sake of tourism, with little regard for negative sociocultural, ecological and economic impacts (Murphy, 1985). Observers argue that this 'unplanned' form of tourism is still practised and promoted in many areas by politicians who believe that economic growth should always be at the forefront of development and by others who will gain financially by the growth of tourism (Getz, 1987).

This trend appears to be changing throughout the world, however, giving way to more sustainable forms of tourism as planners are beginning to realize that the industry's impacts are most vivid in destination communities and that destination residents are an essential part of the tourism product (Simmons, 1994; Davidson and Maitland, 1999). Principles, such as equity, efficiency, integration, balance, harmony, and ecological and cultural integrity are more effectively encouraged when community

©CAB *International* 2003. *Tourism in Destination Communities*
(eds S. Singh, D.J. Timothy and R.K. Dowling)

members are allowed to participate in tourism planning and development, when collaboration and cooperation are allowed to occur, and when tourism is developed in an incremental fashion. This chapter aims to examine these forms of destination planning and develops a normative model that will guide tourism planners, with special reference to the developing world.

Scales of Planning

Scale is an important consideration in tourism planning. Scale refers to the level at which we are representing reality in our thinking, or at which we are trying to understand things (Hall, 2000: 54). Tourism can be planned at many scales, including international, national, regional, destination or local, and site specific. Most planning that occurs at the site-specific and local levels is oriented towards land use and physical development (Inskeep, 1991; Gunn, 1994; Hall, 2000). As one moves up the scale, however, this form of planning becomes more difficult owing to the extensive spatial nature of the area in question to the extent that at the international level, planning is more policy oriented in areas of environment, transportation and promotion (Hall, 2000). Plans prepared at any scale often focus exclusively on that scale, disregarding efforts at lower, equivalent or higher levels of administration elsewhere (Pearce, 1995: 239). Pearce (1995) gives the example of the tourism and recreation development plans of the 1980s in The Netherlands. Each province prepared a tourism plan with a narrow perspective on its own boundaries, ignoring the effects and potentials of projects in neighbouring provinces, which resulted in several problems, including a severe overestimation of total national demand for tourism.

International, or supranational, planning, as mentioned previously is usually limited to areas of policy instead of physical or spatial development, although several supranational policies have implications for physical planning at national, regional and site levels (e.g. the World Heritage Convention) (Hall, 2000). International planning involves the governments of at least two countries working in concert to achieve common goals, usually in terms of environmental protection, marketing and promotion, and transportation systems. International economic communities, or trading blocs, provide a useful and increasingly common framework within which international tourism planning can be accomplished. For example, the European Union has been successful in enacting supranational legislation pertaining to environmental protection within the realm of tourism. The Association of Southeast Asian Nations has seen significant success since the late 1980s in its promotional efforts where the region as a whole is promoted and marketed to potential visitors through multi-nation cooperative efforts. Finally, the Closer Economic Relations agreement between Australia and New Zealand has been instrumental in bringing about significant changes in air transportation between the two countries to their mutual advantage.

National tourism planning is often done at a conceptual or strategic level, where countrywide tourism plans are formulated. These plans commonly form the basis for tourism policy, transportation and infrastructure development, education campaigns, and the allocation of financial resources (Smith, 2000). Sometimes national-level plans are involved in spatial development to the extent that development regions are identified and targeted for intense expansion and promotion. Such was the case in Indonesia in the 1990s, where the national tourism development plan examined the existing tourism levels and needs of all 27 provinces and made recommendations pertaining to which areas should be targeted for intensive tourism development, and which ones should not. One of the primary aims of this exercise was to spread the positive economic benefits more equitably throughout the country.

Planning at the national level, though, is sometimes difficult in large countries. Difficulties arise where planning is being done in a vast country in both area and population, because the needs of many diverse provinces and regions must be met. This is problematic because in many cases national-level planning takes place with complete disregard for the needs and aspirations of lower-level governments and communities. Within this context, Tosun (2001) argued that tourism planning in developing countries is usually done at the national level in isolation from the interests of local communities and governments, lacking coordination, two-way communication, and involvement by local communities.

Regional planning generally includes activities initiated by state or provincial governments. According to Smith (2000), plans may cover the entire area of political jurisdiction or a smaller area within subnational boundaries, and the definition of the area in question is usually defined by the study objectives. In general, regional plans should fit within the broader scope of national plans in order to maintain harmonious relations between national and regional governments. In Indonesia, for example, planning occurs at two administrative levels in the regional context: regional and provincial. While regional governments do not exist in Indonesia, regional planning does take place. It simply refers to activities that involve more than one province in areas that overlap provincial boundaries.

Destination planning involves the delineation of physical development within specified geographic contexts (Smith, 2000), although these contexts are typically difficult to define (Hall, 2000). New purpose-built resort areas may be planned from the ground up, and many examples of this exist (Inskeep and Kallenberger, 1992), while other established tourist destinations may be planned for specialized issues such as heritage management, environmental conservation, marketing and human resource supply. In most cases, it is hardly ever too late to initiate tourism plans in destination areas, despite the tolls taken on the communities in the past. Sometimes planning is a response to past and potential negative and positive impacts. Hundreds of examples exist where established tourism communities decide to plan for rejuvenation (e.g. Atlantic City, USA; Niagara Falls, Canada/USA; Yogyakarta, Indonesia), reorientation or reinvention (e.g. Leavenworth, USA; St Jacobs, Canada), and heritage conservation and urban regeneration through tourism (e.g. Singapore; London; Venice).

Project or site planning endeavours focus on very specific attractions, services and sites in destination areas and tend to relate to physical enhancements, such as restoring historic monuments, building interpretive centres, paving parking lots, constructing ticket booths, erecting hotels, and installing additional lighting or other infrastructure features. These site-specific plans are quite easy to complete and implement, so they have gained favour in the eyes of public planners. In areas of the world that are now beginning to implement sustainable planning principles, such as Yogyakarta, Indonesia, site-specific plans are seen to contribute to meeting the objectives of regional and provincial plans, thereby contributing to the achievement of long-term development goals. By way of example, the 1992 Central Java and Yogyakarta Cultural Tourism Development Plan acknowledged the importance of specific site projects around Yogyakarta. As part of this, individual plans were drafted for Kota Gede and Kasongan handicraft villages, Kaliurang mountain retreat, and beaches south of the city, wherein recommendations were made to develop these locations physically and spatially for the future of tourism (UNESCO/UNDP, 1992).

Planning Approaches in Destination Communities

Comprehensive tourism development, where all aspects of regional tourism (e.g. facilities, services, institutional elements, etc.) are planned and coordinated in a holistic manner, has been strongly advocated in the literature. In this way, tourism is seen as an interdependent system that needs to be planned and developed in an organized and inclusive manner (Inskeep, 1991; Dowling, 1993; Pearce, 1995; Hall, 2000). Gunn (1994) argues that all elements of regional tourism (e.g. lodging, attractions, information, transportation and marketing) need to be coordinated to avoid conflicts between industry subsectors. While this view is important within the context of tourism, it has received its share of critics in the past, who highlight the virtual impossibility of including all elements of regional systems in the planning process at one time (Hudson, 1979; Mitchell, 1989).

Other scholars have argued for the need to integrate tourism into the broader development strategy of a country or region (Inskeep, 1991; Marcouiller, 1997). In this sense, tourism should not be planned alone. Instead it should be planned within a more extensive development framework (Baud-Bovy, 1982; Marcouiller, 1997). Such an approach, experts suggest, will increase efficiency, equity, and adaptability, as components of the industry are planned together and integrated into regional development goals.

Participatory (community-based) planning

Community-based tourism is viewed as a more sustainable approach to development than traditional mass tourism (Murphy, 1985, 1988), for it allows host communities to free themselves from the hegemonic grasp of outside tour operators and powerful leaders at the national level. In fact, Woodley (1993: 137) argues that participatory tourism development is 'prerequisite to sustainability'. Grass-roots empowerment is seen to develop the industry in harmony with the 'needs and aspirations of host communities in a way that is acceptable to them, sustains their economies, rather than the economies of others, and is not detrimental to their culture, traditions or, indeed, their day-to-day convenience' (Fitton, 1996: 173). This argument, that the host community's goals and desires for tourism should be at the forefront of development, has acquired a significant following among development specialists in recent years (e.g. Murphy, 1988; Inskeep, 1991; Prentice, 1993; Bramwell and Sharman, 2000). According to Long (1993), if destination residents are not involved in the tourism growth process, implementing even the most well-meaning and well-planned development programmes will be obstructed by the very people who were supposed to be involved. According to Murphy (1985: 153), 'Tourism . . . relies on the goodwill and cooperation of local people because they are part of its product. Where development and planning do not fit in with local aspirations and capacity, resistance and hostility can . . . destroy the industry's potential altogether.'

This approach to planning recognizes that the private and public sectors, the host community, advocacy groups and business representatives are all interdependent stakeholders in a complex and dynamic tourism domain, where no single individual or group can resolve strategic tourism issues by acting single-handedly. Jamal and Getz (1995) argue that to achieve sustainability, stakeholders must work together to meet common objectives.

Based in part on the work of Friedmann (1992), Scheyvens (1999) conceptualizes empowerment in tourism as being economic, psychological, social and political (Table 10.1). Economic empowerment allows residents and entire communities to benefit financially from tourism. Psychological empowerment is vital for developing self-esteem and pride in local cultures, traditional knowledge and natural resources. Social empowerment assists in maintaining a community's social equilibrium and has the power to lead

Table 10.1. Types of community empowerment in tourism development. Source: after Scheyvens (1999).

Type	Signs of empowerment
Economic	Tourism brings long-term financial benefits to a destination community. Money is spread throughout the community. There are notable improvements in local services and infrastructure.
Psychological	Self-esteem is enhanced because of outside recognition of the uniqueness and value of their culture, natural resources and traditional knowledge. Increasing confidence in the community leads members to seek out further education and training opportunities. Access to jobs and cash leads to an increase in status for usually low-status residents, such as women and youth.
Social	Tourism maintains or enhances the local community's equilibrium. Community cohesion is improved as individuals and families cooperate to build a successful industry. Some funds raised are used for community development initiatives like education and roads.
Political	The community's political structure provides a representational forum through which people can raise questions and concerns pertaining to tourism initiatives. Agencies initiating or implementing the tourism ventures seek out the opinions of community groups and individual community members, and provide chances for them to be represented on decision-making bodies.

to cooperation in important areas like education and health care. Finally, political empowerment is best manifest in representational democracy where people can make their opinions known and raise concerns about development initiatives. True political empowerment requires that agencies and groups that initiate tourism projects seek contributions from community members and other stakeholders in decision-making (Arnstein, 1969; Friedmann, 1992).

Incorporating these ingredients of empowerment, community-based tourism can be viewed in at least two ways: public participation in decision-making and local involvement in the benefits of tourism (Timothy, 1999b). Participation in decision-making means that residents have opportunities to voice their own hopes, desires and fears for development and contribute to the planning process from their own expertise and experiences, thereby gaining a meaningful voice in the organization and administration of tourism (Timothy, 2002). While relatively few residents of developing countries have experiences as tourists, they have plenty of familiarity with local sociocultural and environmental conditions.

Representing a step in this direction, development specialists now see the value of indigenous knowledge and environmental management practices (Berger, 1996; Boonzaier, 1996; Strang, 1996; Dei, 2000) and argue that answers to many difficult questions about host environments can be found in the communities themselves, for in most instances, traditional societies do not see themselves as unconnected from nature. Indigenous systems of pastoralism, hunting and agriculture are frequently the most sustainable forms of resource management (Timothy, 2002). The Maasai people of East Africa, for example, have long used

> large areas for extensive grazing in ways that have sustained natural ecosystems and allowed relatively harmonious co-existence of wildlife and people. The Maasai did not hunt except in severe famine. In the past, they limited forage offtake levels by restricting access to grazing and water at certain seasons. They practiced rotational grazing and the opportunistic movement of herd to take advantage of spatially and seasonally erratic rainfall.
>
> (Berger, 1996: 184)

Timothy (2002) argues that in cultural terms, local control of decision-making is crucial because residents have a greater tendency to plan in a way that is more in harmony with cultural traditions – something that can be important in building ethnic pride. Exogenous power, however, results in negative impacts because outsiders cannot understand in as much depth the traditional approaches to unique situations. When control lies in the hands of external forces, community cohesion and cooperative spirit diminish, and practices such as unhealthy competition and individualism have a tendency to replace the traditional emphasis on group welfare (Berger, 1996). Baez (1996) suggests that the success of tourism in Monteverde, Costa Rica, is a result of the local people being in control and working in groups towards the common good, as prescribed by social conventions. This results in more harmonious relationships throughout the community, consistency and solidarity.

Resident involvement in planning also allows communities to protect sacred spaces from irreverent tourists, and gives a voice to locals who have traditionally been under-represented (e.g. women and ethnic minorities) (Timothy, 2001). Such segments of society must be given a louder voice in planning and policy making if the goals of sustainability are to be realized, for they are an important part of society and are affected directly by the existence of tourism (Timothy, 2002).

For reasons of harmony, equity, and holistic growth, tourism planning should also include other stakeholders, in addition to residents, such as advocacy groups, public agencies, business associations and non-governmental organizations (NGOs). It is now widely accepted that planning and development must include all parties at the grass-roots level (Murphy, 1988; Simmons, 1994; Scheyvens, 1999; Tosun, 1999, 2000).

So far this discussion has highlighted the need for community involvement in tourism development, but uncertainty is common regarding how this can be done. Many techniques have been designed to involve residents in decision-making. For instance, Gill (1996) examines the value of informal gatherings of small groups of community members in a moderated, though relaxed, situation in homes throughout the community. Similarly, Fitton (1996) explains the 'planning for real' method, which is a form of town meeting that involves bringing the community together before the planning process begins. Community members, rather than hired planners, mediate meetings so that an exchange of ideas between residents is the primary driving force. Participants are provided with map- and situation-based scenarios where they can indicate where they believe the most problematic locations for tourists are and where they think new services and infrastructure are needed. When the session is complete, an in-depth round-table discussion is held where residents can continue to discuss, debate and learn about their interests and concerns for tourism. This approach allows even the less outspoken community members to participate and is an excellent tool for informing the planning process (Timothy, 2002). These types of techniques are important in developing tourism, for 'clearly, if communities do not want to be involved in tourism it is difficult and counter-productive to insist' (Fitton, 1996: 169).

Another method that has found considerable success is household surveys (Haywood, 1988; Simmons, 1994; Timothy, 2002). These help identify issues that are important to an area, focus on the needs of the community, and draw attention to opportunities for improvement. It gives nearly everyone in the community an opportunity to participate and encourages them to think about tourism and its accompanying issues in depth (Fitton, 1996: 170). One example introduced by Fitton (1996) comes from Llanthony, a small community in southern Wales, where the approaches to community participation as described above made clear that residents were unwilling to choose tourism as a tool for economic development. They considered outside visitors to be too ignorant about their community and too disruptive to everyday functions. In contrast, the same exercises demonstrated how several rural communities in South Pembrokeshire, Wales, strongly supported tourism, as long as residents would remain in control. Since the 1980s, communities in the region have been involved in the development of new tourism opportunities, which has resulted in fiscal benefits to the local area and a strong community commitment to tourism (Timothy, 2002).

The other part of participatory tourism, taking part in the benefits of tourism, means that residents will gain personally from the industry's development. Community tourism planning should also include creating opportunities for people to own businesses, to work in industry-related employment, to receive training, and to be educated about the role and effects of tourism in their regions (Timothy, 1999b). Small-scale, locally owned businesses are an example of this form of empowerment. These types of establishments result in more direct benefits to residents and allow little to leak to outside interests (Smith, 1998; Hatton, 1999). Likewise, small-scale businesses require more local involvement, and are more culturally and ecologically sensitive because they tend to place less stress on local environments (Long and Wall, 1995). Very often, as tourism increases, scale will also necessarily have to increase with the up-scaling of facilities and services, which nearly always involves loans and investments from external sources. In recent years, however, sustainability advocates have argued that keeping tourism at a small scale will remain more financially and economically viable in the long-term than rapid mass tourism development (e.g. Mowforth and Munt, 1998). Increasingly more places are beginning to realize this, and their attitudes are changing to reflect that rapid economic growth is not always the desired effect if it means losing local control of the industry. This has certainly been the case so far in the Toledo Ecotourism Association villages of southern Belize (Timothy and White, 1999) and several other similar community projects throughout the world (Fitton, 1996; Lipscomb, 1998).

By way of example, Hatton (1999) describes the Huangshan Mountain region of China, which has experienced remarkable community-based tourism in recent years. While the form of government in place in China has historically precluded popular participation in tourism decision-making, strides are being made to include residents in the benefits of tourism at least. From its inception, the Huangshan tourism development initiative has benefited local residents. For instance, during its development of infrastructure, the Huangshan Mountain Scenic Development Area (HMSDA) committee actively guided and encouraged locals to construct supplementary tourist facilities, services and attractions. This has resulted in increased community incomes and regional prosperity in recent years. As part of these efforts, the HMSDA worked closely with villagers to establish a tourist attraction based on the local wildlife – monkeys. While the area has always been known for spectacular natural beauty, few tourists were attracted there until the monkey reserve was created. Now, thousands of tourists visit each year, generating millions of RMB Yuan. This and other developments have had major impacts on the region. The monkey park created many local jobs which brought economic stability and regular wages. Villagers have used tourism receipts to invest in educational facilities and financial aid for children who might not otherwise afford an education. Assistance to elderly and disabled residents has also been funded through the project (Hatton, 1999).

An additional component of community involvement in the benefits of tourism is education, or increased awareness (Timothy, 1999b, 2002). Although residents of developed countries may have valuable insight from their experiences as both hosts and guests, people in less-developed regions have scant first-hand knowledge about being tourists, since few have ever had opportunities to travel outside their home regions. None the less, Din (1993) argues that action by locals in tourism initiatives and plans requires some degree of knowledge and understanding about tourism. The old adage, knowledge is power, is true in this context, for when local people understand the process of tourism planning and development, as well as the multitudes of opportunities in which they can participate, they have the potential to become more powerful agents in the tourism development process (Lynn, 1992; Din, 1993; Tosun and Jenkins, 1998; Timothy, 2000).

Some destination communities are making important strides in building awareness of tourism among local populations. Recently, Yogyakarta, Indonesia, has attempted to educate its residents about the prospective benefits of tourism and their potential role in its development. Efforts were under way in the mid-1990s to heighten public awareness of tourism through official educational campaigns. The educational crusade involved various media, such as television advertisements, newspapers and brochures that were circulated throughout the community. Additionally, short courses in foreign languages and cultures, small business management, and accounting were offered by the local tourism development office to community members who were most likely to be involved with tourists (e.g. taxi and pedicab drivers, guest house and restaurant owners, and street vendors) (Timothy, 2000).

Incremental growth

Another strategy is incremental growth, which was recognized early on by Lindblom (1965) as a means of assuring that changes can be made as development processes unfold. In tourism this means that once a plan has been drafted and recommendations made, development options are selected carefully, implemented gradually and monitored regularly until goals have been met. Even when goals are achieved, the incremental view recommends continuous monitoring to assure that development upholds ecological and cultural integrity. Such a practice was stressed by Baud-Bovy (1982) because of the economic, political and social vagaries of tourism over time. In most cases, incrementalism applies best to the spatial planning that typically occurs at destination and site-specific levels. The strength of this approach is that it allows higher levels of predictability and flexibility (Getz, 1987; Tosun and Jenkins, 1998). Incremental development ensures adaptability and promotes efficiency because it allows for adjustments in the development process if events or issues appear which were not previously foreseen and which may negatively affect the successful development of tourism. According to Rondinelli (1982: 66), this method will:

allow policy makers and managers to readjust and modify programs and projects as more is learned about the conditions in which they are trying to intervene. Planning and implementation must be regarded as mutually dependent activities that refine and improve each other over time, rather than as separate functions.

This practice is efficient in that it may save time, effort and money if problems can be predicted and avoided as the planning process unfolds. This will allow the mitigation of these problems by predicting changes and allowing adjustments to the long-term implementation of plan recommendations as the needs arise.

Incremental development grew out of a general dissatisfaction with traditional central control, which often focused on rapid development and limited flexibility. Traditionally, a great deal of emphasis was placed on preparing the master plan as the end product of a planning endeavour. The incremental approach, however, maintains that planning is a dynamic and continuous process, which must be flexible while guiding the way to meeting development objectives (Inskeep, 1991; Cullingworth and Nadin, 1994).

Few places in the world today can be used as clear examples of incremental tourism development (Timothy, 1998b), primarily because this relatively new concept in tourism has had limited time to be tried and tested. However, several examples of this do exist around the world where long-range planning is done in a way that spreads physical/spatial and some other forms of development initiatives into 'development periods' of 5, 10 or 20 years. In fact, most modern-day tourism plans adopt this approach as a means of being able to monitor progress and to assure the feasibility of development programmes (Inskeep, 1991; Inskeep and Kallenberger, 1992; Gunn, 1994).

Collaborative/cooperative planning

In order to achieve comprehensive tourism development, as described here, cooperation between planning sectors at various scales is necessary. Timothy (1998a) describes five types of cooperation that need to exist in developing sustainable tourism:

1. Between government agencies (e.g. department of transportation and department of agriculture);
2. Between the private and public sectors (e.g. hotel sector and ministries of tourism);
3. Between different levels of administration (e.g. national and provincial);

4. Cross-border cooperation between same-level polities (e.g. state and state); and

5. Between private-sector services (e.g. tour guides and food services).

While some argue that this can be achieved, at least to some degree (Nunn and Rosentraub, 1997), such an array of collaborative efforts is difficult to achieve because 'there is no other industry in the economy that is linked to so many diverse and different kinds of products and services as is the tourism industry' (Edgell, 1990: 7). After Timothy's (1998a) work, the following sections examine the benefits and costs of each of the five types of cooperation highlighted above.

Coordinated efforts between public agencies can decrease misunderstandings and conflict related to overlapping goals and actions. According to Spann (1979: 411, cited in Hall, 1994), coordination 'refers to the problem of relating units or decisions so that they fit in with one another, are not at cross-purposes, and operate in ways that are reasonably consistent and coherent'. In addition, government agencies continually compete for scarce operating funds. Efficiency might be improved if agencies would coordinate their development efforts. So much money in so many cases is wasted on overlapping and parallel projects, that in theory such cooperative efforts would mean less money spent, and more funds available for other purposes.

As mentioned earlier, tourism involves a wide range of services and facilities, many of which are owned and operated by individuals and private companies. Regional tourism, however, must be regulated, promoted and physically developed – responsibilities that usually fall under the auspices of government agencies. As a result, cooperation between the private and public sectors is crucial. The public sector is dependent on private investors and the private sector relies on government approval of projects. In the developed world, tourism is largely controlled by the private sector, while in most developing areas, governments play a larger role in the industry's development.

To achieve success in comprehensive planning, collaboration between different levels of government jurisdiction is necessary. For example, local initiatives commonly require approval and fiscal support from national governments, although examples exist where successful projects have been conceptualized and operationalized at the local level without interference from above (Timothy and White, 1999). Likewise, initiatives at the national level might require the involvement of lower-level governments, such as states, provinces and counties, because development usually requires some degree of place-specific knowledge, and lower-order administrative frameworks are often seen as useful tools for disseminating information, building consensus, and filtering project funding.

In places where cultural and natural tourism resources extend across the territory of two or more autonomous polities, cross-border collaboration is vital. While planning traditions in most parts of the world have been restricted by political boundaries, cross-frontier tourism planning at both subnational and international levels is on the rise as neighbouring destinations are beginning to understand the value of networking to develop, conserve and promote common resources (Richard, 1993; Timothy, 1998a). Cross-border partnerships are vital in areas where resources lie across or adjacent to national borders, for they may encourage a more balanced use of resources and a standardized system of conservation. In short, cross-border collaborative efforts can place sustainable development goals and objectives in a more holistic and equitable framework. Within this context, Kjos (1986: 22, 26) argues that as destination planners,

> we need to learn what is happening on the other side of the border. We need to learn what plans are contemplated and why, and then to sit down and see what we can do to reach some form of cooperation and mutually acceptable solutions . . . Our planning world does not end at the border.

Finally there is the issue of cooperation between private sector services, including industry organizations (e.g. hotel associations) and NGOs. These forms of collaboration can increase efficiency levels and provide a stronger basis for working with the public sector to meet the demands of private industry and lobby groups. In common with collaboration between government agencies, private sector interests can eliminate overlap, and potentially offer a bigger and better product when they work together, particularly in areas of promotion and marketing.

The International Peace Garden (IPG) on the USA–Canada border is a good example of some of these types of cooperation. This park is divided between two nations, and several levels of government agencies are involved in its functioning. The IPG is owned and operated privately by International Peace Garden Incorporated (IPG Inc.) and administered by a board of directors that is comprised equally of Canadian and American representatives. From its inception, the IPG was a meeting of minds between the US and Canadian governments. Since its foundation, the IPG's daily operation requires constant bi-national collaboration, monitoring and concession, particularly in the areas of law enforcement, conservation, human resources, promotion and marketing, and infra-structure development. One example of concessions deals with human resources. Both countries have agreed to permit citizens of the other country to work visa-free anywhere within the park boundaries on either side of the international border. Another example is the importing of consumer products. In common with the human resource issue, because the park entrance is located between the customs stations of both countries, goods brought into the IPG from the USA or Canada never have to pass through the other country's inspections. Thus, all goods brought into the park are exempt from customs duties and can be used without restraint on both sides of the border within the park (Timothy, 1999a).

The IPG also requires cooperation between different levels of government and private and public sectors. The transportation department of Manitoba maintains the roads on the Canadian side of the park, while North Dakota's transportation office handles the roads on the US side. Likewise, each federal and provincial/state government's regulations pertaining to conservation are in place on each side, which in some places might create significant problems. Here, however, it does not. Owing to its ability to collaborate between various administrative levels, IPG Inc. has experienced notable planning and management success as a private company working within the framework of two sets of national and provincial/state laws (Timothy, 1999a).

Participatory, Incremental, Collaborative/Cooperative (PIC) Planning

This review of prominent theories and paradigms associated with community planning in general and tourism planning in particular has provided the basis for developing a normative model of destination community tourism planning. Figure 10.1 presents three substantive principles, which according to the research literature, ought to be paramount in the tourism planning process if the goals of sustainability are to be met in communities where the tourist experience takes place. This model takes the acronym PIC, reflecting three broad strategies described previously and recommended in the community planning literature, namely participation, incremental development and collaboration/cooperation. Each of these comprises principles that are considered by researchers and practitioners to be necessary in effective planning.

As the model indicates, these approaches and principles are not meant to replace the traditions of procedural planning (i.e. the step-by-step planning process). Instead, the PIC principles should function as the broader context within which the rational comprehensive planning steps should be taken. Participatory and collaborative/cooperative principles can and ought to be included at each step in the process, while rules of incrementalism fit best towards the end of the process when plans have been drafted and recommendations made.

This model is process-oriented, not directly product-oriented. The assumption here is that if the PIC principles, which fall well within

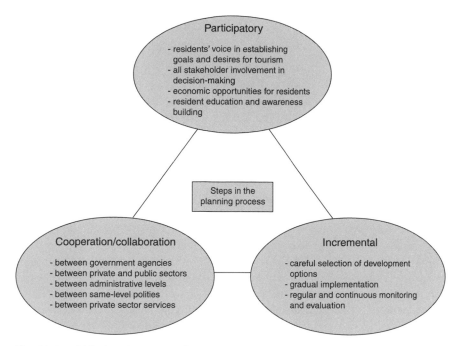

Fig. 10.1. PIC planning principles.

the purview of sustainable tourism, are utilized by destination communities and their planners, a sustainable product will result. Thus, in the context of tourism, sustainability of the industry itself and the sociocultural, physical and economic environments of destination communities will be more likely.

Obstacles to the PIC Planning Model

Although this PIC model is based on normative views of tourism development and supports the principles of sustainability as gleaned from the planning and tourism planning literature, the model is obviously not perfect, nor is its implementation without challenges. The examples described in this chapter and most advocates of community tourism planning highlight the positive effects of participatory planning, while very few ever point out the potential problems and constraints related to it. This section aims to highlight some of the problems that exist in attempting to operationalize the model described in Fig. 10.1. Timothy (1998a, 1999b, 2002) has outlined several constraints to the PIC model described above. Some of the following is adapted from his work.

Inadequate representation

Bramwell and Sharman (2000: 27–28) highlight three sets of issues
concerning the community approach to tourism planning: scope of
participation, intensity of participation and degree of consensus
(Table 10.2). From this framework, several challenges become clear. First
is the issue of representation. True community participation cannot
be achieved if the range of community participants is not adequately
representative of the entire population. Secondly, a related concern is
whether or not adequate numbers of community representatives from
various stakeholder groups are involved in planning and policy making.
Thirdly, is the degree to which community participants are involved
in open, meaningful dialogue. In some parts of the world, this is done
officially, but public consultations sometimes amount to little more than
tokenism to satisfy outside observers. Fourthly, is a concern about how
often destination stakeholders are included in dialogue and council
meetings. Finally, there is the extent of consensus among community
participants in the planning process. Consensus is often fragile and
differences of opinions among stakeholders may result in stalemates to
the extent that important issues may remain unsolved. Sometimes such
differences are brought about by external forces (Parker, 1999) and
accentuated by inequalities between stakeholders (Bramwell and Sharman,
1999). None the less, consensus is not absolutely essential, for there will
nearly always be some community members who do not want tourism, or
who fight against its effects.

Table 10.2. Issues affecting community participation in tourism planning.
Source: after Bramwell and Sharman (2000).

Sets of issues	Specific issues
Scope of community participation	• The extent to which the range of participation by the community is representative of all relevant stakeholders • The numbers of people who participate from among the relevant stakeholders
Intensity of participation by the community	• The extent to which all community participants are involved in direct, respectful and open dialogue • How often community stakeholders are involved • The extent to which all participants learn from each other
Degree to which consensus emerges among community members	• The extent to which community participants reach a consensus about issues and politics • The extent to which consensus emerges across the inequalities

Traditions of power

One of the most significant obstacles to the PIC approach is traditional power structures, which are still strong in many traditional societies. It is common in developing regions for a limited number of people or one individual from the privileged class to have all the voice in social decision-making. This has led to the belief among leaders and community members at large that representational democracy, from the Western perspective at least, is unnecessary (Haywood, 1988; Tosun, 2000). Thus, traditions of power distribution exclude most population groups from decision-making and commonly preclude them from participation in the benefits of tourism. This is particularly the case for women and ethnic minorities, who throughout history have been considered socially marginal in systems governed by patriarchal rulers (Timothy, 2001). In the area of collaboration and cooperative planning, conventional power structures have long reinforced traditional sectoral divisions between economic and social sectors and resulted in political boundary-restricted planning practices (Timothy, 1998a). Imbalances in power relations also create obstacles to the practice of incremental development. Flexibility, one of the basic premises of incrementalism, is sometimes stifled when decisions cannot be made at very local levels, even when problems occur (Timothy, 1998b).

On the island of Java these traditions of authority still dominate modern society and heavily influence Indonesia's political structure. That political and social authority is allowed to rest in the hands of one individual, or power centre, enabled the concentration of power in the hands of President Suharto and his cronies for more than 30 years (Suryadinata, 1997). To break from this socio-political order in Javanese culture is a sign of rebellion and would be insulting to one's superiors. Much of this probably comes from the reluctance of people in positions of control to share their decision-making power. Reed (1997: 589) argues that people in tourism planning 'who traditionally hold power may resist its redistribution, thereby hindering attempts for collaboration'.

When there is a power differential between stakeholders, problems arise pertaining to equal representation. True collaborative and community-based planning can be best achieved when power is more evenly spread among stakeholders (Gray, 1989; Parker, 1999) (see Hall, Chapter 6 this volume).

Advocacy groups sometimes frown on participatory planning and collaboration. Critics argue that collaboration may lead to a loss of agency power for resource managers, and environmental groups fear that environmental laws will be bypassed by community-based collaboration. Some observers fear that small minorities have the potential to stifle collaborative processes or veto actions that might be in the broader community and national interest (Selin, 1999: 271).

Lack of awareness

Another hindrance to community-based tourism is a lack of awareness in many destination regions. Owing to the comparative infancy of tourism in many places, adequate local expertise has yet to be developed. A lack of proper experience and training among public-sector decision makers commonly gets in the way of community input into development processes. It has also been blamed for a lack of collaborative planning, for local leaders are sometimes unaware of the need for, and possible benefits of, cooperation. Additionally, owing to bureaucratic confusion, the rights of local leaders to collaborate across political lines are commonly unclear.

There is also a lack of understanding among residents about tourism, which may keep some people from becoming involved (Tosun, 2000). For example, villagers on some Pacific islands have an interest in attracting tourists, but they cannot identify with foreigners' desire to visit their rural communities (Lipscomb, 1998). Based on interviews with community members and small tourism entrepreneurs in Yogyakarta, Indonesia, Timothy (1999b) concluded that there is a sense of inadequacy among citizens for participating in tourism decision-making. Sometimes these attitudes are utilized by planners as excuses for not involving the public in planning. For example, according to one government official interviewed, 'the people are not prepared to participate in tourism planning'. Faced with these prospects, leaders simply turn to elites who are already in positions of power for input into the planning process.

Economics and time

From an economics perspective, inadequate public funding is a major limitation to community tourism planning. Budgetary constraints among local governments increase dependence on national administrators and foreign corporations, which has a tendency to increase outside control of local resources and industry initiatives. Additionally, a common thought among decision makers is that public participation, especially in the area of stakeholder dialogue, is a luxury that cannot be afforded in both temporal and financial terms (Tosun, 2000). Likewise, poverty and social standing may keep people from becoming involved in decision-making. It is difficult to incite enthusiasm among community members for setting long-term goals and enacting broad-based policies when their immediate survival is most important (Timothy, 1999b).

Lack of public funds are also a constraint to incremental development. In many developing destinations, many plans never make it to the implementation stage. Often the money allocated for development is spent on plan and policy formulation with the result that insufficient capital is left to implement the plan's recommendations. The idea of continuous monitoring is also affected by lack of funds, for if money has been available to implement recommendations initially, there usually is not enough to continue monitoring the project (Timothy, 1998b).

As noted earlier, site-specific physical planning is the preferred approach to planning in many developing countries owing to its fast and conspicuous nature. This type of planning can be done with relative ease and in relatively short periods of time. Collaborative and incremental planning usually require significant time commitments, which makes it a lower priority among tourism officials (Timothy, 1998a).

Peripherality

In communities located at the edge of national space or in otherwise physically isolated areas, a constant struggle exists to be included in national-level development efforts in both developed and developing countries. In many places, peripheral areas are viewed by politicians as unimportant in national efforts to modernize and develop. This results in a lack of managerial support and financial assistance for programmes like tourism because it is much more common for populations and communities located in core areas and industrial interiors to be favoured. This attitude among leaders leads to the marginalization of residents' opinions and concerns during policy development and planning. Thus, as Timothy (2002) argues, it is not surprising that national-level policies are often at odds with the needs and priorities of distant communities. Despite this prevalent attitude, limited numbers of countries, such as Canada and New Zealand, have made remarkable strides in involving some of their more spatially disadvantaged groups in tourism negotiations.

Conclusion

This chapter has presented a normative model of destination community tourism planning. This PIC approach to planning recommends three primary elements that should be integrated into the planning process, namely community participation, incremental development and cooperation/collaboration. It is important in participatory planning to include community members in decision-making processes, but in addition, input from other stakeholders (e.g. lobby groups, business people, etc.) is vital. Despite the importance of community control, few examples exist today where the host community actually controls tourism, although as the cases presented in this chapter show, there is evidence that this might be changing. Participation also should entail building awareness of the industry throughout the community and providing opportunities for residents to benefit economically and socially from tourism, for tourism planning will be better equipped to meet the demands of sustainable development when community members have a voice and when they profit from tourism. Likewise, incremental development promotes efficiency and adaptability, for it allows changes to be made in plan implementation when unforeseen events occur. Cooperation between government agencies, private and public sectors, different levels of administration, same-level administrations, and private-sector services is also an important element of planning that has potential to promote sustainability and improve efficiency.

In summary, destination community planning is about community empowerment. All of the elements discussed above lead to this theme. Such a grass-roots approach should lend power to the people who are most affected by tourism. The knowledge base of indigenous communities remains largely unused in tourism planning in many parts of the world, but the approach recommended here has the potential to change this. The PIC approach to tourism development planning is not a simple matter. In fact it is an alternative to traditional highly centralized, opaque and *ad hoc* planning approaches to tourism. As a result, the implementation of this proactive approach, which requires participation of stakeholders, decentralization of power and transparency in decision-making, may face political and bureaucratic obstacles particular to developing countries.

None the less, as tourism matures, particularly in developing destinations, and as people begin to understand the impacts of tourism better, destination community empowerment will no doubt intensify. When opportunities are provided for locals to participate in decision-making, gain from tourism, control tourism through incremental development, and build partnerships through various levels of cooperation, communities will begin to share in the benefits of tourism rather than simply suffering its consequences.

References

Arnstein, S.R. (1969) A ladder of citizen participation. *Journal of the American Institute of Planners* 35(4), 216–224.

Baez, A.L. (1996) Learning from experience in the Monteverde Cloud Forest, Costa Rica. In: Price, M.F. (ed.) *People and Tourism in Fragile Environments.* John Wiley & Sons, Chichester, pp. 109–122.

Baud-Bovy, M. (1982) New concepts in planning for tourism and recreation. *Tourism Management* 3, 308–313.

Berger, D.J. (1996) The challenge of integrating Maasai tradition with tourism. In: Price, M.F. (ed.) *People and Tourism in Fragile Environments.* John Wiley & Sons, Chichester, pp. 175–197.

Boonzaier, E. (1996) Negotiating the development of tourism in the Richtersveld, South Africa. In: Price, M.F. (ed.) *People and Tourism in Fragile Environments.* John Wiley & Sons, Chichester, pp. 123–137.

Bramwell, B. and Sharman, A. (1999) Collaboration in local tourism policy-making. *Annals of Tourism Research* 26, 392–415.

Bramwell, B. and Sharman, A. (2000) Approaches to sustainable tourism planning and community participation: the case of the Hope Valley. In: Richards, G. and Hall, D. (eds) *Tourism and Sustainable Community Development.* Routledge, London, pp. 17–35.

Cullingworth, J.B. and Nadin, V. (1994) *Town and Country Planning in Britain.* 11th edn. Routledge, London.

Davidson, R. and Maitland, R. (1999) Planning for tourism in towns and cities. In: Greed, C.H. (ed.) *Social Town Planning.* Routledge, London, pp. 208–220.

Dei, L.A. (2000) Community participation in tourism in Africa. In: Dieke, P.U.C. (ed.) *The Political Economy of Tourism Development in Africa.* Cognizant, New York, pp. 285–298.

Din, K. (1993) Dialogue with the hosts: an educational strategy towards sustainable tourism. In: Hitchcock, M., King, V.T. and Parnwell, M.J.G. (eds) *Tourism in South-East Asia.* Routledge, London, pp. 327–336.

Dowling, R.K. (1993) An environmentally-based planning model for regional tourism development. *Journal of Sustainable Tourism* 1(1), 17–37.

Edgell, D.L. (1990) *International Tourism Policy.* Van Nostrand Reinhold, New York.

Fitton, M. (1996) Does our community want tourism? Examples from South Wales. In: Price, M.F. (ed.) *People and Tourism in Fragile Environments.* John Wiley & Sons, Chichester, pp. 159–174.

Friedmann, J. (1992) *Empowerment: the Politics of Alternative Development.* Blackwell, Cambridge, Massachusetts.

Getz, D. (1987) Tourism planning and research: traditions, models and futures. In: *Proceedings of the Australian Travel Workshop.* Australian Travel Workshop, Bunbury, Western Australia, pp. 407–448.

Gill, A.M. (1996) Rooms with a view: informal settings for public dialogue. *Society and Natural Resources* 9, 633–643.

Gray, B. (1989) *Collaborating: Finding Common Ground for Multiparty Problems.* Jossey-Bass, San Francisco.

Gunn, C. (1994) *Tourism Planning: Basics, Concepts, Cases,* 3rd edn. Taylor and Francis, Washington, DC.

Hall, C.M. (1994) *Tourism and Politics: Policy, Power and Place.* John Wiley & Sons, Chichester.

Hall, C.M. (2000) *Tourism Planning: Policies, Processes and Relationships.* Prentice Hall, Harlow.

Hatton, M.J. (1999) *Community-based Tourism in the Asia-Pacific.* Canadian International Development Agency, Ottawa.

Haywood, K.M. (1988) Responsible and responsive tourism planning in the community. *Tourism Management* 9, 105–118.

Hudson, B.M. (1979) Comparison of current planning theories: counterparts and contradictions. *Journal of the American Planning Association* 45(4), 387–398.

Inskeep, E. (1991) *Tourism Planning: an Integrated and Sustainable Development Approach.* Van Nostrand Reinhold, New York.

Inskeep, E. and Kallenberger, M. (1992) *An Integrated Approach to Resort Development: Six Case Studies.* World Tourism Organization, Madrid.

Jamal, T.B. and Getz, D. (1995) Collaboration theory and tourism planning. *Annals of Tourism Research* 22, 186–204.

Kjos, K. (1986) Trans-boundary land-use planning: a view from San Diego County. In: Herzog, L. (ed.) *Planning the International Border Metropolis: Trans-Boundary Policy Options in the San Diego-Tijuana Region.* Center for US–Mexican Studies, University of California, San Diego, pp. 22–26.

Lindblom, C.E. (1965) *The Intelligence of Democracy.* Free Press, New York.

Lipscomb, A.J.H. (1998) Village-based tourism in the Solomon Islands: impediments and impacts. In: Laws, E., Faulkner, B. and Moscardo, G. (eds) *Embracing and Managing Change in Tourism: International Case Studies.* Routledge, London, pp. 185–201.

Long, V.H. (1993) Techniques for socially sustainable tourism development: lessons from Mexico. In: Nelson, J.G., Butler, R.W. and Wall, G. (eds) *Tourism and Sustainable Development: Monitoring, Planning, Managing.* Department of Geography, University of Waterloo, Waterloo, Ontario, pp. 201–218.

Long, V.H. and Wall, G. (1995) Small-scale tourism development in Bali. In: Conlin, M.V. and Baum, T. (eds) *Island Tourism: Management Principles and Practice.* John Wiley & Sons, Chichester, pp. 237–257.

Lynn, W. (1992) Tourism in the people's interest. *Community Development Journal* 27(4), 371–377.

Marcouiller, D.W. (1997) Toward integrative tourism planning in rural America. *Journal of Planning Literature* 22(3), 338–357.

Mitchell, B. (1989) *Geography and Resource Analysis,* 2nd edn. Longman, London.

Mowforth, M. and Munt, I. (1998) *Tourism and Sustainability: New Tourism in the Third World.* Routledge, London.

Murphy, P.E. (1985) *Tourism: a Community Approach.* Methuen, New York.

Murphy, P.E. (1988) Community driven tourism planning. *Tourism Management* 9, 96–104.

Nunn, S. and Rosentraub, M.S. (1997) Dimensions of interjurisdictional cooperation. *Journal of the American Planning Association* 63(2), 205–219.

Parker, S. (1999) Collaboration on tourism policy-making: environment and commercial sustainability on Bonaire, NA. *Journal of Sustainable Tourism* 7(3/4), 240–259.

Pearce, D. (1995) Planning for tourism in the 1990s: an integrated, dynamic, and multiscale approach. In: Butler, R.W. and Pearce, D. (eds) *Change in Tourism: People, Places, Processes.* Routledge, London, pp. 229–244.

Prentice, R. (1993) Community-driven tourism planning and residents' preferences. *Tourism Management* 14, 218–227.

Reed, M.G. (1997) Power relations and community-based tourism planning. *Annals of Tourism Research* 24, 566–591.

Richard, W.E. (1993) International planning for tourism. *Annals of Tourism Research* 20, 601–604.

Rondinelli, D.A. (1982) The dilemma of development administration: complexity and uncertainty in control-oriented bureaucracies. *World Politics* 35(1), 42–72.

Scheyvens, R. (1999) Ecotourism and the empowerment of local communities. *Tourism Management* 20, 245–249.

Selin, S. (1999) Developing a typology of sustainable tourism partnerships. *Journal of Sustainable Tourism* 7(3/4), 260–273.

Simmons, D.G. (1994) Community participation in tourism planning. *Tourism Management* 15, 98–108.

Smith, R.A. (2000) Tourism planning and development in Southeast and South Asia. In: Hall, C.M. and Page, S. (eds) *Tourism in South and Southeast Asia: Issues and Cases.* Butterworth Heinemann, Oxford, pp. 104–114.

Smith, V.L. (1998) Privatization in the third world: small-scale tourism enterprises. In: Theobald, W.F. (ed.) *Global Tourism,* 2nd edn. Butterworth Heinemann, Oxford, pp. 205–215.

Spann, R.N. (1979) *Government Administration in Australia.* Allen and Unwin, Sydney.

Strang, V. (1996) Sustaining tourism in far north Queensland. In: Price, M.F. (ed.) *People and Tourism in Fragile Environments.* John Wiley & Sons, Chichester, pp. 109–122.

Suryadinata, L. (1997) Democratization and political succession in Suharto's Indonesia. *Asian Survey* 37(3), 269–280.

Timothy, D.J. (1998a) Cooperative tourism planning in a developing destination. *Journal of Sustainable Tourism* 6(1), 52–68.

Timothy, D.J. (1998b) Incremental tourism planning in Yogyakarta, Indonesia. *Tourism Recreation Research* 23(2), 72–74.

Timothy, D.J. (1999a) Cross-border partnership in tourism resource management: international parks along the US–Canada border. *Journal of Sustainable Tourism* 7(3/4), 182–205.

Timothy, D.J. (1999b) Participatory planning: a view of tourism in Indonesia. *Annals of Tourism Research* 26, 371–391.

Timothy, D.J. (2000) Building community awareness of tourism in a developing country destination. *Tourism Recreation Research* 25(2), 111–116.

Timothy, D.J. (2001) Gender relations in tourism: revisiting patriarchy and underdevelopment. In: Apostolopoulos, Y., Sönmez, S. and Timothy, D.J. (eds) *Women as Producers and Consumers of Tourism in Developing Regions.* Praeger, Westport, Connecticut, pp. 235–248.

Timothy, D.J. (2002) Tourism and community development issues. In: Sharpley, R. and Telfer, D.J. (eds) *Tourism and Development: Concepts and Issues.* Channel View Publications, Clevedon, pp. 149–164.

Timothy, D.J. and White, K. (1999) Community-based ecotourism development on the periphery of Belize. *Current Issues in Tourism* 2(2/3), 226–242.

Tosun, C. (1999) Towards a typology of community participation in the tourism development process. *International Journal of Tourism and Hospitality* 10(2), 113–134.

Tosun, C. (2000) Limits to community participation in the tourism development process in developing countries. *Tourism Management* 21, 613–633.

Tosun, C. (2001) Challenges of sustainable tourism development in the developing world: the case of Turkey. *Tourism Management* 22(3), 285–299.

Tosun, C. and Jenkins, C.L. (1998) The evolution of tourism planning in third-world countries: a critique. *Progress in Tourism and Hospitality Research* 4, 101–114.

United Nations Educational, Scientific and Cultural Organization (UNESCO)/United Nations Development Programme (UNDP) (1992) *Cultural Tourism Development, Central Java – Yogyakarta: Final Report.* UNESCO/UNDP, Yogyakarta.

Woodley, A. (1993) Tourism and sustainable development: the community perspective. In: Nelson, J.G., Butler, R.W. and Wall, G. (eds) *Tourism and Sustainable Development: Monitoring, Planning, Managing.* Department of Geography, University of Waterloo, Waterloo, Ontario, pp. 135–146.

Community Attitudes: Tourism Development in Natural Environments

11

ROSS K. DOWLING

School of Marketing, Tourism and Leisure, Edith Cowan University, Joondalup, Australia

Introduction

Participation by host communities in tourism planning and development is fundamental to the process (Cooper and Wanhill, 1997; Richards and Hall, 2000). Travis (1980: 82) states that 'the host population and local services are important in themselves and are incidentally basic resources in relation to tourism'. UNEP (1986) advocated that tourism should be subject to environmental planning and management taking into account the well-being of the local population, which too often has had to accept a large influx of tourists without having had a voice in such development. The public now demand that their concerns be incorporated into the decision-making process. This has resulted in the emergence of public participation programmes and requirements that environmental impact statements be prepared.

Liu *et al.* (1987) carried out a major study of resident perceptions of the impact of tourism on the environment in Hawaii, North Wales and Turkey. Residents of Hawaii and North Wales gave protection of the environment the highest priority. It was ranked higher than cultural benefits, social costs and even economic benefits. Conclusions drawn from the study were that the impact of tourism on the environment is of universal concern; different cultures view the ways environmental and negative impacts of tourism are perceived differently; destination communities perceive many of the benefits brought by tourism, such as the preservation of historic sites; and it is important to incorporate the perceptions of host communities when evaluating the effects of tourism development for planning purposes.

©CAB *International* 2003. *Tourism in Destination Communities*
(eds S. Singh, D.J. Timothy and R.K. Dowling)

General public participation in planning is important for a variety of reasons. They include gaining attitudes and perceptions of residents' views on their environment, tourism development, community aspirations and on the tourists themselves. Dasmann *et al.* (1973: 115) suggested that 'the more local people benefit from tourism, the more they will benefit from a commitment to preserve the environmental features which attract tourism'.

A second reason for community consultation is because not all communities are in favour of tourism development. Therefore tourism planning should always be carried out in close collaboration with the local inhabitants who are most likely to be affected. de Kadt (1979) lamented that he knew of no country that evaluated alternative approaches to tourism for the purpose of selecting one that promised to maximize social benefits to hosts. He recommended community controlled, forward-looking planning as opposed to typical remedial planning. Within a few years Murphy (1985) and Getz (1986) echoed the emphasis on community participation for its own gain.

A third reason for community consultation is because it is the local people who have much to lose or gain from policy decisions. UNEP (1986: 2) suggested that 'tourism planning should always be carried out in close collaboration with the local inhabitants who are most likely to be affected'. Murphy (1983) asserted that tourism thrives on a community's resources and therefore it must take into consideration the opinions of the residents of a destination area. He added that there is a growing awareness of tourism's dependency on and responsibility to the local community. Consequently it is advocated that future planning be undertaken from the perspective of a community industry, one that is responsible to the community it is selling. This is also endorsed by Getz (1986), who suggested that a tourism development plan should include statements on what tourism is expected to contribute to more general goals including community development, enhancement of cultural identity, social welfare, the provision of leisure opportunities, as well as the provision and maintenance of living amenities.

The fourth aspect of gaining community views during the planning process is to gauge the perceptions of hosts (residents) to guests (tourists). Mathieson and Wall (1982) suggested that planners should consider the conflicting opinions of members of the community, and Romeril (1989) asserted that destination cultures vary in their degree of robustness or resilience to the impact of tourists. Many individuals involved in the tourist industry are likely to welcome tourists, whereas others may resent their presence and behaviour.

In summary, the participation in tourism development by the host community, especially in regard to issues of the physical environment, provides a more balanced approach than traditionally oriented development ones. Research into community attitudes towards tourism is reasonably well developed although incorporation of such views into the planning process is far less common (Pearce, 1989). However, it is essential for this to occur in order to ensure environmental conservation, minimization of unacceptable impacts, community growth and acceptance of tourism. Tourism planning must reduce any conflicts between visitors and the environment as well as between visitors and residents as each competes for the same amenities (Knopp, 1980). Much of this potential conflict may be resolved if resident and tourist opinions are sought and heeded when planning is carried out. A proactive stance by tourism has greater opportunities than the present reactive position in most communities (Gunn, 1987). Therefore an important part of any tourism development process is the seeking out of the views of the host community on tourism's physical, social and cultural issues. To achieve this it is important to understand the different approaches to the environment. This chapter now outlines various approaches to the environment and tourism, then describes how the community in a World Heritage Region in Western Australia views tourism development and how it impacts on the local natural environment and social fabric.

The Environment

The environment simply means 'our surroundings'. Generally, however, the term is used to refer to the earth's physical environment, which comprises both biophysical and human-made elements. The biophysical environment, sometimes referred to simply as the physical environment, is the biosphere or outer layer of the earth. It is made up of the atmosphere (air), hydrosphere (water) and lithosphere (land). The biosphere contains all living organisms and the variations among living organisms is referred to as biological diversity or biodiversity. The biophysical environment includes both terrestrial (land) and marine (water) environments divided into three major climatic zones – the polar, temperate and tropical regions. In the higher (polar) latitudes temperature is the most important defining characteristic, whereas in the temperate and tropical zones precipitation determines differentiation. Within each of the major climatic regions are a number of different environments (or ecosystems). These include deserts, grasslands and forests.

Approaches to the environment

People differ over how serious environmental problems are owing to their different perspectives of the world (Miller, 1994). Such views come in many forms but the two most common vary according to whether or not humans are placed at the centre of things. Two examples are the human-centred (anthropocentric) view that underlies most industrial societies and the ecocentric (life-centred) outlook. Key principles of the human-centred approach are that humans are the planet's most important species and are apart from, and in charge of, the rest of nature. It assumes the earth has an unlimited supply of resources to which human access in general is through use of science and technology. Other people believe that any human-centred world view, even stewardship, is unsustainable. They suggest that our world views must be expanded to recognize inherent or intrinsic value to all forms of life, that is, value regardless of their potential or actual use to humankind. This is a life-centred or ecocentric view in which humans believe that it is useful to recognize biodiversity as a vital element of the earth for all life forms.

The ecocentric perspective believes that nature exists for all of earth's species and that humans are not apart from, or in charge of, the rest of nature. In essence it posits that humans need the earth, but the earth does not need humans. It also suggests that some forms of economic growth are beneficial and some are harmful. Humankind's goals should be to design economic and political systems that encourage sustainable forms of growth and discourage, or prohibit, forms that cause degradation or pollution. A healthy economy depends on a healthy environment.

Given this understanding then, sustaining the earth requires every person to make a personal commitment to live an environmentally ethical life. By extension, its application to natural area tourism is that governments, the tourism industry, operators, tourists and the local communities should all play a part in not only conserving natural areas but also their enhancement. In doing this, the very resource base, which underpins the natural area, will be protected and will be able to be utilized in a sustainable manner that fosters environmental, social and economic well-being.

Conserving the environment

The conservation of the natural environment can occur in a number of ways at the community level including the adoption of a bioregional approach, as well as the advocacy of an educative ethic. The former focuses on fostering an understanding of the local geographic area where communities live as being part of a natural region or bioregion. A bioregion is a unique life territory with its own soils, landforms, watersheds, microclimates, native plants and animals, and other distinctive natural characteristics. Bioregional living is an attempt to understand and live sustainably within the natural cycles, flows and rhythms of a particular place. For local communities it means being clear on its environmental uses and impacts in regard to energy, water, waste, etc. Often traditional, rural and/or remote communities understand these things better than newer, more urbanized societies.

The central impulse of environmental education is to help develop communities that are knowledgeable of, concerned about, and motivated to do something for, the environment. This involves empowering people to be knowledgeable about their natural, social and economic environments, be concerned about their environmental problems, and be motivated to act responsibly in enhancing the quality of their environment as well as their lives. Thus sustaining the physical environment at the community level requires people to make personal commitments individually and collectively to live an environmentally ethical life. The rationale for this is based on the premise that this should occur not because it is required by law but because it is right. This right is couched in our individual and collective responsibility to the environment, the earth and all living things on it. This is known as the environmental ethic and there are a number of steps communities can take in order to promote this approach (see Fennell and Przeclawski, Chapter 8 this volume). They include evaluating our view of the physical environment by comparing the state it is in to its natural condition. Communities should also become more ecologically informed through sharing environmental knowledge and awareness with others to build a collective understanding of the natural world.

Communities that hold or adopt an ecocentric view of their surroundings are better able to work with it to engender a sustainable future. Important components in this approach include the view that the physical environment exists for all species and that humans are not set apart from, or in charge of, the rest of nature. As mentioned previously, it is underpinned philosophically by the view that: 'Humans need the earth, but the earth does not need humans'. Therefore, the goals of tourism development in destination communities should be to design economic and political systems that encourage sustainable forms of growth that bring equitable economic and social benefits to all people both now and in the future. It is argued here that a healthy economy depends on a healthy environment. Such a sustainable view is based on a number of major principles that include interconnectedness, intrinsic value, conservation, inter-generational equity and individual responsibility.

Tourism

Hall (1991) states that tourism is the temporary, short-term travel of non-residents to and from a destination. It may have a wide variety of impacts on the destination, the transit route, and the source point of tourists. Tourism may also influence the character of the tourist, and this is primarily for leisure or recreation, although business travel is also important. A central part of the tourism experience usually focuses on leisure and recreational activities. Tourism is usually viewed as being multi-dimensional, possessing physical, social, cultural, economic and political characteristics.

Tourism in the 21st century will not only be the world's biggest industry, it will be the largest by far that the world has ever seen (Page and Dowling, 2001). As it grows the tourism industry will need to embrace greater responsibility for its impacts, be they economic, social or environmental. The World Tourism Organization indicates that tourists of the 21st century will be travelling further afield on their holidays. China will be the world's most popular destination by the year 2020, and it will also become the fourth most important generating market. Other destinations predicted to make great strides in tourism are Russia, Thailand, Singapore, Indonesia and South Africa. Product development and marketing will need to match more closely, based on the main travel motivators of the 21st century, the three Es: entertainment, excitement and education.

Types of tourism

Tourism can be seen as either mass or alternative tourism. The former is characterized by large numbers of people seeking some degree of replication of their own cultures in institutionalized settings with little cultural or environmental interaction in authentic settings. Alternative tourism is sometimes referred to as 'special interest' tourism or 'responsible' tourism, and it is usually taken to mean alternative forms of travel that place emphasis on greater contact and understanding between residents and tourists, as well as between tourists and the environment (Smith and Eadington, 1992).

The development of the environmental movement in the 1980s coincided with the development of, and increases in, the availability and range of holiday types that inferred a greater level of environmental awareness than is associated with mass tourism. Alternative tourism can be broadly defined as forms of tourism that set out to be consistent with natural, social and community values and which allow both hosts and guests to enjoy positive and worthwhile interaction and shared experiences (Wearing and Neil, 1999).

Cater (1993) notes that alternative tourism comprises small-scale, locally owned activities. She suggests that these contrast with mass tourism, which is often characterized by large-scale multinational concerns, typified by repatriation of profits to offshore countries. Other characteristics of alternative tourism include its focus on minimizing negative environmental and social impacts, links to other sectors of the local economy (e.g. agriculture), and the retention by local people of tourists' expenditures. Finally, alternative tourism also fosters the involvement of local people in the decision-making process and includes them in the tourism development process. Using these criteria, alternative tourism surpasses purely a concern for the physical environment that typifies green tourism, to include economic, social and cultural considerations. Thus, alternative tourism can be viewed as being synonymous with the concept of sustainable tourism development (Holden, 2000), and it is especially relevant to tourism in destination communities.

Sustainable tourism

Natural areas have always attracted people, and with the advent of modern travel, humans are now visiting places all over the planet. Tourism to natural areas is booming, and it has been estimated to have risen from approximately 2% of all tourism in the late 1980s to about 20% of all leisure travel today (The Ecotourism Society, 1998; Weaver and Oppermann, 2000; Newsome *et al.*, 2001; Page and Dowling, 2001). The World Tourism Organization (WTO) concurs with this latter figure and suggests that natural area tourism is now worth US$20 billion a year (WTO, 1998). Thus, natural area tourism is undergoing explosive growth and as such it has the capability to change both natural areas and tourism itself. Here, this phenomenon is explored from the standpoint that natural area tourism can be beneficial to individuals, regions and countries, provided it is planned, developed and managed in a responsible manner.

The growing concern for conservation and the well-being of the environment over the last two decades has moved far beyond the realms of a concerned few, into the wider public arena. At the same time there has been a corresponding upsurge in tourism all over the world, leading to mass tourism. With this unparalleled growth of both, it was inevitable that one day they would meet and interact. In natural areas, where tourism either exists or is proposed, there is the potential for both beneficial and adverse environmental and sociocultural impacts to occur. Thus, there are two streams of thought regarding the environment–tourism relationship. The first is that the natural environment is harmed by tourism and hence the two are viewed as being in conflict. The second is that the two have the potential to work together in a symbiotic manner where each adds to the other.

The environment–tourism relationship has been the subject of considerable debate for the last three decades. The International Union for the Conservation of Nature and Natural Resources (IUCN, now known as the World Conservation Union) first raised the nature of the relationship when its director general posed the question in a paper entitled: *Tourism and environmental conservation: conflict, coexistence, or symbiosis?* (Budowski, 1976).

Thirteen years later the question appeared to remain unanswered when Romeril (1989) posited the question 'Is tourism and the environment in accord or discord?'. Thus the environment–tourism relationship may be viewed from one of two standpoints: that it is either in conflict or symbiosis. Either point of view may be adopted and defended but it is argued here that no matter which standpoint is espoused, the way to reduce conflict or increase compatibility is through understanding, planning and management that is grounded in environmental concepts and allows for sustainable development.

The environment–tourism relationship is grounded in the concepts of the sustainable use of natural resources as fostered by the World Conservation Strategy (IUCN, 1980) and the sustainable development strategy of the World Commission on Environment and Development (WCED, 1987). This environmental–development link often includes tourism as a bridge. The basis of this partnership is resource sustainability, and tourism must be fully integrated with the resource management process. This will require the adoption of resource conservation values as well as the more traditional development goals. Central to the goals of environmental conservation and resource sustainability is the protection and maintenance of environmental quality. To achieve this primary goal requires an awareness that is based on environmental protection and enhancement yet fosters the realization of tourism potential.

Drumm (1998) points out that local communities view ecotourism as an accessible development alternative which can enable them to improve their living standards without having to sell off their natural resources or compromise their culture. In the absence of other sustainable alternatives, their participation in ecotourism is often perceived as the best option for achieving their aspiration of sustainable development (see Scheyvens, Chapter 12 this volume). Drumm (1998) outlines a number of options for communities wanting to become involved in tourism development. They include:

1. Renting land to an operator to develop while simply monitoring impacts.
2. Working as occasional part-time or full-time staff members for outside operators.
3. Providing services such as food preparation, guiding, transport or accommodation to operators.
4. Forming joint ventures with outside operators with a division of labour, which allows the community to provide most services, while the operator takes care of marketing.
5. Operating fully independent community tourism programmes.

He adds that in each case, full community involvement in all stages of planning and management is essential to ensure healthy development.

Tourism's Impacts

Impacts can be either positive or negative. In most of the current literature tourism's impacts on the physical environment have been seen in a negative light. Wall (1994) notes that ecotourism attracts attention to natural treasures, thereby increasing the pressures upon them. Hvenegaard (1994) describes a number of adverse environmental impacts caused by tourism. They include overcrowding, overdevelopment, unregulated recreation, pollution, wildlife disturbances and vehicle use. However, the positive benefits of the environment–tourism relationship have also been considered for over two decades. Tourism and the environment are interrelated and it is argued that there are a number of reasons why conservation should seek the support of tourism. These include the fact that tourism provides conservation with an economic justification, it is a means of building support for conservation, and it can bring in resources for conservation (Phillips, 1985).

Tourism can generate positive impacts directly and indirectly by increasing political and economic support for natural area conservation and management. Thus, there is considerable support for the notion that regional tourism can support both conservation of physical environments as well as social and economic benefits to local communities.

While economic impacts may be measured and quantified to identify financial and employment effects, social and cultural impacts on visitors and host communities are often only considered when tourism development leads to local opposition (Page and Dowling, 2002). The attitudes of a host community's residents are a key component in identifying, measuring and analysing the impact of tourism. Resident perceptions of tourism may be one factor in shaping the attractiveness of a destination, and negative attitudes may be one indicator of an area's ability (or inability) to absorb tourism.

Doxey's (1975) Index of Tourist Irritation (Irridex) illustrates how the interaction of tourists and residents may be converted into different degrees of irritation. He argued that residents' responses would change in a predictable manner, passing through four stages – euphoria, apathy, annoyance and antagonism. However, at any one point in time, a community will be characterized by a range of views and grouping them into a simplified model such as Doxey's does not recognize local diversity (Page and Dowling, 2002). Communities with a history of exposure to tourism adapt to accommodate its effects, so that attitudes may change through time, and it is argued that communities can simultaneously hold both positive and negative attitudes towards tourism.

The sociocultural environment also serves as both an attraction and a recipient of tourism's impacts on host communities (Lindberg and McKercher, 1997). If the impacts become adverse the sustainability of local tourism will be in danger. For the tourism industry, the main concerns are to ensure the local population are not alienated or adversely impacted to the point that they may want to affect the local resource base or deny future access to the resource, over which they are the custodians.

One of the key elements of tourism is that it should be beneficial, which also raises issues related to the degree of control local people have over ecotourism ventures, highlighting the need to consider the empowerment of local communities (Ashley and Roe, 1998; Scheyvens, 1999). If positive attitudes to tourism are to be fostered, then destination communities should receive economic and social benefits. These include improved cultural appreciation and understanding, cultural heritage, and local pride (Ross and Wall, 1999).

It is also important that local residents decide what level of tourism they want (i.e. self-determination), what cultural practices they wish to share, and where tourists will be allowed to go. Several levels of involvement are possible, from full community development of facilities, to partnerships or joint ventures with the industry (Brandon, 1996). The process should include raising the awareness of probable tourism impacts so that residents can make informed decisions regarding the desirability of tourism.

Thus tourism development should only be considered successful if local communities have some measure of control over it and if they share equitably in the benefits emerging from ecotourism activities (Scheyvens, 1999). Scheyvens suggests that positive benefits of tourism on local communities should embrace both conservation and development at the local level.

Conservation-supporting Approaches

A central tenet in the planning and development of tourism in regions is that it should support conservation of the biophysical environment in those areas. This can be achieved either directly through the involvement of visitors in environmental protection and enhancement activities or indirectly through the generation of fees to fund local conservation activities. The key lies in the establishment of adequate revenue collecting through fees as well as by the emplacement of effective tourism management.

A code is a set of expectations, behaviours or rules written by industry members, government or non-government organizations (Holden, 2000). Their principal aim is to influence the attitudes and behaviour of tourists or the tourism industry. Codes may be informal and adopted by a group, or more formal and instituted for industry members and/or tourists. A code of ethics provides a standard of acceptable performance, often in written form, that assists in establishing and maintaining professionalism (Fennell, 1999) (see Fennell and Przeclawski, Chapter 8 this volume).

The WTO has adopted a global code of ethics for tourism (WTO, 2000). It includes principles outlining a sustainable approach to tourism development for destinations, governments, tour operators, developers, travel agents, workers and travellers themselves.

The following section examines these issues and concepts empirically in the context of Western Australia.

The Gascoyne Region, Western Australia

The Gascoyne region is situated on the coast of Western Australia (WA) approximately 1000 km north of Perth and has a number of outstanding, and in some cases unique, biological and geological phenomena (Dowling, 1991). The region's natural environment is protected by a number of national and marine parks and reserves that are administered by the WA State Government's Department of Conservation and Land Management (CALM). However, there is increasing concern for the region's environment especially owing to the pressures placed on it by tourism.

The region covers an area of $141,000 \text{ km}^2$ and is sparsely populated (14,000 people). It is divided into four local government areas, including the shires of Carnarvon, Exmouth, Shark Bay and Upper Gascoyne (Fig. 11.1). The principal town is Carnarvon with a population of 7000, about 30% of whom are Aboriginal. Other population centres are Exmouth (3000), Denham (1000) and Gascoyne Junction (100). The region's economy is based on pastoralism, horticulture, fishing, mining, tourism and defence. Tourism is the fastest growing industry in the Gascoyne region and its demand is being monitored by the WA Tourism Commission. In 2000 there were 401,600 tourists who generated Aus\$100 million in revenue. The need for increased attractions, facilities and developments has been highlighted in the region's Tourism Development Plan and is further emphasized by the widespread expansion of existing facilities and current proposals for resorts and marinas.

Since 1988 a longitudinal study has been evaluating the social and environmental impacts of tourism on the region's resources. Part of the approach incorporates the views and perceptions of the host community of the area's natural environment, tourism, and the relationship between the two. It is this segment of a much broader study that is briefly presented here. Data have been gathered by face-to-face interviews with residents over a 12-year period from January 1990 to January 2001 (e.g. Dowling, 1990, 1993, 1996, 1999, 2000). During that time over a dozen surveys have sampled residents randomly from areas representative of Gascoyne demographics. A total of 1200 residents were sampled, comprising 647 males and 553 females with a wide range of education levels and occupations. Respondents ranged in age from 14 to 73 years and had lived in the area for

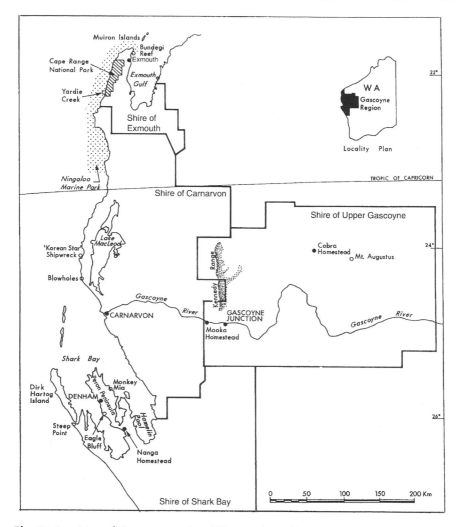

Fig. 11.1. Map of Gascoyne region, Western Australia.

an average of 12.6 years (Fig. 11.2). Their reasons for living there include job opportunities or employment (61%), a desirable place to live (25%), being born in the region (9%) or a desirable place to retire (5%).

Community attitudes

The social fabric of the Gascoyne community is rapidly changing. Retired people from Perth seeking a leisure life in the sun are joining long-term

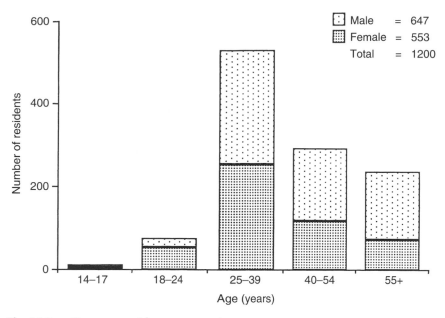

Fig. 11.2.   Gascoyne residents surveyed.

residents. In addition, the number of tourists is rapidly increasing each year. The long-term residents do not like either group much. When asked whether he was happy with the tourists visiting the area, a local fisherman replied, 'We don't like 'em and that's that' (Raffaele, 1989: 65). However, an early survey of residents indicates that they have considerable contact with tourists either directly through their job (40% agree), in public (33%) or as guests in their home (Dowling, 1993). The majority of residents point out that tourists do not diminish their enjoyment of the area (66%) and do not place a burden on the local services (61%). Those that do feel there is a burden on their community (24%) indicate that this is in relation to police and medical services as well as water supplies. Other problems stated include the increase in litter as well as congestion both in towns and at key recreational facilities such as boat ramps.

Residents agree that tourism generates more money for the local people than other commercial activities (72%), suggesting that it distributes economic benefits 'more evenly' than commercial fishing, mining or pastoralism. As tourism in the area increases so does the number of outsiders coming either to invest or work in the industry. For example, the local Shire Council of Shark Bay, which for years held back the tide of tourism, is now taking a more proactive stance in regard to tourism development and promotion (Dowling, 1996).

There was strong agreement by the Gascoyne residents (73% agree) that the environment in general needs greater protection (Table 11.1). Although there was a clear call for greater environmental protection in the region, respondents were split on their views as to whether there should be more national and marine parks. Many thought that there were enough already (42%) while others felt that there should be more (31%). Respondents who felt that the environment is looked after well stated that this is due to the efforts of local residents, pastoralists and fishermen. Others stated that credit should be given to the CALM, and a few noted that tourists help to look after the environment.

Those who felt that there were enough national and marine parks and reserves in the region already noted the many existing parks and reserves including Shark Bay Marine Park, Francois Peron National Park and Hamelin Pool Marine Reserve (Dowling and Alder, 1996). Also at the time of some of the earlier surveys there were proposals by the Federal Government to nominate Shark Bay in the southern part of the region as a World Heritage Area (Dowling, 1990). This caused consternation among the local residents who thought they were losing a certain degree of autonomy. At one fiery public meeting held on the issue, 299 residents out of the 300 present voted against the World Heritage proposal (Chubb, 1988) suggesting instead the implementation of the state-generated Shark Bay Region Plan (SPC and CALM, 1988). The bay was designated as a World Heritage Region in December 1991.

Table 11.1. Destination community residents' perceptions of the environment–tourism relationship in selected studies. Results from 1200 members of the host community in the Gascoyne region from 1990 to 2001.

Rank	Factor[a]	Mean[b]	Percentage[c]
1	Tourism should be integrated with conservation in the region	4.391	87.8
2	Tourism developments should be encouraged provided they do not conflict with the environment	3.917	78.3
3	The environment needs greater protection	3.645	72.9
4	The economic gains of tourism are just as important as the protection of the environment	3.357	57.9
5	There should be more national and marine parks in the region	2.112	42.2
6	Tourism does not harm the environment	1.175	23.5

[a]Factors are ranked by means of combined values.
[b]Scale ranges from 1 = strongly disagree to 5 = strongly agree.
[c]Percentage agreeing are those answering 4 or 5.

Residents who felt there were already a sufficient number of parks and reserves suggested that the real issue was not a question of more parks but rather one of greater protection of the existing ones. A large number of respondents suggested the need for more on-site management by increasing the number of park rangers (by CALM) and fisheries inspectors (WA Department of Fisheries). Others suggested the establishment of a public environmental awareness programme with increased interpretive information in the form of leaflets and signs.

The local community agreed that the economic gains of tourism are just as important as the protection of the environment (58%). They strongly supported tourism in the Gascoyne region (Table 11.2) indicating that tourists do not diminish their enjoyment of the area (66%). Most have considerable contact with tourists either directly through their job or as guests in their home (Fig. 11.3). For other residents their relationship with tourists is either limited to contact in public places or is reasonably little or none at all.

As mentioned previously, residents felt that tourism's economic benefits for the local community are generated 'more evenly' than pastoralism, commercial fishing or mining. Others added that the economic future of the region is closely tied to tourism; however, those who disagree (12%) state that economic benefits are derived for only a relatively few people, mostly the towns' business people, and that tourism pushed up the cost of living for locals. Residents also stated unequivocally that tourism in their region is based on its natural resources (89%); however, a lesser number believed the region's environment was well looked after (51% agree, 23% disagree).

Table 11.2. Destination community members' opinions of tourism. Results from 1200 members of the host community in the Gascoyne region from 1990 to 2001.

Rank	Factor[a]	Mean[b]	Percentage[c]
1	Tourism is based on its natural resources in the region	4.455	89.1
2	Tourism generates more money for the local people than other commercial activities	3.590	71.8
3	Tourists do not diminish my enjoyment of the area	3.285	65.7
4	The environment of the region is well looked after	2.570	51.4
5	Tourism is a burden on local services	1.650	33.0

[a]Factors are ranked by means of combined values.
[b]Scale ranges from 1 = strongly disagree to 5 = strongly agree.
[c]Percentage agreeing are those answering 4 or 5.

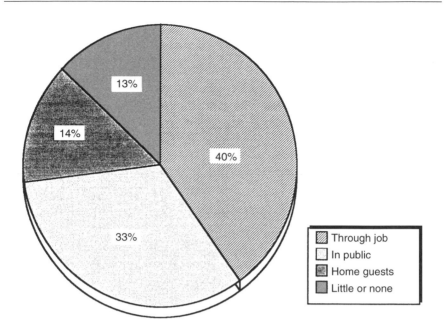

Fig. 11.3. Destination community contact with tourists.

Of the four major commercial activities in the area, the residents agreed that the most environmentally compatible one is tourism (83% agree) ahead of pastoralism (62%), commercial fishing (55%) and mining (19%). Residents point to overfishing, pastoral overstocking and the possibility of oil spills as reasons for incompatibility. Overall they viewed the activities as having a higher level of compatibility than the tourists and they also differed in their second preference by scoring fishing ahead of pastoralism. This is understandable as the livelihood of more people in the region is dependent on this commercial activity. Tourism is generally supported as long as adequate planning is carried out and on-site management provided.

The residents considered the main attractions of the region to be the pleasant climate (80% agree), the opportunities for fishing (71%) and the relaxed lifestyle (63%). Most of the community's recreational activities take place in the outdoor marine environment. The most popular ones are fishing, swimming and sailing. Others include boating, whale and turtle watching, and off-road driving. Recreational activities favoured by a minority included bush walking, snorkelling, cycling, diving, surfing, seashell collecting and scuba diving.

The community gave a low level of support to the statement that tourism does not harm the environment (23%, see Table 11.1). They suggest that the effects of a number of regional activities associated with recreation and tourism are environmentally harmful (Table 11.3). These include littering (84%), overfishing (75%) and undersized fishing (64%), disturbance to and/or destruction of landforms, fauna and flora, as well as water and noise pollution. The community ascribes many of these activities to tourists rather than themselves. Those causing the litter are suggested to be campers and fishermen littering the bays, reefs and beaches with decapitated fish, offal, plastic bait bags and fish hooks. However, Carnarvon residents in particular, apportion most of the blame for unsightly litter in their shire to other members of the community (Dowling, 1993).

Other areas noted for their litter are the roadside verges that are suggested as being strewn with a whole host of items including glass, tins, plastic and other rubbish. Camping sites and roadside rest areas are also identified as attracting litter, some of which is human excrement. Suggestions to overcome this despoilation of the countryside include the need for more bins especially at rest areas and camping sites, more shire litter officers, banning of the sale of non-returnable drink bottles, more anti-litter signs, and a programme of public awareness.

The second most noted regional recreational and touristic activity suggested as causing harm to the environment is overfishing and undersized fishing. Those against these detrimental activities especially single out 'net' and 'trap' fishing as well as the overuse of portable freezers to take fillets out of the region. Like the litter problem, the community attributes most of the blame to the tourists. Reasons suggested for this include net fishing from beaches, taking fish out of season, disregard for bag limits, and ignorance of the laws. Suggestions for reducing the problems include the need for more fisheries inspectors, education, a ban on freezers and more stringent bag limits. The third most noted harmful suite of activities was the disturbance of sand dunes (35%), the destruction of vegetation

Table 11.3. Destination community members' opinions of the effects of adverse environmental activities. Results from 1200 members of the host community in the Gascoyne region from 1990–2001.

Rank[a]	Activity	Percentage
1	Litter	84
2	Overfishing	75
3	Undersized fishing	64
4	Disturbance of sand dunes	35
5	Destruction of vegetation	31
6	Disturbance of wildlife	21
7	Anchor damage to reef	20
8	Water pollution	16
9	Noise pollution	15

[a]Factors are ranked by percentage responses.

(31%) and the disturbance of wildlife (21%). These are caused mainly by four-wheel-drive (4WD) vehicles near the beaches and popular campsites.

The local community suggests a number of environmentally appropriate tourism activities for the region (Table 11.4). The major ones are photographic tours, fishing and diving. Others are also sanctioned, especially activities that can be controlled by responsible operators. Uncontrolled activities associated with the indiscriminate use of 4WD vehicles were not supported. Residents agreed that tourism developments should be encouraged, provided they do not conflict with the environment (78%, see Table 11.1).

Many suggested the importance of ensuring that the regional environmental character and social fabric should not be destroyed by tourism. Low-key tourist developments were preferred (88%). Suggestions included more camping and caravanning facilities especially outside the national parks, more boat launching ramps and moderately priced tourist accommodation. Also advocated was the need for tourist developments to blend in with their surroundings. Marinas (26%) are preferred to resorts (22%), but large-scale tourist developments received very little support (6%). It was also advocated that such developments should be concentrated in existing developed areas to ensure that environmental impacts are minimized. This lends support to a similar suggestion made by the State's tourism and environmental departments (WATC/EPA, 1989).

The community gave overwhelming support (88%) for the integration of tourism and conservation (Table 11.1). One resident commented that 'tourism development is inevitable so it needs to be controlled and directed with careful negotiation by both local Shire authorities and State

Table 11.4. Destination community members' opinions of the environmentally compatible activities. Results from 1200 members of the host community in the Gascoyne region from 1990 to 2001.

Rank[a]	Activity	Percentage
1	Photographic tours	82
2	Fishing	71
3	Diving	70
4	Cycling	68
5	Yachting	67
6	Windsurfing	65
7	Boating	61
8	Heritage trails	60
9	Wildlife tours	52
10	Canoeing	49

[a]Factors are ranked by percentage responses.

departments such as CALM'. Therefore it is evident that CALM should have a larger degree of input into the future planning and management of environmentally related tourism activities and developments. This should ensure that the concept of sustainable development is applied in the region, allowing tourism to grow and environmental conservation and protection to be achieved.

Discussion

The Gascoyne case study findings are consistent with several earlier surveys on resident views of the environment–tourism relationship (e.g. Liu *et al.*, 1987; Schlüter and Var, 1988; see Table 11.5). However, in some it has been divergent. Examination of the findings confirms the earlier ones that host communities perceive tourism as improving the local economy and not causing a burden on local services. This latter view is also endorsed by their belief that tourism does not diminish the residents' enjoyment of the area. Their agreement with the statement that 'the economic gains of tourism are just as important as the protection of the environment' concurs with the

Table 11.5. Destination community members' perceptions of the environment–tourism relationship in selected studies.

Statement	Hawaii[a]	Wales[a]	Turkey[a]	Argentina[b]
Positive impacts				
Creates more parks for local residents	51.3	65.0	76.4	
Has not contributed to environmental decline	49.6	56.5		45.6
Helps protect areas of built environment	47.5	50.9		
Helps protect areas of historic building		86.8		
Negative impacts				
Increases littering	51.7	84.9	87.9	97.0
Increases traffic problems	47.9	98.1		
Increases congestion in parks, etc.	38.0	45.3		49.0
Increases congestion in shopping centres	41.4	44.0		
Increases vandalism	43.1	50.9		
Increases noise pollution	12.7	30.4		63.6
General				
Long-term planning can control impacts of tourism on the environment	90.4	66.9	[85.4][c]	87.5
A lower standard of living is worth the cost of environmental protection	41.2	58.5		
More money should be spent on environmental protection than tourism promotion	61.7	62.3		54.7

[a]Hawaii, USA; North Wales; and Istanbul, Turkey – after Liu *et al.* (1987).
[b]Argentina – adapted from Schlüter and Var (1988).
[c]Square brackets indicates an answer to a similar statement.

earlier findings that they do not wish to see their standard of living drop in order to obtain increased environmental protection. Gascoyne residents do not share the view that tourism helps protect the environment (23% agree; previous studies 51%) and they strongly support the increased protection of the environment. However, the survey confirms the previous findings that destination communities perceive a number of negative environmental impacts caused by tourism. Littering is cited as the foremost problem but the residents take a lot of the blame for it themselves. When asked if tourists cause it the residents only rank it fifth out of nine adverse environmental impacts.

In terms of planning and management, the Gascoyne host community survey is in accord with the previous findings that long-term planning can control the impacts of tourism on the environment (81% agree). The support for this statement was the highest overall and is very similar to that of the previous four surveys (83%). The Gascoyne community also believes that tourism developments should be encouraged providing they do not conflict with the environment (78%). While the residents were not asked if tourism creates more parks for themselves, they did not give a high level of support to the suggestion to add more parks to the region (42%). It is argued that this is due to the large number of existing and proposed parks and reserves already in the region.

Conclusion

The future of sustainable tourism development in host communities lies in its planning and management in local economic, social and physical environments. Careful planning enables developers and managers of tourism to protect the natural environment and bring about a greater understanding of it. The key lies in the activity of planning *for* natural areas rather than solely planning *in* them. This is best carried out in an inclusive manner that embraces the interest of, and input by, key stakeholders, namely host community members themselves. In addition, sustainable development should be iterative and flexible to allow objectives and strategies to be achieved while still providing a means for consistent management.

There are several ways to manage tourism development in biophysical environments, some of which focus on site management, while others focus on visitor management techniques. One key strategy is zoning in which activities are separated by either space and/or time. Management includes the strategies and actions taken to protect or enhance natural areas in the face of impacts from tourism activities. Strategies are defined as general approaches to management, usually guided by an objective, for example, reserving and/or zoning a natural area as a national park. A strategy can also be a group of actions, for example, site management and its associated actions.

Planning and management need to reflect a balanced approach to how natural resources are used and include local communities in the development process. A more 'sustainable' approach to tourism development is required, and it is through destination community tourism that this may be achieved (Dowling, 1998). While it is imperative that the earth's environmental elements are not perceived solely as attributes, the reality is that if natural areas are to survive they must be 'valued' more through developments such as tourism. Often it is only tourism that will provide the basis for conservation of such areas. So while there is undoubted concern at the increasing demand for tourism to natural areas, this just maybe the one activity that ensures their continued survival. Therefore, the interplay of understandings that a host community can bring to bear on sustainable development within its biophysical environments is a fundamental prerequisite for responsible tourism growth.

References

Ashley, C. and Roe, D. (1998) *Enhancing Community Development in Wildlife Tourism: Issues and Challenges.* International Institute for Environment and Development, London.

Brandon, K. (1996) *Ecotourism and Conservation: a Review of Key Issues.* World Bank, Washington, DC.

Budowski, G. (1976) Tourism and environmental conservation: conflict, coexistence, or symbiosis? *Environmental Conservation* 3(1), 27–31.

Cater, E. (1993) Ecotourism in the third world: problems for sustainable tourism development. *Tourism Management* 85, 90–96.

Chubb, P. (1988) Earth and fire. *Time Australia* 28 November, 14–41.

Cooper, C. and Wanhill, S. (eds) (1997) *Tourism Development: Environmental and Community Issues.* John Wiley & Sons, Chichester.

Dasmann, R.F., Milton, J.P. and Freeman, P.H. (1973) *Ecological Principles for Economic Development.* John Wiley & Sons, Chichester.

de Kadt, E. (ed.) (1979) *Tourism: Passport to Development.* Oxford University Press, Oxford.

Dowling, R.K. (1990) *Tourism and the Environment in the Gascoyne Region, Western Australia: an Interim Report on Resident and Tourist Opinions.* Environmental Science, Murdoch University, Perth.

Dowling, R.K. (1991) *The Gascoyne Environment: a Regional Description of the Natural and Cultural Environment.* Environmental Science, Murdoch University, Perth.

Dowling, R.K. (1993) Tourist and resident perceptions of the environment–tourism relationship in the Gascoyne Region, Western Australia. *GeoJournal* 29(3), 243–251.

Dowling, R.K. (1996) Visitor management in Shark Bay, Western Australia. In: Hall, C.M. and McArthur, S. (eds) *Heritage Management in Australia and New Zealand: the Human Dimension*, 2nd edn. Oxford University Press, Melbourne, pp. 160–169.

Dowling, R.K. (1998) Harnessing the benefits of regional ecotourism development: lessons from Western Australia's nature-based tourism strategy. In: Weir, B., McArthur, S. and Crabtree, A. (eds) *Developing Ecotourism into the Millennium, Proceedings of the Ecotourism Association of Australia 6th National Conference*. Bureau of Tourism Research, Canberra, pp. 31–35.

Dowling, R.K. (1999) Developing tourism in the environmentally sensitive North West Cape Region, Western Australia. In: Singh, T.V. and Singh, S. (eds) *Tourism Development in Critical Environments*. Cognizant, New York, pp. 163–175.

Dowling, R.K. (2000) Visitors' views of an icon ecotourism site. In: *Proceedings of the Ecotourism Association of Australia 8th National Conference, Ecotourism – Changing the Nature of Australia, 2–5 November*. Lorne and Phillip Island, Victoria.

Dowling, R.K. and Alder, J. (1996) Shark Bay Western Australia: managing a coastal world heritage area. *Coastal Management in Tropical Asia: a Newsletter for Practitioners* 6, 17–21.

Doxey, G.V. (1975) A causation theory of visitor resident irritants: methodology and research inferences. In: *The Impact of Tourism, Proceedings of the Sixth Annual Conference of The Travel and Tourism Research Association*. The Travel and Tourism Research Association (TTRA), San Diego, pp. 195–198.

Drumm, A. (1998) New approaches to community-based ecotourism management. In: Lindberg, K., Epler Wood, M. and Engeldrum, D. (eds) *Ecotourism: a Guide for Planners and Managers*, Vol. 2. Ecotourism Society, North Bennington, Vermont, pp. 197–213.

Fennell, D.A. (1999) *Ecotourism: an Introduction*. Routledge, London.

Getz, D. (1986) Models in tourism planning: towards integration of theory and practice. *Tourism Management* 7, 21–32.

Gunn, C.A. (1987) Environmental designs and land use. In: Ritchie, J.R.B. and Goeldner, C.R. (eds) *Travel, Tourism and Hospitality Research: a Handbook for Managers and Researchers*. John Wiley & Sons, New York, pp. 229–247.

Hall, C.M. (1991) *Introduction to Tourism in Australia: Impacts, Planning and Development*. Longman Cheshire, Melbourne.

Holden, A. (2000) *Environment and Tourism*. Routledge, London.

Hvenegaard, G.T. (1994) Ecotourism: a status report and conceptual framework. *The Journal of Tourism Studies* 5(2), 24–35.

IUCN (1980) *World Conservation Strategy: Living Resource Conservation for Sustainable Development*. International Union for the Conservation of Nature and Natural Resources, United Nations Environment Programme/World Wildlife Fund, Gland, Switzerland.

Knopp, T.B. (1980) Tourism, the local interests and the function of public lands. In: Hawkins, D.E., Shafer, E.L. and Rovelstad, J.M. (eds) *Tourism Planning and Development Issues*. George Washington University, Washington, DC, pp. 225–237.

Lindberg, K. and McKercher, B. (1997) Ecotourism: a critical overview. *Pacific Tourism Review* 1, 65–79.

Liu, J.C. Sheldon, P.J. and Var, T. (1987) Resident perception of the environmental impacts of tourism. *Annals of Tourism Research* 14, 17–37.

Mathieson, A. and Wall, G. (1982) *Tourism: Economic, Physical and Social Impacts.* Longman, London.

Miller, G., Jr (1994) *Living in the Environment: Principles, Connections, and Solutions.* 8th edn. Wadsworth, Belmont, California.

Murphy, P.E. (1983) Tourism as a community industry: an ecological model of tourism development. *Tourism Management* 4, 180–193.

Murphy, P.E. (1985) *Tourism: a Community Approach.* Methuen, New York.

Newsome, D., Moore, S. and Dowling, R.K. (2001) *Natural Area Tourism: Ecology, Impacts and Management.* Channel View, Clevedon.

Page, S. and Dowling, R.K. (2002) *Ecotourism.* Pearson, Harlow.

Pearce, D.G. (1989) *Tourist Development.* 2nd edn. Longman, London.

Phillips, A. (1985) Opening address. In: *Tourism, Recreation and Conservation in National Parks and Equivalent Reserves,* Proceedings of a European Heritage Landscapes Conference. Peak Park Joint Planning Board, Derbyshire, UK.

Raffaele, P. (1989) Shark Bay. *Australian Geographic* 14, 54–77.

Richards, G. and Hall, D. (eds) (2000) *Tourism and Sustainable Community Development.* Routledge, London.

Romeril, M. (1989) Tourism and the environment: accord or discord? *Tourism Management* 10, 204–208.

Ross, S. and Wall, G. (1999) Ecotourism: towards congruence between theory and practice. *Tourism Management* 20, 123–132.

Scheyvens, R. (1999) Ecotourism and the empowerment of local communities. *Tourism Management* 20, 245–249.

Schlüter, R. and Var, T. (1988) Resident attitudes toward tourism in Argentina. *Annals of Tourism Research* 15, 442–445.

Smith, V.L. and Eadington, W.R. (eds) (1992) *Tourism Alternatives: Potentials and Problems in the Development of Tourism.* University of Pennsylvania Press, Philadelphia.

SPC and CALM (1988) *The Shark Bay Region Plan.* The State Planning Commission and the Department of Conservation and Land Management, Perth.

The Ecotourism Society (1998) *Ecotourism Statistical Fact Sheet.* Ecotourism Society, North Bennington, Vermont.

Travis, A.S. (1980) The need for policy action. In: OECD (ed.) *The Impact of Tourism on the Environment.* Organization for Economic Cooperation and Development, Paris, pp. 79–97.

United Nations Environment Programme (UNEP) (1986) Carrying capacity for tourism activities, special issue. *UNEP Industry and Environment Newsletter* 9(1), 1–2.

Wall, G. (1994) Ecotourism: old wine in new bottles? *Trends* 31(2), 4–9.

WATC/EPA (1989) *The Eco Ethics of Tourism Development.* Western Australian Tourism Commission and the Environmental Protection Authority, Perth.

World Commission on Environment and Development (WCED) (1987) *Our Common Future: Report of the World Commission on Environment and Development.* Oxford University Press, Oxford.

Wearing, S. and Neil, J. (1999) *Ecotourism.* Butterworth Heinemann, Oxford.

Weaver, D. and Oppermann, M. (2000) *Tourism Management.* John Wiley & Sons, Brisbane.

WTO (1998) Ecotourism: now one-fifth of market. *World Tourism Organization News,* January–February, 6.

WTO (2000) *Sustainable Development of Tourism: a Compilation of Good Practices.* World Tourism Organization, Madrid.

Local Involvement in Managing Tourism   12

REGINA SCHEYVENS

Geography Programme, Massey University, Palmerston North, New Zealand

Introduction

This chapter centres around a very important question: who should manage tourism in destination communities? In the past, tourism development has been dominated by private sector interests, a prescription that does not always bode well for local communities. It is argued that it is not sufficient to state that host communities should gain material benefits from tourism development in their area but, rather, that they have a right to have some control over the tourism process. This is a somewhat radical idea if one considers the predominant roles of host communities in tourist areas to date as, for example, service providers, sellers, craftspeople and even ethnic 'attractions' in their own right. Rarely have they had considerable control over the rate or the manner in which tourism progresses within their communities. It is thus essential to consider the multiple ways in which host communities need to be empowered if they are to have a genuine and influential role in managing tourism in their areas in the future (see Johnston, Chapter 7 this volume; Timothy and Tosun, Chapter 10 this volume). Questions also need to be raised about appropriate forms of tourism development in host communities, including issues of scale and the nature of tourism development.

This chapter simultaneously recognizes that other stakeholders must play their part to facilitate the involvement of host communities in tourism management. Governments can set in place an enabling policy environment for small-scale tourism enterprises controlled at the local level, provide support for local community members to establish viable business enterprises, and establish a regulatory environment to ensure that private sector interests do not impinge on social well-being or the integrity of the natural environment. The private sector can encourage involvement of local community members in tourism associations and on tourism boards, and it can engage in partnership relationships whereby community members work alongside and thus learn from the skills and experience of the business community. Non-governmental organizations (NGOs), meanwhile, can engage in capacity building work and facilitate the empowerment of host community members so that they have the knowledge and confidence to assert their opinions about appropriate tourism development. After examining these issues the chapter concludes by looking at the need to move beyond the 'passive' involvement of local communities in tourism development.

Putting Community Tourism Management into Practice

Limited management roles for host communities in the past

Throughout the world host communities play an integral role in the tourism industry. What they typically lack, however, is the power to influence the nature and direction of tourism development. As Campbell (1999: 536) notes, '. . . the level of choice exercised by host communities in becoming a destination is questionable with tourism in general, and particularly in developing countries'. Thus in worst case scenarios, host communities are actively disadvantaged by tourism occurring in their own backyards, which is why the term 'host' can be hotly contested (see Singh *et al.*, Chapter 1 this volume). For example, in many contexts indigenous peoples have been displaced from land so that national parks or wildlife areas can be created (Adams, 1990). In such cases the rewards of subsequent tourism development are typically pocketed by outside tourism operators and the government, while local people must deal with diminished livelihood options (Bell, 1987). This situation has been played out in the Chiawa communal lands of Zambia, which border the Zambezi River. Here, the chief granted up to 20 tourism operators the rights to lease land along the river banks and bordering the Lower Zambezi National Park in the hope that this would bring much wanted investment and jobs to the region. The government, not the community, collects lease money from these operators. Most of the guests are higher spending tourists who engage in fishing expeditions, canoe safaris, game drives and other nature-tourism activities. In practice, while some young men have received work at the lodges which have been established, there have been few other flow-on benefits of tourism for the local community. Meanwhile, their access to certain prime sites along the river bank has been impeded, fishing activities

have been interrupted by speed boats, and crop damage by wild animals – the major draw card for tourists – continues to impinge severely on the well-being of these largely impoverished people.

While better scenarios see host communities benefiting economically from servicing tourists, it is still rare to find examples of communities exerting real control over the tourism process. Indeed, there seems to be an assumption that host communities do not need to have any control over tourism development. Even the World Tourism Organization's *Global Code of Ethics for Tourism*, released in 2000, only discusses the right of communities to benefit from, not to manage, tourism, and for private developers to inform communities of their plans, not to consult with them before drawing up any plans (see Table 12.1). In such an environment, it is unlikely that the priorities and interests of host communities will be central concerns in tourism planning and management.

As mentioned above, the private sector typically dominates in terms of controlling the process of tourism development. This is particularly of concern in the context of Third World destinations and small countries in general whose development is strongly influenced by overseas investors (Britton, 1982; Brohman, 1996). There is a global economic concentration

Table 12.1. How host communities feature in the global code of ethics for tourism. Source: World Tourism Organization, http://www.world-tourism.org/

Article 5: Tourism, a beneficial activity for host countries and communities

(i) Local populations should be associated with tourism activities and share equitably in the economic, social and cultural benefits they generate, and particularly in the creation of direct and indirect jobs resulting from them.

(ii) Tourism policies should be applied in such a way as to help to raise the standard of living of the populations of the regions visited and meet their needs; the planning and architectural approach to and operation of tourism resorts and accommodation should aim to integrate them, to the extent possible, in the local economic and social fabric; where skills are equal, priority should be given to local manpower.

(iii) Special attention should be paid to the specific problems of coastal areas and island territories and to vulnerable rural or mountain regions, for which tourism often represents a rare opportunity for development in the face of the decline of traditional economic activities.

(iv) Tourism professionals, particularly investors, governed by the regulations laid down by the public authorities, should carry out studies of the impact of their development projects on the environment and natural surroundings; they should also deliver, with the greatest transparency and objectivity, information on their future programmes and their foreseeable repercussions and foster dialogue on their contents with the populations concerned.

of wealth in tourism, witnessed by the domination of the package tour sector by a small number of key players with advanced forward and backward linkages, which enable them to control aspects of the industry. For example, company mergers taking place in the UK are likely to result in just four tour companies controlling up to 90% of outbound charter capacity. These companies do not just own tour operators in Britain and abroad, they also own hotels, self-catering accommodation, airlines, cruise ships and retail chains (O'Connor, 2000). As noted by the managing director of Sunvil Holidays, Neil Josephides, such dominance is not necessarily in the interests of 'host' countries such as his home, Cyprus. 'Thomson combined with Preussag will control 20 to 30 per cent of tourism to Cyprus. Tourism represents over 20 per cent of the country's Gross Domestic Product, so the operators don't just control the hoteliers, they control the country. It's very depressing' (cited in O'Connor, 2000: 5).

While the state can play an important role in regulating the activities of private developers and thus can protect the interests of host communities, the neo-liberal agenda dominating economic systems in many parts of the world has promoted the opening up of national economies to foreign investment and a minimalist role for the state (Brohman, 1995). Some governments have been under direct pressure from the International Monetary Fund to adopt policies that will earn them money to pay back mounting debts, and in this context they tend to assume that more money will be earned by attracting mass tourists and those who can afford luxury goods and services. This is despite the fact that such forms of tourism often lead to a country's dependence on foreign products, foreign investment and foreign skills, resulting in repatriation of resultant profits (Baskin, 1995; Britton and Clark, 1987). In addition to communities having little control over luxury or mass tourism, few of the economic benefits 'trickle down' to be of significance to local residents.[1] The case of governments prioritizing large-scale tourism development is clearly played out in Indonesia, where luxury tourism has been promoted as a strategy for modernization. Also while the national policy supports resort development and hotels with star ratings, providing every encouragement to foreign investors, small-scale tourism initiatives are officially meant to be supported by the ill-equipped and less powerful local and provincial governments (Dahles and Bras, 1999).

If Third World governments wish to facilitate equitable involvement of local communities in the tourism industry, they may have to consider more carefully small-scale tourism initiatives, which can offer numerous benefits

---

[1] There are exceptions, however, whereby communities do gain significant economic benefits from luxury tourism. Thus in Fiji, some local clans have favourable lease agreements with hotel and resort developers who have built on their land.

to host communities. Presently, for example, a number of countries actively discourage 'undesirable' elements, including backpackers, despite the fact that local communities may gain much from servicing this end of the market (Wilson, 1997; Hampton, 1998). Thus, Botswana places itself in an ambiguous situation when they have a policy that, while denigrating budget tourists, aims simultaneously to 'provide local communities with direct and indirect benefits from tourism activities' (Little, 1991: 6). In most cases it is not realistic for impoverished rural communities to cater to higher end tourists, as they do not usually have the necessary range of skills, experience or resources.

Why communities need to be empowered to have a management role

Clearly most destination communities currently do not dictate the terms or conditions on which tourism takes place in their home areas, yet it is they who must live with the direct consequences of tourism. Such consequences often include negative social and environmental impacts, even in situations where communities are benefiting economically from tourism.

To ensure a strong likelihood of economic, political and social benefits of tourism accruing to host communities, Ashley and Roe (1998: 25) stress the need for *full* participation. Full participation can be said to occur where communities supply the majority of goods and services to tourists, have considerable input into planning decisions, and they collectively manage common resources. This latter point is particularly relevant in situations whereby tourism is based on natural and cultural features, such as a marine reserve or forest park, which face multiple use demands. When tourism ventures are largely dependent on local cultural and natural resources, and are locally managed, this allows communities to 'participate with equity in the [tourism] process' (Lillywhite and Lillywhite, 1991: 89g).

Empowerment should be a precursor to community involvement in tourism, as it is a means to determining and achieving socioeconomic objectives. As Akama (1996: 573) argues in the Kenyan context, 'the local community need to be empowered to decide what forms of tourism facilities and wildlife conservation programmes they want to be developed in their respective communities, and how the tourism costs and benefits are to be shared among different stakeholders'.

Thus, access to information pertaining to the pros and cons of tourism and how it may impact upon their lives is important for host communities, particularly for those in less developed countries where information flows are often poor. Some of the questions local communities may want to consider include:

• What forms of tourism are desirable in our community?

- How can we ensure that a majority of benefits from tourism accrue locally?
- What measures need to be in place to ensure tourism takes place in a controlled manner?
- How can we ensure that tourism does not undermine our culture, our society, or existing livelihood activities in this community?

Empowerment is not an easily defined concept, yet it is a term that has been enthusiastically adopted by agencies with diverse social and political aims because it is both attractive and seen as politically correct. The following framework, which specifies four dimensions of empowerment (economic, social, psychological and political), helps explain what empowerment can mean for host communities involved in tourism as well as how disempowerment may manifest itself (Scheyvens, 1999). It demonstrates multiple ways in which communities need to be empowered if they are to have at least some management control over tourism and secure maximum benefits from engaging in tourism initiatives.

Economic empowerment

Economic gains from involvement in both formal and informal sector activities can lead to empowerment for host communities, but what is more important than the total amount of these economic benefits is the spread of the benefits. Recent studies suggest that local elites, particularly men, often co-opt and come to dominate community-based development efforts, thereby monopolizing the economic benefits of tourism (Mansperger, 1995; Sindiga, 1995; Wilkinson and Pratiwi, 1995; Akama, 1996). Economic empowerment also requires that diversification be maintained in terms of the livelihood options of many communities where tourism is periodic and cannot provide regular, reliable incomes.

For a community to be economically empowered it will need secure access to productive resources in a tourism area. This is particularly important in the case of common property resources and in situations whereby protected areas have been established. Conversely, where natural resources, such as rainforests, reefs or wild animals have become a tourist attraction, but in so doing indigenous peoples' rights to harvest resources from the area have been undermined and they have failed to gain significant economic benefits from tourism, it can be argued that economic disempowerment has occurred. For example, in Kenya, 20 out of 25 national parks could otherwise be used for agricultural or pastoral activities (Sindiga, 1995). Cater (1993: 88) argues that if they undermine local livelihoods, national parks '. . . cannot be regarded as truly sustainable practices because they pay little regard to the needs of the host population in either the short or long term'.

Social empowerment

Social empowerment refers to a situation wherein a community's sense of cohesion and integrity has been confirmed or strengthened through its involvement in tourism. Social empowerment is perhaps most clearly a result of tourism when profits are used to fund social development projects identified by the community, such as water supply systems or health clinics, in the local area. On the other hand, social disempowerment may occur if tourism results in crime, begging, perceptions of crowding, displacement from traditional lands, loss of authenticity or prostitution. Inequities in the distribution of tourism's benefits, described under 'economic empowerment' above, can also lead to social disempowerment through feelings of ill-will and jealousy they may foster. For example, one village chief in Yap, Federated States of Micronesia, kept all of the entrance fees to his village for himself. This led some community members to feel that 'money is making people stingy and therefore harming community spirit' (Mansperger, 1995: 90).

Psychological empowerment

Psychological empowerment ideally should mean that a community's confidence in its ability to participate equitably and effectively in tourism planning, development and management is maximized. This may involve capacity-building and reinforcement of the self-worth of community members so that they can play an active role in decision-making or power-sharing processes with external stakeholders (Mander and Steytler, 1997: 5). Yet this psychological dimension of empowerment has rarely been given credence in the literature on community involvement in tourism.

A host community that is optimistic about the future, has faith in the abilities of its residents, is relatively self-reliant, and demonstrates pride in traditions and culture can be said to be psychologically powerful. Tourism that is sensitive to cultural norms and builds respect for local traditions can, therefore, be empowering for local people. In many small-scale, less industrialized societies, preservation of aspects of tradition is extremely important in terms of maintaining a group's sense of self-esteem and well-being. On the other hand, tourism that undermines customs by, for example, interfering with the integral relationship between a group of people and its land, may have devastating effects (Mansperger, 1995). According to Norberg-Hodge's (1991: 81) work with Ladakhi people in the Himalayan region, the 'psychological pressure to modernize', which comes from exposure to tourists and other aspects of Western society, can undermine the self-esteem of indigenous peoples. Feelings of apathy, depression, disillusionment or confusion in the face of tourism development could suggest that psychological disempowerment has occurred.

Political empowerment

It is at this level of empowerment that the issue of community management of tourism most clearly comes to the fore. If community members are to be politically empowered by involvement in tourism, their voices and concerns should guide the development of any tourism initiative from the feasibility stage through to its implementation. Because of the existence of diverse interest groups within a community, framed by factors such as class, gender, caste, age and ethnicity, it is important that democratic structures that encourage involvement of a range of interest groups are in place. The meaning of 'democracy' may, however, waver from conventional Western interpretations (Timothy, 1999). In any case it is certainly helpful if a particular society has a strong tradition of community organization that accommodates the interests of diverse groups.

A village development committee or a local tourism board can provide suitable representation and help protect local interests. In Bali, for example, Wall and Long (1996) explain how a strong tourism organization was initiated in one neighbourhood where home-stays were common. Its aims were to promote tourism in the area, to protect the local environment and to address any issues that concerned the community, including the in-migration of outside entrepreneurs. Forming organizations, or working through traditional organizational structures, can certainly help communities gain greater control over tourism development in their areas and give them political strength to deal with outsiders, including the private sector and government officials (Ashley and Garland, 1994).

To exert some control over tourism development, community representatives may also need to participate in broader bodies such as regional tourism associations or park boards. In other cases, they may wish to form associations with a mandate to lobby actively against forms of tourism they feel are contrary to local interests, such as all-inclusive resorts, or to stand up against foreign control of tourism. In Goa, India, for example, Jagrut Goenkaranchi Fauz (JGF), has a campaign named 'Our homes – their holidays', which focuses on the need for strong local input into tourism planning to ensure that tourism does not undermine residents' access to essential services and infrastructure, including water and electricity. A further campaign targets labour practices of the luxury hotels, attempting to ensure that workers gain the security of permanent jobs and wages rather than being exploited by being employed under trainee status and earning only tips (Herald News Desk, 1999).

Appropriate Forms of Tourism: Issues of Scale and the Nature of Tourism Development

Another issue critical to understanding the management of host community tourism is scale. Small-scale initiatives have gained much support in discussions of community involvement in tourism because they are more likely to be owned and managed locally and thus provide greater local benefits than tourism enterprises controlled by outsiders (Britton and Clark, 1987; Oppermann, 1993; Dahles and Bras, 1999). For example, tourists in Samoa are often serviced by basic accommodation facilities and food provided by local families, thus local ownership and participation characterize Samoan tourism. According to Twining-Ward and Twining-Ward, 1998: 270), this leads to a '. . . more socially equitable and ecologically sustainable tourism industry' than that found in neighbouring Fiji where much of the industry is foreign-owned.

Essentially, when local people can meet many of the needs of tourists themselves, they are more likely to retain some control over tourism. Controlling one's own enterprise is a positive step in the direction of self-determination for people otherwise dependent on the tourism industry for menial jobs or handouts, and is more likely to lead to self-fulfilment. There is a notable difference, for example, for an individual '. . . between being a cleaner in a large international hotel compared with being the owner of a small *losmen* [homestay], cooking and serving at tables in their own place' (Hampton, 1998: 650). Thus Wilson (1997: 69) is concerned that a growing emphasis on luxury tourism development in Goa, India, which has traditionally been characterized by small family businesses catering for the domestic and backpacker markets, may undermine local development:

> . . . this focus on up-market tourism is out of keeping with the present structure of the tourism industry in Goa, which is mainly low-budget and served by a multitude of small hotels, guest-houses, rented rooms, and a host of ancillary services. . . . The danger here is that control over up-market tourism could pass out of indigenous hands into foreign ownership and that these multinationals might be . . . less sensitive to . . . social, cultural, and environmental issues.
>
> (Wilson, 1997)

Thus, protests by the well-developed anti-tourism lobby in Goa have aimed at mass rather than independent tourists, even though it is the latter group which have given the area its 'hippy haven' reputation. A well-publicized case of Goan people throwing rotten fish and cow dung at tourist buses, for example, was instigated by small-scale local entrepreneurs, who felt that charter-package tourism was putting them out of business by providing for all of the needs of tourists (accommodation, transport and food) in a single outlet (Wilson, 1997).

If tourism moves 'up scale' in an area, local people can lose important economic advantages as well as control over tourism enterprises. This is certainly a concern in Pangandaran, a fishing village in Java, which has developed into a beach resort. As noted by Wilkinson and Pratiwi (1995: 295), Pangandaran may not retain the feeling of being a village for long, particularly as tourism development here has been identified as a major priority by the government. Major land ownership changes have started to occur with both a proposal for a golf course and the development of a five-star hotel on what was previously communal village land.

Such dramatic changes will have the greatest effect on lower-class people – the poor. Many of them live on and cultivate household crops on *tanah negara* (the nation's land) which appears slated for tourism development. They face the possibility of being displaced from their homes and losing employment in their informal sector jobs *as the tourism product moves up-scale* and creates demands for higher standards of facilities and services (Wilkinson and Pratiwi, 1995: 295, emphasis added).

As shown in Table 12.2, however, while community enterprises certainly offer opportunities for residents to manage tourism on their own terms, other configurations, such as joint ventures with private-sector partners, also enable host communities to play a management role.

Whether destination communities always see small-scale or alternative forms of tourism as preferable to mass or luxury tourism should also be questioned. Thomlinson and Getz (1996) argue that while small-scale tourism is perceived to fit in well with the philosophy of alternative tourism, such as ecotourism, in practice mass tourism may be the preferred option if it brings in more money to local communities. It may also be true that some communities prefer mass tourism that involves, for example, one bus load of tourists per day coming to them at a set time for a cultural performance and to buy crafts and then returning to their hotels, rather than tourism where outsiders come to stay in their village, as the latter is more culturally invasive. Other communities may be concerned that small-scale enterprises simply cannot compete with larger tourism ventures. Thomlinson and Getz (1996) note such a case from Central America whereby a small operator felt its operation was being pushed out by larger operators. They concluded that while 'small is beautiful in the context of ecotourism . . . small is also vulnerable' (Thomlinson and Getz, 1996: 197).

Thus it is likely that while some host communities will wish to pursue small-scale, alternative forms of tourism, others will prefer mass or resort tourism. It is in the latter cases, however, that concerns are more likely to arise about the lack of community control over tourism. Two case studies from southern Africa serve to illustrate this point, while also explaining the complexity of choices facing local communities when they get involved in tourism. In the case of Phinda, local communities were lured by the status of being involved in a luxury lodge tourism project as well as the

Table 12.2. Opportunities for host communities to be involved in the management of tourism. Source: adapted from Ashley and Roe (1998: 8).

Type of enterprise or institution	Opportunities for management roles by locals	Examples
Private business run by outsider(s) or local entrepreneur	• written agreement over nature and extent of the enterprise • agreement over benefits for the wider community	• tours of natural features in the area to take place only at set times and to be postponed during community rituals • no more than two bus loads of tourists to visit an attraction within the community in a day • jobs for local people or donations to a community fund based on the number of visitors
Community enterprise	• collectively owned and managed • collectively owned but individually managed	• community campsite run by a management committee • craft centre owned by the community but managed by an individual with business training
Joint venture between community and private operator	• revenue sharing agreement • participation in decision-making	• community has equity in lodge and representatives sit on board of directors • community leases land for tourism development and set conditions upon which development may proceed
Tourism planning body or conservation authority	• consultation • representation • participation	• local consultation in regional tourism planning • community representatives on tourism board or parks board

employment options this would bring, even though it meant the private sector would fully manage and control the venture. In the case of the Sunungukai ecotourism camp, however, while the community members manage the campsite on their own, and this is a great source of pride to them, their economic achievements have been poor to date.

Conservation Corporation Africa at Phinda Reserve, South Africa

Conservation Corporation Africa (CCA), established in 1990, has become the largest private company in South Africa involved in wildlife tourism. Their 17,000 hectare Phinda wildlife reserve in southern Maputaland houses four luxury lodge complexes, and tourists have the choice of a range of activities including game viewing, canoeing, fishing and bird watching. According to CCA's promotional material, 'Phinda is acclaimed as South Africa's most responsible wildlife tourism project, with its goals of wilderness restoration and community participation' (Conservation Corporation Africa, 1997: 17).

Phinda is not a joint venture with local communities in which they have a direct say in the management of tourism or a share of profits from the reserve. However, CCA does aim to bring direct benefits to locals for the very pragmatic reason that with almost 30,000 economically disadvantaged people living around the reserve, community participation is vital to ensure support for Phinda's conservation efforts (Carlisle, 1997). There are several ways in which CCA benefits the communities surrounding Phinda. First, CCA has improved the livelihood options of many local people. Phinda employed 350 people in 1998, most of them locals. All employees who have worked at Phinda for over 6 months are involved in training programmes, some of which cover basic skills such as literacy and numeracy. CCA has also supported local entrepreneurs, helping one to establish a brick-making business which originally sold bricks for the first lodge at Phinda, and allowing another to set up a charcoal making business in the reserve using wood that needed to be cleared. Phinda's management also allows sustainable rates of harvesting of certain plants from the reserve, including medicinal plants, wood and thatch (Cherry, 1993). Secondly, CCA has involved community representatives in discussions on certain issues, such as where to locate boundary fences and how to deal with the perceived threat of lions to local cattle. Finally, CCA has established a development fund, the Rural Investment Fund (RIF), thus showing how 'a private company can act as a catalyst in mobilising funding for community projects' (Wells, 1996: 44). The RIF has three aims:

1. To ensure that ecotourism is endorsed by local communities;
2. To promote rural economic development; and
3. To advance conservation frontiers (Conservation Corporation Africa, 1997: 23).

Through the fund, private and bilateral donors can contribute to community development projects in communities near to CCA developments (Wells, 1996: 44). To date this money has been used to build 20 school rooms and a clinic, to purchase a computer and generator for one school, and to provide training for members of development committees and community leaders. Much of the funding has come from CCA guests, who are taken on tours of local communities at their own request. CCA's contribution to the RIF is its management and administration of the fund.

While surrounding communities have undoubtedly been economic beneficiaries of the Phinda development, they do not share in the control or management of what goes on within the reserve. Community representatives are consulted only when Phinda management sees fit to do so and only on certain issues. Even in the case of resource harvesting, for example, Phinda employees determine what offtake levels are sustainable, not necessarily in consultation with the communities concerned, and when harvesting may take place.

Sunungukai ecotourism camp, Zimbabwe

The Sunungukai ecotourism camp, established in 1993, is a venture initiated under Zimbabwe's renowned CAMPFIRE (Communal Areas Management Programme For Indigenous Resources) scheme (Chalker, 1994). CAMPFIRE is a unique initiative that involves the Department of National Parks and Wildlife Management, NGOs and indigenous communities living on communal lands. It explicitly sets out to empower local communities by allowing them to manage natural resources in their area and to determine how they can benefit economically from these resources. Rather than the more common CAMPFIRE initiatives, which involve leases to safari companies to carry out restricted hunting on communal lands, Sunungukai represents a new breed of non-consumptive ecotourism initiatives entirely managed by local communities.

A picturesque site on the banks of the Mazoe River is home to the Sunungukai camp, which consists of four community-built chalets and a campsite. Visitors can either have their meals provided or they can prepare food themselves. The camp adjoins the Mupfurudzi Safari Area so there is the possibility of taking guided walks into the park to see cave paintings or to view animals. Other activities include fishing, bird watching, swimming, walks to view hippos and crocodiles along the river and cultural tours of the adjoining village. Most visitors come to Sunungukai for the opportunity to relax and experience rural life in Zimbabwe.

While initial revenue for the construction materials was provided through CAMPFIRE and the New Zealand High Commission, residents of the five villages surrounding the site were also given the opportunity to have a financial share in the project by paying Z$10 each and providing free labour for construction and maintenance, thus becoming 'members'. In 1998 there were 65 members, most of whom lived in one of the three villages closest to the camp. All members are eligible to vote for a management committee for the camp, which meets every month to check progress on camp activities and plan new activities. They also discuss how they think any revenue from the venture should be spent and then present their ideas to general meetings of members for further discussion.

Community cohesion was enhanced when the camp was first developed because all members worked together in contributing their labour to construct the chalets and to ensure the venture's eventual opening. Members are very proud of the campsite and chalets they have built and even non-members say they feel honoured that people have come out of their way to visit them and learn about their way of life. Their enthusiasm has been expressed in the warmth with which they greet visitors: 'this is the reflection of a healthy community and it attracts or at least impresses tourists' (R. Friesen, unpublished data, 1997). However, a lack of financial success at Sunungukai has led to disinterest among many members. It took 4 years, until 1997, for Sunungukai to realize sufficient profit to be able to distribute a modest dividend of Z$120 to each of its members. Small amounts of money have also been generated for community projects and further development of the camp. Those who have gained most financially from this development have been the three direct employees of the camp, and a few casual guides. The camp's poor economic performance has also led to general members being suspicious about the activities of their elected management committee.

Poor occupancy (see Table 12.3) is the main reason for low returns from the camp. This has led to serious doubts being raised about the economic viability of non-lease tourism ventures, such as the Sunungukai development (Murphree and Nyika, 1997). Despite management committee members receiving training in areas such as marketing and strategic planning, only *ad hoc* efforts have been made in these areas in the past. While committee members have ideas for future improvements, including provision of more activities for tourists and development of camp facilities, they often do not know how to work effectively to achieve their aims. Weak planning is of concern because an effective planning process is 'essential for ensuring community proprietorship' (Murphree and Nyika, 1997: 5). Similarly, although positive commentaries in the *Rough Guide* and *Lonely Planet* guide books and an award in the British Airways Tourism for Tomorrow competition have been good for publicity, the only marketing strategy

Table 12.3. Occupancy rates at Sunungukai Camp, June 1997–May 1998. Source: Sunungukai Visitors' Book.

Date	Visitor numbers	Occupancy %
1997		
June	13	2.7
July	19	4.0
August	13	2.7
September	22	4.6
October	10	2.1
November	13	2.7
December	8	1.7
1998		
January	21	4.4
February	6	1.3
March	21	4.4
April	6	1.3
May	10	2.1

being pursued in 1998 was the production of brochures. Yet when the author visited the CAMPFIRE head office in Harare during this time it had run out of brochures completely.

Undoubtedly, effective management of the camp is hindered by a number of logistical matters. While Sunungukai is located only 2 hours by car from the capital, Harare, the journey by public bus, which is used by many independent travellers, is considerably longer, and the last 4 km are a rough dirt road. There are no telephones or two-way radios in the immediate area and thus it is difficult to book a chalet or campsite in advance. Finding Sunungukai can also be problematic because the Ministry of Transport knocked down signs for the camp which did not comply with its specifications.

Such logistical difficulties combined with the host community's lack of business, marketing and service industry skills has led some commentators to suggest that lease or joint venture projects, whereby the expertise of experienced operators can be drawn upon, are more likely to secure long-term economic benefits for the community. For example, Morrison and Robinson (1995) raise the possibility of tendering the camp so that it would be run by an outside tourist operator with appropriate expertise, which would possibly lead to an increase in visitor numbers and thus improve the financial return to the community. They note, however, that this is not desirable if the community wishes to retain control over the enterprise. 'Community management and control, if financially viable, offers not only pecuniary benefits but also gives the community skills and confidence useful for future development' (Morrison and Robinson, 1995: 6). Thus, leasing the camp to an outside operator would effectively undermine the main benefits that members have gained from Sunungukai so far – retaining control of the project and gaining pride from its (albeit humble) successes.

A comparison of Phinda reserve and Sunungukai camp shows that achieving an ideal of economic viability and sustainability, as well as control over a tourism venture, may be difficult for many communities. Communities that attempt to manage their own enterprise may find that short-term economic returns are poor, and that they require a wide range of business and marketing skills just to manage daily operations. Isolation and a lack of communications technology often provide additional constraints. On the other hand, such ventures offer greater opportunities for community empowerment than those in which land is simply leased to an outside operator, or a joint venture in which the community has equity, and therefore shares in profits, but essentially has little power overall. It is important, therefore, not to reject the potential of these initiatives largely on the basis of economic performance without adequately considering how the reasons behind the lack of financial success could be addressed.

The pros and cons must be carefully weighed therefore before decisions as to what forms of tourism to pursue are made by the communities.

Whatever a community decides, it is likely that the benefits it gains will be considerably enhanced if it has support from other stakeholders involved in tourism development.

Other Stakeholder Support

Wherever possible, community members need information about the potential changes tourism can bring, both good and bad, before deciding whether to support tourism development in their area (Scheyvens, 2002). Government officers and NGOs can assist with such information gathering by organizing study tours for community members to visit existing community tourism enterprises. Seeing for themselves the visual impacts of tourism and discussing with service providers the potentials and pitfalls of their ventures can be a very illuminating exercise for people who may only have considered the economic benefits tourism can bring them.

If a community decides to proceed with a tourism venture, institutional support may be needed if proposed business ventures are to be successful (Baskin, 1995: 111). This institutional support from governments, NGOs and/or the private sector, can involve provision of information, networking opportunities and capacity building through skills training. Capacity building must be of high quality and of an ongoing nature, however. Those who are trained need the confidence to put their new skills into practice, the faith of members of the wider community who may be suspicious of new management styles and business practices, and ongoing support from professionals. Sending a few community members on various one-week training courses and expecting them to return home and become skilled marketers or business managers virtually overnight, is simply unrealistic. It may also be appropriate to engage qualified professionals, such as lawyers and small business experts, to provide advice when appropriate. For example, legal experts were hired to help the Makuleke people in South Africa win a land claim involving part of the renowned Kruger National Park (Tapela and Omara-Ojungu, 1999). They also scrutinize any contracts put forward by private sector interests wishing to collaborate with the community. Appropriate information and assistance can help to overcome the disadvantage that most host communities face when engaging with the tourism sector. The crux of the problem is that 'the local destination remains relatively isolated from the international market, receiving tourists but not understanding or playing any part in controlling the terms on which, and the processes by which, they arrive' (Goodwin *et al.*, 1997: 5).

The relatively independent position of the NGO sector places it in an important position to support the interests of communities involved in tourism. In addition to providing information and access to resources not available locally, NGOs can act in advocacy roles. They can also work with community organizations to establish ongoing monitoring of the positive and negative impacts of tourism, to determine whether or not tourism as it is being pursued is offering an appropriate form of development for the community (Joppe, 1996: 479). Independent researchers can also assist here by giving community members the opportunity to be involved in relevant research that takes place. During the author's fieldwork in 1998, an interesting example was observed where the Makuleke community insisted that outside researchers employ young people from the area as assistants to help develop their research skills.

Governments can play an important role in directing the nature of tourism within their country, as discussed above. They can either take a 'hands-off' approach and just let tourism develop according to international demand and the marketing strategies of travel agencies and tour operators, as was the case with Cyprus, or they can try to attract particular types of tourists whom they feel will bring the most benefits, and least harm, to their country. Thus, examples were provided earlier of governments that had tried to control the nature or volume of tourism by focusing exclusively on higher-end tourists. If they wish to support local development, however, and ensure that communities have a role in managing tourism rather than simply providing labour in tourism enterprises owned and controlled by outsiders, governments ought to encourage other forms of tourism. Policies of the past, such as discouraging backpackers or failing to promote local tourism enterprises, simply undermine development options for host communities. In Papua New Guinea the tourist office operating in the early 1980s offered no support to guest house owner-operators, choosing instead to refer visitors to large-scale, Western-style hotels (Ranck, 1987: 165). Strategies governments could use to support small-scale ventures, include making available start-up capital and business advice, and promoting a wide range of tourism options rather than just those appealing to mass or luxury tourists.

In addition, supportive legislation is necessary to enable communities to establish viable enterprises. For example, restrictive building codes may mean that it would be too expensive to establish accommodation facilities up to government standards even when in reality, a basic traditional house with the addition of bathroom facilities would suffice. Indeed, this may carry added appeal for some tourists. In the Solomon Islands, where building codes are based on Western standards, local artisans cannot meet the requirements of the building code if they use traditional construction methods and materials, available locally at little cost. If building regulations were adhered to, a small-scale tourism venture would cost around US$100,000 (Sofield, 1993: 737). Similarly, in some countries official tourist guides need to pass extensive written tests to gain a government endorsement, thus disqualifying illiterate or semi-literate guides who may be excellent at their trade.

Finally, governments have a responsibility to regulate tourism development to ensure that the private sector developers do not impinge on the well-being of local communities and environments (see Fennell and Przeclawski, Chapter 8 this volume). Tourism will only proceed in a sustainable manner if it is controlled by the public sector at the local level. 'Local authorities, through the production of integrated plans and development control powers, are best placed to assess the characteristics of the local environment and the priorities, needs and attitudes of local people to tourism' (Hunter 1995: 92).

The following two cases demonstrate the need for support from other stakeholders if communities are to maximize the benefits they can gain from involvement in tourism. The first one looks at ecotourism in Ostional, Costa Rica, to show how careful government planning and more information for local people is needed to create an environment of active community participation and control over tourism. The second case of Noah's cultural tours in Zimbabwe illustrates how government (at the local level in this case), NGO, and private sector interests combined to assist an individual in establishing and managing an effective cultural tourism enterprise in his home community.

Ecotourism in Ostional, Costa Rica

Ostional beach lies within Ostional Wildlife Refuge, which is a nesting ground for olive ridley sea turtles. Relatively low, but steadily increasing, numbers of tourists interested in wildlife protection visit this site, which therefore seems an ideal location for an alternative tourism initiative with strong community involvement. However, although the local population of just under 400 people whose village is located within the reserve has a high level of community organization, they have played a small role in tourism development, and therefore have reaped few of the benefits of tourism in the area.

Campbell (1999) asserts that this lack of community participation and management in tourism is a result of two factors. First, the community has received no support from the government. Instead the government's only interest in tourism in the area has been to collect taxes from accommodation providers and extract entrance fees from visitors entering the turtle refuge area. While the University of Costa Rica has a research laboratory within the refuge, its only concern has been minimizing the impacts of tourism on the nesting patterns of the turtles. Secondly, the community lacks information and experience relating to tourism development. Thus, even though many local residents feel that tourism is positive for local development, they have difficulty identifying the economic opportunities tourism could provide them. In fact, 82% of respondents identified two or fewer opportunities. Furthermore, they did not have a realistic idea of constraints to their participation in tourism initiatives, as only 11% felt that monetary issues might stand in their way and 5% recognized that there were legal impediments, such as restrictions on land use within the reserve (Campbell, 1999).

Thus while theoretically ecotourism in Ostional offers great potential for community involvement through provision of food, accommodation, and guiding services, it is likely that tourism initiatives will be dominated by individual entrepreneurs, both Costa Ricans and foreigners, in the future, with very little community control.

Noah's cultural tours, Zimbabwe

Chimanimani is a mountainous and extremely scenic area in the eastern Highlands of Zimbabwe, which attracts many foreign and domestic tourists. Noah Majuta is a 24-year-old man who decided to establish a tour guiding service when he realized there was little chance of gaining other employment in the Chimanimani area. He was from a poor family and now had a wife and child to support in his newly adopted village, 'Old Location'.

While Noah initiated his own guided hiking venture in 1996, it was only with outside assistance that he developed the most successful aspect of his business to date: cultural tours. It is generally assumed that visitors to Africa are there to see the wildlife and scenery, but when a British volunteer working for the Chimanimani District Council conducted a survey of visitors to Chimanimani, she found that many respondents wanted to see a village and learn about the Shona people, who constitute the largest ethnic group in Zimbabwe (Helen Steward, Voluntary Service Overseas, Chimanimani, June 1998, personal communication). She then assisted Noah in developing a suitable tour. As they walk to Noah's village, visitors are told about the local flora and fauna and the use of plants in traditional society, before sharing a meal with Noah's family. Visitors learn how food is traditionally grown, prepared and cooked, how houses are constructed using traditional materials, and about Shona customs. Comments in the visitors' book show that guests appreciate broadening their visit to Africa by experiencing not just nature and wildlife, but local living conditions and cultural norms as well. For example, 'all through our journey in Africa we were looking for tours where we could learn about traditions and traditional ways of life. We were lucky to come here and find your tour' (comment in Noah Majuta's Visitors' Book, 1997).

Despite having no telephone or transport of his own, Noah has managed to secure a regular supply of customers in the tourist season with the help of private sector interests. Noah is one of the only indigenous people who is a member of the Chimanimani Tourist Association, as most tourism enterprises in the area are owned by whites. The Association's information office distributes brochures about Noah's tours. They and a nearby hotel also take bookings on his behalf, so Noah checks in with them daily to see if he has customers.

Through her work at the local council, the British volunteer was also helping Noah expand his enterprise so that it could benefit the village more widely, rather than just his family. After several months of running the cultural tours Noah recognized that not everyone in the village understood why he was bringing foreign people there and that this had generated some suspicion and jealousy. He saw the need to secure the approval and support of the entire village for his enterprise and decided a good way of doing this would be to contribute a percentage of his revenue to a central fund. Initial talks with the elected village committee revealed that they were very enthusiastic about developing tourism in the village. They were particularly happy that Noah was willing to pay a percentage of his takings into a fund that could be used to support villagers during times of need, for example, when arranging funeral ceremonies or if someone required urgent medical attention. Possibilities for expanding the business in the future, including overnight stays in Old Location and visits to artisans and specialists in the village, such as the traditional healer or drum maker, were also raised by the volunteer and have been discussed with the village committee. This would lead to visitors' money being spread more widely around the village, particularly if craft items were made available for sale.

Conclusions

This chapter has discussed possibilities for host communities to play a management role in tourism, rather than assuming that they should be satisfied with simply gaining economic benefits from tourist activity. Other chapters in this volume have demonstrated that economic gains do not always compensate for the social, cultural and environmental impacts of tourism in destination communities. Undoubtedly the tourism industry in many countries is dominated by foreign ownership and capital with little meaningful local involvement. There is a strong rationale for host communities to play a role in managing tourism when they are the ones faced with the most direct consequences of poorly planned and managed tourism. Strategies to maximize community member/stakeholder control over the rate and manner of tourism development in their home areas can follow no simple formula, however, especially when these communities lack power, resources and experience in relation to other stakeholders.

It has been shown that the form and nature of tourism can play a major role in influencing whether or not communities will be able to play a management role. This is more likely to occur if tourism remains small scale and caters to the budget market, and less likely as resort development, other forms of luxury tourism and mass tourism come to dominate. In the latter cases it may be appropriate for host communities to establish partnership arrangements with private sector interests so they can share experience and resources. However, there is a danger here, as in the case of Phinda reserve, that while benefiting economically from such arrangements, destination communities will have to surrender any hopes of controlling the tourism enterprise.

While rhetoric from the private sector, conservation agencies, and government tourism is generally supportive of a role for communities in the management of tourism, this may not always be based on an interest in securing active participation. For example, support for 'participation of local communities', can simply be:

- A public relations guise (useful in advertising brochures, such as Conservation Corporation Africa's publicity).
- A means of placating the community to ensure they do not jeopardize the venture.
- Politically expedient (e.g. as in the present climate in South Africa where reparations are being made for past alienation of black people from their land and their consequent impoverishment).

The passive participation approach sees local communities as beneficiaries, receiving a handout to secure their loyalty or to appease them. Active participation, on the other hand, recognizes that communities need to be empowered with a knowledge of their choices and options regarding management of natural resources and tourism development, so that they can decide what options to pursue and how they wish to pursue them (Koch, 1994; Timothy, 1999). Only when local people take the initiative to change systems themselves (for which they need psychological empowerment) and establish more equitable structures (a sign of social and political empowerment), can active participation occur (Wells, 1996: 4).

It is important to realize that by including local communities as more active participants in tourism development, it is likely that there will be increasing conflicts between them and other stakeholders, including the government (Wells, 1996: 3). Finding effective ways of resolving such conflicts will be critical to the long-term success of such ventures. Tourism ventures can also be a source of division within communities, causing fractures in their complex yet delicate arrangement of individuals and social groups. In the case of Sunungukai Camp, for example, only a proportion of residents from the five surrounding villages chose to become members of this tourism initiative and thus had the chance to benefit directly from it. Nevertheless there are successful examples of tourism ventures that have bridged social and cultural divisions, bringing widespread benefits to local people (e.g. Barkin and Pailles, 1999).

As it is clear that in many cases destination communities are at a disadvantage in relation to the skills, experience and knowledge of tourism processes necessary to play an active role in managing tourism, it would be useful for future studies to expose examples of collaborative arrangements that have been organized to overcome these disadvantages. Particularly pertinent would be examples of arrangements that secure a strong role for communities in actually managing tourism to their areas, not just playing the role of beneficiaries.

References

Adams, W.M. (1990) *Green Development: Environment and Sustainability in the Third World.* Routledge, London.

Akama, J. (1996) Western environmental values and nature-based tourism in Kenya. *Tourism Management* 17, 567–574.

Ashley, C. and Garland, E. (1994) *Promoting Community-Based Tourism Development.* Ministry of Environment and Tourism, Windhoek.

Ashley, C. and Roe, D. (1998) *Enhancing Community Involvement in Wildlife Tourism: Issues and Challenges.* International Institute for Environment and Development, London.

Barkin, D. and Pailles, C. (1999) NGO–community collaboration for ecotourism: a strategy for sustainable regional development. *Tourism Recreation Research* 24(2), 69–74.

Baskin, J. (1995) Local economic development: tourism – good or bad? In: *Tourism Workshop Proceedings: Small, Medium, Micro Enterprises.* Land and Agriculture Policy Centre, Johannesburg, pp. 103–116.

Bell, R.H. (1987) Conservation with a human face: conflict and reconciliation in African land use planning. In: Anderson, D. and Grove, R. (eds) *Conservation in Africa: People, Policies and Practice.* Cambridge University Press, Cambridge, pp. 79–101.

Britton, S.G. (1982) The political economy of tourism in the third world. *Annals of Tourism Research* 9, 331–358.

Britton, S. and Clarke, W.C. (eds) (1987) *Ambiguous Alternative: Tourism in Small Developing Countries.* University of the South Pacific, Suva.

Brohman, J. (1995) Universalism, Eurocentrism, and ideological bias in development studies: from modernisation to neoliberalism. *Third World Quarterly* 16(1), 121–140.

Brohman, J. (1996) New directions in tourism for the third world. *Annals of Tourism Research* 23, 331–358.

Campbell, L. (1999) Ecotourism in rural developing communities. *Annals of Tourism Research* 26, 534–553.

Carlisle, L. (1997) Conservation Corporation: an integrated approach to ecotourism. In: Creemers, G. (ed.) *Proceedings of a Workshop on Community Involvement in Tourism.* Natal Parks Board and KwaZulu-Natal Tourism Authority, Pietermaritzburg, pp. 6–7.

Cater, E. (1993) Ecotourism in the third world: problems for sustainable tourism development. *Tourism Management* 14, 85–90.

Chalker, B. (1994) Ecotourism: on the trail of destruction or sustainability? A minister's view. In: Cater, E. and Lowman, G. (eds) *Ecotourism: a Sustainable Option.* John Wiley & Sons, Chichester, pp. 87–99.

Cherry, M. (1993) Phinda: making ecotourism profitable for the people. *Sunday Times* (Johannesburg), 30 May, p. 35.

Conservation Corporation Africa (1997) *Conservation Corporation Africa.* CCA, Johannesburg.

Dahles, H. and Bras, K. (eds) (1999) *Tourism and Small Entrepreneurs: Development, National Policy and Entrepreneurial Culture – Indonesian Cases.* Cognizant Communications, New York.

Goodwin, H., Kent, I., Parker, K. and Walpole, M. (1997) *Tourism, Conservation and Sustainable Development: Volume 1 – Comparative Report.* Final Report to the Department for International Development, London.

Hampton, M.P. (1998) Backpacker tourism and economic development. *Annals of Tourism Research* 25, 639–660.

Herald News Desk (1999) JGF will oppose upmarket tourism. *The Herald* (Bangalore), 27 September.

Hunter, C. (1995) Key concepts for tourism and the environment. In: Hunter, C. and Green, H. (eds) *Tourism and the Environment: a Sustainable Relationship?* Routledge, London, pp. 52–92.

Joppe, M. (1996) Sustainable community tourism development revisited. *Tourism Management* 17, 475–479.

Koch, E. (1994) *Reality or Rhetoric: Ecotourism and Rural Reconstruction in South Africa.* United Nations Research Institute for Social Development, Geneva.

Lillywhite, M. and Lillywhite, L. (1991) Low impact tourism: coupling natural/ cultural resource conservation, economic development, and the tourism industry. In: Kusler, J.A. (ed.) *Ecotourism and Resource Conservation: a Collection of Papers,* Vol. 1. International Symposium on Ecotourism, Miami, Florida, pp. 89a–89r.

Little, A.M. (1991) *The Impact of Tourism on the Environment and the Culture of the Local Population.* Institute of Natural Resources, Pietermaritzburg.

Mander, M. and Steytler, N. (1997) *Evaluating Eden: Assessing the Impacts of Community Based Wildlife Management – the South African, Lesotho and Swaziland Component. Phase 1.* The World Conservation Union and International Institute for Environment and Development, London.

Mansperger, M.C. (1995) Tourism and cultural change in small-scale societies. *Human Organization* 54(1), 87–94.

Morrison, K. and Robinson, J. (1995) Sunungukai Camp Recommendations. Unpublished report, November 1995, Dalhousie University, Halifax.

Murphree, M. and Nyika, E. (1997) *Investigation into the Performance of Non-Lease Tourism Projects in the Communal Lands of Zimbabwe.* IRT/SPECISS Consulting Services, Harare.

Norberg-Hodge, H. (1991) *Ancient Futures: Learning from Ladakh.* Rider, London.

O'Connor, J. (2000) The big squeeze. *In Focus,* Summer, 4–5.

Oppermann, M. (1993) Tourism space in developing countries. *Annals of Tourism Research* 20, 535–556.

Ranck, S.R. (1987) An attempt at autonomous development: the case of the Tufi guest houses, Papua New Guinea. In: Britton, S. and Clarke, W.C. (eds) *Ambiguous Alternative: Tourism in Small Developing Countries.* University of the South Pacific, Suva, pp. 154–166.

Scheyvens, R. (1999) Ecotourism and the empowerment of local communities. *Tourism Management* 20, 245–249.

Scheyvens, R. (2002) *Tourism for Development: Empowering Communities.* Prentice Hall, Harlow.

Sindiga, I. (1995) Wildlife-based tourism in Kenya: land use conflicts and government compensation policies over protected areas. *Journal of Tourism Studies* 6(2), 45–55.

Sofield, T. (1993) Indigenous tourism development. *Annals of Tourism Research* 20, 729–750.

Tapela, B.N. and Omara-Ojungu, P.H. (1999) Towards bridging the gulf between wildlife conservation and rural development in post-apartheid South Africa: the case of the Makuleke community and the Kruger National Park. *South African Geographical Journal* 81(3), 148–155.

Thomlinson, E. and Getz, D. (1996) The question of scale in ecotourism: case study of two small ecotour operators in the Mundo Maya region of Central America. *Journal of Sustainable Tourism* 4(4), 183–200.

Timothy, D.J. (1999) Participatory planning: a view of tourism in Indonesia. *Annals of Tourism Research* 26, 371–391.

Twining-Ward, L. and Twining-Ward, T. (1998) Tourism development in Samoa: context and constraints. *Pacific Tourism Review* 2, 261–271.

Wall, G. and Long, V. (1996) Balinese homestays: an indigenous response to tourism opportunities. In: Butler, R.W. and Hinch, T. (eds) *Tourism and Indigenous Peoples.* International Thomson Business Press, London, pp. 27–48.

Wells, M.P. (1996) *The Economic and Social Role of Protected Areas in the New South Africa.* Overseas Development Institute, London; and Land and Agriculture Policy Centre, Johannesburg.

Wilkinson, P.F. and Pratiwi, W. (1995) Gender and tourism in an Indonesian village. *Annals of Tourism Research* 22, 283–299.

Wilson, D. (1997) Paradoxes of tourism in Goa. *Annals of Tourism Research* 24, 52–75.

Presenting Destinations: Marketing Host Communities

13

GIANNA MOSCARDO AND PHILIP PEARCE

Tourism Program, James Cook University, Townsville, Queensland, Australia

Introduction

The term Sami refers to the Lapp people of northern Finland near the Arctic Circle. Christmas is the peak visitor season in this region. In December 1996 young members of the Sami community distributed handouts to foreign tourists bearing the headlines 'Indigenous people's protest', 'Stereotyped people', 'Fake Fake Fake' and 'Let's protect Sami culture' (Saarinen, 1998). The pivotal feature about this local community call to action was the perceived false representations of a community. In particular, the contested representation involved Sami people in traditional dress posing in activities such as herding reindeer or gutting fish. Saarinen notes, however, that the traditional dress is equivalent to formal Western clothing, so the idea of wearing it to herd reindeer or to undertake fishing tasks is ridiculous. Even further, a number of the tourism images involved non-Sami women wearing the traditional dress in a suggestive manner, thus transforming the exotic into the erotic in an exploitative rendition of Sami culture.

This chapter deals with both the contentious issues and the opportunities in the marketing of host communities for tourism. It commences with an overview of the diversity of this phenomenon. The extent of the phenomenon is linked to a perspective on communities, which emphasizes the tensions and contested values at work in human social groups. This perspective, it will be argued, provides more insight for understanding marketing issues in tourism than a view of communities as geographically-based harmonious systems. Next a brief but broad view of the scope of contemporary marketing is considered. Here, the emphasis is on viewing marketing as multifaceted, including but extending beyond promotional issues and embracing product, price and distribution systems as a part of the necessary discussion. Tourism studies have been frequently directed towards sustainability issues in the last decade (Ryan and Page, 2000). The core links between the marketing of communities for tourism and sustainable tourism issues are developed, and four case studies are described. Together with the sustainable tourism perspectives, the cases provide a basis for reviewing the benefits and opportunities, as well as the conflicts and costs, likely to be associated with the marketing of destination communities. In a penultimate integrative section, one theoretical thread running through the work discussed will be highlighted. This integrative approach can be broadly described as social representations theory (Moscovici, 1984, 1988). The final section of the chapter focuses on contemporary marketing practices noting the relevance of approaches such as societal marketing for harnessing the strengths and avoiding the pitfalls in the process of presenting communities.

Diversity of the Phenomenon

Cautionary and sometimes value-laden polemics on the problems caused by tourism frequently focus on the exploitation of poor isolated ethnic communities by multinational tourism interests (Boum, 1998; Carling, 1998). There are, however, several dimensions and categories of host communities that need to be considered and which expand the range of the topic under discussion. Some of these dimensions include the size and economic well-being of the host community being portrayed, the relationship of the host community or enclave to its society or national culture and the coherence and existing awareness of the message being marketed. Carling (1998) reports on the identity struggle of the mountain people of the northern Philippines, and Boum (1998) notes that rural Moroccans profit little from the promotion and marketing of regional attractions. Butler (1998) highlights the success of the tartan mythology for Scotland, while Judd (1995) stresses the power of image making to reshape futures of urban centres in the USA. Clearly all of these examples are communities of a sort and an analysis based only on a sample of the smaller ethnic communities frequently studied in the anthropology of tourism literature will be likely to yield rather different inductive findings than a focus on developed or larger scale groups (Smith, 1978; Crick, 1989; Harrison, 1992).

The discussion in this chapter considers a broad diversity of host community types. Further, it follows a framework for defining a community that is more than a simple nexus of people living in a place (see Boyd and

Singh, Chapter 2 this volume). In particular, as Burr (1991) has argued, there are conceptualizations of communities that emphasize different features. For example, a human ecological approach considers a community to be any geographically specified, well-adapted group with distinctive characteristics. By way of contrast a social system approach to community considers what roles exist and how institutions, governance and group membership are managed. Another option with its derivations in the work of Mead (1934) stresses an interactional approach where the processes that create and alter community structure are highlighted. A further approach, referred to as the critical perspective, considers the power of key groups in community decision-making and emphasizes the tensions and opposing forces at work in communities.

A definitional emphasis combining the critical and interactionist perspective and which goes beyond a basic or implicit human ecological mould of communities will be used in this discussion. The value of stressing the view that communities are dynamic, that there are competing forces and different powers at work, seems to be particularly applicable to some of the contested representations involved in tourism marketing. For example, Law discussing the promotion of tourism in English cities notes:

> Who is pushing tourism? Who has the strategic vision for urban tourism? . . .
> with the rise of public–private partnerships for promotion, members of
> the private sector have come to occupy positions of influence. What kind
> of background do they have and what kind of vision do they have? (in short)
> . . . How does a city decide what image it wants to project?
>
> (Law, 1996: 251)

The kinds of questions raised by Law will be explored throughout this chapter.

Contemporary Marketing

One of the features of tourism studies is the diversity of disciplinary backgrounds of the researchers who contribute to the principal journals in the field (Jafari, 1990; Pearce, 1995). In particular the researchers who have been prominent in commenting on destination communities in tourism have often had an anthropological or sociological disciplinary orientation (van den Berghe, 1994; Robinson and Boniface, 1997; Yamashita *et al.*, 1997). One of the difficulties accompanying these contributions is that some of the key authors venture into discussing marketing-related issues with an everyday rather than a professional understanding of marketing. For example, in his detailed work on the marketing language of tourism, Dann (1996) implicitly conceives of marketing as being almost entirely focused on promotional efforts, particularly involving the print media.

In this discussion of the marketing of destination communities, the use of the marketing concept will extend beyond the use of marketing simply to mean promotion. Both within the larger marketing field and within tourism marketing texts there is widespread agreement that marketing embraces product selection and development, promotion, pricing decisions and the use of distribution systems to inform customers and intermediaries (Seaton and Bennett, 1996; Middleton, 1998; Lewis and Chambers, 2000). How might this broader and now commonplace marketing concept shape the focus of the work on marketing host communities? There are several additional emphases that can be explored in case study material to pursue this wider framework. In particular, sensitivity to the components of the host community that are emphasized for tourism warrants attention. Additionally, little discussion exists in the anthropological literature on the pricing features of destination community-related tourism. It is possible to predict that there may be different levels of community acceptability to tourism according to pricing and revenue-based determinants.

Further, the distribution systems chosen to promote tourism fall outside the coverage of much of the existing analysis of destination community studies. Again, perhaps owing to the ease of accessibility of material, many tourism researchers primarily consider the direct channel of communication to the visitor such as brochures (Zeppel, 1997) rather than the information designed for wider channels of distribution such as those reported by Lewis and Chambers (2000) as affiliations, consortia, reservations companies, incentive houses, representation companies, travel agents, tour operators and wholesalers, discount brokers and international distribution systems. At this stage in the development of an understanding of how host communities are marketed there are few case studies and little comprehensive academic consideration of the full business dimensions and systems of marketing. Wherever possible the case studies explored in this chapter are assessed with this multifaceted approach to marketing rather than simply emphasizing promotional components.

A Sustainability Framework

The fable of Rip van Winkle relates the story of a character who has fallen asleep for 20 years and awakes to a changed world where he struggles to recognize his new surroundings. A tourism researcher suffering a Rip van Winkle-style fate in the early 1980s would undoubtedly be challenged by at least two dominant trends of the moment: (i) the rise of the Internet and electronic tourism; and (ii) the dominance of the sustainability theme in tourism writing. The principles and details of the sustainability emphasis are, arguably, stronger in Australia, New Zealand, Canada, Great Britain and Europe than they are in the USA (Swarbrooke, 1999).

Table 13.1. Goals and characteristics of ecologically sustainable tourism.
Source: Pearce *et al.* (1996).

Goals
To improve material and non-material well-being of communities.
To preserve inter-generational and intra-generational equity.
To protect biological diversity and maintain ecological systems.
To ensure the cultural integrity and social cohesion of communities.

Characteristics
Tourism which is concerned with the quality of experiences.
Tourism which has social equity and community involvement.
Tourism which operates within the limits of the resource – this includes
   minimization of impacts and use of energy and the use of effective waste
   management and recycling techniques.
Tourism which maintains the full range of recreational, educational and cultural
   opportunities within and across generations.
Tourism which is based upon activities or designs which reflect the character of a
   region.
Tourism which allows the guest to gain an understanding of the region visited
   and which encourages guests to be concerned about, and protective of, the
   host community and environment.
Tourism which does not compromise the capacity of other industries or activities
   to be sustainable.
Tourism which is integrated into local, regional and national plans.

Ecologically sustainable tourism (EST) is usefully defined through an understanding of its goals and a description of its characteristics. Table 13.1 sets out the key goals and characteristics of EST as described in the Australian Government's ESD (Ecologically Sustainable Development) Working Group Report for Tourism (1991).

Lane (1991), Middleton (1998) and Swarbrooke (1999), among others, have further discussed the characteristics listed in Table 13.1 focusing on communities. Some notes of caution are beginning to emerge in this discussion of sustainable tourism concepts and the sociocultural and community sphere. A first point, repeated by a number of authors, is that while the community is given much attention in the goals of ecologically sustainable tourism, the language of EST emphasizes biological and biophysical considerations, thus marginalizing the importance of social and community issues in the debate (Pigram, 1990; Pearce, 1993). It can be argued that if the EST emphasis in tourism focuses only on biophysical processes and does not consider community impacts then it will gradually lose power as an organizing system for tourism thinking and become synonymous with environmental impact assessment.

A second note of caution may stem from a perceived research inability to measure and assess the community concerns. This perspective places the community response issues into the 'too hard' and 'subjective' category, raising the spectre of interdisciplinary territorial disputes about the quality and acceptability of research in different fields (Becher, 1989). A further emerging thought in sustainability of communities is to highlight the adaptability and dynamic nature of cultural and subcultural groups. Yamashita *et al.* (1997: 26) observe, 'but important as issues of sustainability may be they are still only part of the picture in considering the future of tourism . . . much of the development is due to local creativity . . . attempts to preserve only pristine culture are misplaced'.

As an amplification of these incipient notes of concern about the sustainability framework, Hollinshead (1999) asks a series of questions about the representations of the US state of Texas. He states:

> Fundamentally then, the subject of interest is whom does the state of Texas belong to i.e. whom do state decision-makers in public culture, history and heritage appear to represent and privilege (if anyone?) when they make their large and small representation decisions.
>
> (Hollinshead, 1999: 65)

The most challenging element of the sustainability debate is at core a political one. When the goals and characteristics of sustainable tourism are built on such phrases as:

- 'to improve the material and non-material well-being of communities';
- 'to ensure the cultural integrity and social cohesion of communities'; and
- 'tourism which has social equity and community involvement';

the further challenge is to ask by whose definition, from whose perspective is the community improving its well-being, its social and cultural integrity and its equity? Robinson (1997) echoes these concerns in a study of the provincial industrial cities of the UK where tourism is an agent of change and urban management is employed increasingly as the traditional industrial tasks of these communities fade. He argues that there is a passive community in these cities, a segment of 'other' people, who are beginning to ask questions as their cities are re-shaped. The questions, inherently linked to the sustainability and benefits goals outlined above are comments on the new tourist buildings and museums of industrialized heritage. 'What the hell's this?' 'What use is that?' and 'Why can't the money be better spent?'

The following sections describe four case studies that will be used to highlight issues in the tourism marketing of host communities. These cases are approached bearing in mind the emphases on community power and interaction discussed earlier, the wider view of the meaning of marketing and the framework of sustainability, and accompanying questions about its applicability.

The case studies were chosen to reflect considerable diversity in the types of community being marketed for tourism. Additionally, they are all supported by some quality research information. The first case study is of an Aboriginal group, the Tjapukai in northern Australia. The second is about a Mexican community, San Cristobel, the third is of Scotland, and the final case is from central Java, Indonesia. The fieldwork and material for these cases have all been collected in the last decade, but in some cases recent additional events can be added to the discussion. The cases are chosen to emphasize the diversity of geographic scale, developed and developing countries, recent and long-standing examples of tourism promotion and with examples of both ethnic tourism and broader based tourism traditions.

The Tjapukai Cultural Experience

The information for this case study comes from the reports by the manager of the commercial entity (Freeman, 2000) together with published work on the visitor markets and tourism products (Moscardo and Pearce, 1999) and a wider community tourism appraisal (Pearce *et al.*, 1996).

The Tjapukai people of the North Queensland region are one of a number of Aboriginal communities who traditionally inhabited the area. After a period of displacement and suffering from colonizing pressures and hostilities, the remnant Aboriginal community consists of less than 1000 people distributed around the small towns of the area. Tourism for this community was originally developed through a structured theatre show celebrating traditions of Aboriginal dance. In 1996 a larger tourist attraction in a 10-acre landscaped setting was built. This expanded version of the attraction is referred to as the Tjapukai Cultural Park and features three core sections, a history theatre, a creation theatre with a laser light show, and an outdoor landscaped park where the dance performance remains the main attraction. The ownership and control of the attraction is based on a partnership between the traditional Aboriginal people, some of whom work as employees, and external entrepreneurial investment and management.

The Tjapukai Cultural Park with its attendant marketing of the Aboriginal community and culture has parallels with the Amish communities in the USA, various Russian and other enclave communities in western Canada, ethnic tourist attractions in South Africa, and the presentation of First Nations people in North America. The core feature is the use of a tourist attraction as a buffer zone, a contact area to present aspects of a community, while not actually presenting an *in situ* residential group.

From the community marketing perspective the Tjapukai case raises some powerful issues. In terms of product development, the cultural park features a vivid and necessarily ugly account of the historical fate of the Aboriginal community. In visitor appraisals of the attraction this history feature was perceived positively by most visitors, including Australians (Moscardo and Pearce, 1999). It is a small but compelling example that tourism presentations can raise difficult topics successfully. Other cultural components selected for product development include story telling emphasizing the spirituality of the people, food products, dance, painting and music. The key entrepreneurial couple who have worked with the Tjapukai community emphasize that they have made the cultural presentations a success by putting business principles first (Freeman, 2000). The Tjapukai experience is seen as an expensive or high-price style of cultural tourism, the entry charges exceeding that of most other nearby attractions. The business emphasis also includes extensive tourism industry liaison resulting in promotional and trade awards and various forms of packaging with other attractions. The cultural messages and images used in promotional materials are audited by key members of the Tjapukai community, essentially a small group of respected elders.

The benefits of the Tjapukai community appraisal include ongoing employment in the park for local indigenous people as well as the maintenance of two complete dance groups. International travel opportunities for these community members have been rich, with the dance groups being used by the Australian Tourist Commission in Asia, the Americas and Europe. The cultural and political dimensions of the Tjapukai operation have to be set in a national context where reconciliation issues between traditional owners and the Federal Government have been problematic for some time. In this period the Tjapukai presentations have been a leading national example of non-indigenous and Aboriginal partnership. The operation is viable, without being a major commercial success, and attests to the multidimensionality of assessing sustainability in cultural as well as economic and biophysical terms.

San Cristobel, Mexico

The information for this case study comes from the sustained fieldwork of van den Berghe (1994). Working within an ethnographic tradition he provides a full volume of observations, interviews and analyses researching the tourism impacts and developments in this Mexican community over a 30-year period.

San Cristobel and its multi-ethnic people were perhaps fortunate to be bypassed by the Pan-American highway in the 1960s. With the realization by the civic authorities that the architecture of other Mexican communities was changing into a pastiche of Western styles, building codes and restrictions were effectively implemented. van den Berghe reports that the effect is to make San Cristobel charming and attractive to tourists with a small-town feel but with the activity and sophistication of a much larger community. San Cristobel is a relatively inexpensive place to visit. In effect, the comfortable, but not luxurious, facilities in hotels and restaurants service the enthusiastic rather than the indulgent traveller.

In a marketing sense, however, and more pertinent to this chapter, is the changed roles of San Cristobel's Indian community as tourism has grown. The powerful, numerically dominant group in San Cristobel is referred to as the Ladinos. Eurocentric and heirs to the Spanish colonial traditions this group co-existed with the rustic peasant Indian community, the latter frequently being in menial jobs and treated with disdain. With the growth of tourism the Ladinos became aware that high-status visitors were prepared to spend more not to look at the Spanish colonial architecture and heritage exclusively, but rather to see the churches, villages and craft work of the Indian community.

van den Berghe argues that the Ladinos were quick to redefine their attitude to the Indian community, seeing them as a marketable and exploitable commodity. Nevertheless, the popularity of the Indian arts and crafts gradually earned Ladino respect and a strong feature of San Cristobel's marketing in the 1990s reflected Indian themes and heritage. Together these tourism-induced effects have produced major changes in the social relations of San Cristobel's ethnic communities. Through marketing and product identification some of the views of the outside world have changed the views within the town.

The San Cristobel case reveals the interdependence of marketing and management. It was some of the initial administrative actions regarding building codes and designs which assisted San Cristobel's rise to tourism prominence. Furthermore, the sustainability of this colonial heritage remains dependent on not relaxing these codes as the demand for more visitors to the area grows. van den Berghe also suggests a specific tourism carrying capacity figure for ethnic tourism to the now valued Indian villages and community. He suggests a 1% rule; ethnic tourists, he argues, must not exceed 1% of the locals. The basis for this argument is that in small communities modernity accompanies the tourist influx and massive changes will make the product unattractive.

Scotland, UK

The information for this study comes from the work of Butler (1998) together with case studies of other Celtic communities such as Cornwall and Wales (Ireland, 1997) and small-scale studies of Scottish tourism (Downie, 1996).

Scotland has a long-standing tradition of tourism. From the travellers' tales of Dr Johnson through to Royal holiday patronage, it has been involved in hosting visitors for several centuries. As a major historical, ethnic and now administratively distinctive region of the UK, Scotland is associated with a set of images and identities that reach beyond its borders. The large numbers of people living in other countries with deep ties to, and affection for, their Scottish heritage is a major consideration in understanding the marketing of Scotland. Butler adopts the view that the tartan mythology, a collection of dominant images in the promotion of Scotland, has changed relatively little in the last 30 years. He also argues (consistent with the analysis of marketing effort being pursued in this chapter), that the products of Scottish tourism have changed. While the promotional effort for Scotland now uses contemporary technology, there have also been substantial upgrades in the quality of accommodation, food, service levels, adventure tourism opportunities, itinerary design including whisky tours and sports (especially golf) opportunities. Prices too have risen as this service and activity structure attract some independent and better paying customers.

A specific illustration of this kind of product upgrade is reported by Downie (1996). Glasgow and Edinburgh, as Scotland's two largest cities, Downie argues, have been transformed in the last decade. Both centres are sufficiently large and sufficiently well known in Europe to escape the locational anonymity of similar English cities also seeking to transform themselves. Downie reports that an ambitious plan to transform the Royal Mile, the centrepiece of Edinburgh's urban tourism, is partly completed. The pedestrian carriageway was doubled after 1993 and a new linear civic space constructed both for day and night use with an atmospheric array of café bars and street entertainment seeking a cosmopolitan feel. The physical improvements are augmented by a series of marketing and customer care initiatives, particularly responding to short break markets and more trained service personnel. Downie notes that Edinburgh is heavily dependent on repeat visitors, and reinforces the theme that modern Scotland now has the infrastructure to service contemporary visitors even if it continues to build on and use well-established Scottish heritage and tartan themes.

The Scottish case study is broadly relevant to other distinct regional communities in developed countries, some notable examples including Quebec, Wales and Sicily. While the Scottish case has some hallmarks of success, the visitors are coming, infrastructure is being built and old landscapes are finding new uses, there remain some questions about the balance between identity and global culture that were raised in the sustainability overview. Downie enthusiastically reports that the Edinburgh community and street scape is now cosmopolitan. For some community sectors, cosmopolitan may be a desirable description. For others it may mean a homogenization transforming their space into another ordinary European or North American living space. As noted by Yamashita *et al.* (1997), as the detailed implementation of social and cultural sustainability dimensions is pursued, there is a lack of specificity on some points. This is particularly noticeable when terms such as social and cultural cohesion and integrity are able to be defined in starkly different ways with one version emphasizing change and modernity and the other highlighting a continuity of physical and social worlds.

Central Java, Indonesia

The source materials for this case study derive principally from a series of papers edited by Sofield and Tarjana (1995) and reflections on Indonesian tourism by Kagami (1997) and Graburn (1997).

The study area is that based around the city of Surakarta (also known as Solo) in the most heavily populated region of Indonesia. It includes Yogyakarta, which offers access to Borobudur, one of the leading World Heritage Sites in Asia. Unlike the other case studies reported in this chapter, existing levels of tourism to the region are relatively low and with the exception of Borobudur, the marketing of the community at this stage is focused on identifying products for tourism. In common with other rural parts of Indonesia, existing travel is available at all budget levels for affluent Westerners.

Warto (1995), Handajani (1995) and Setyaningsih (1995) all suggest tourism product opportunities in central Java based on historical buildings, food and local ceremonies. They also mention with some consensus that there are restrictions on likely visitor access to some of these ceremonies, sites and local cultural practices. Irawan (1995) and Soemanto (1995) adopt a more utilitarian view in the marketing of Javanese culture and community, stressing the need to develop service standards and attitudes that would facilitate the delivery of the tourism experience. This awareness of some of the human resource capital needs for expanding tourism to the area is noteworthy for sustaining both the business of tourism and the sites themselves.

Kagami (1997) raises some wider sustainability issues in the marketing of Borobudur and Javanese tourism. He notes that a focus on tourism objects, while a necessary part of marketing growth, needs to be considered as part of the definition of local culture and its integration into a national culture. He suggests that one of the great challenges for Indonesia is the integration of local culture into a national one. The promotion of magnificent architectural achievements is heavily endorsed by the Indonesian government and while the focus is on the buildings it appears that local communities support national-level promotion.

Conflict and tension, however, tend to arise when local cultures, whether pertaining to a region or a religious group, are not very well supported in national marketing campaigns. In neighbouring Bali, for example, Kagami notes that the provincial, as opposed to the national, policy of promoting cultural tourism, has strengthened the Balinese self-respect for their own way of life. This has formed a resolve to deflect or oppose the central government's intention to downplay or domesticate local culture.

As a postscript to this academic assessment of community presentations for tourism, the changing circumstances of Indonesian provincial regions such as East Timor and Aceh can be seen as potentially reflecting the struggle for control over cultural presentation and ownership in Indonesia.

Benefits, Opportunities, Conflicts and Costs

Tourism is a distinctive phenomenon partly because it is both a business and a highly social person-to-person activity. Even when a potential customer receives a marketing communication there is an implied connection to another community, an opportunity for personal interaction and experience. It is well established in theories of attitudes that direct experience and personal relevance of communication enhances the likelihood of attention and attitude change. One category of benefits in these case studies of marketing communities seems to be consistent with this theme that tourism can change attitudes. In particular, the Aboriginal tourism enterprise in Australia reported positive attitudes towards a group where it was not entirely predictable that this would be the case. More powerfully the San Cristobel study revealed that the social relations within that Mexican community were modified by the gaze of tourist interest.

Together with some beneficial attitudinal shifts and assessments involved in the marketing of host communities, there are clear infrastructure identification and product development benefits. This can be architectural restoration and preservation, service standards and facilities and new leisure and recreation opportunities. These are significant and powerful features energizing community lifestyles.

The darker, more complex side of marketing destination communities in these case studies rests with the political repercussions for the less powerful community members. Representations of communities that selectively identify distorted features of local societies may make subsections of the community less content, possibly displaced and potentially hostile to planned or existing tourism development.

Social Representations Theory

Some further dimensions that can assist in exploring the features of these cases are provided by a consideration of social representations theory. Expressed succinctly, social representations are:

> Cognitive systems with a logic and language of their own . . . They do not represent simply 'opinions about', 'images of' or 'attitudes towards' but 'theories' or 'branches' of knowledge in their own right, for the discovery and organisation of reality.
>
> (Moscovici, 1973: xiii)

Pearce *et al.* (1996) summarize some of the key features of social representations in Table 13.2. The applicability of the social representations approach to the present chapter lies in its use to understand the effects of host

Table 13.2. Key features of social representations theory. Source: Pearce *et al.* (1996).

1. Social representations are complex meta systems of everyday knowledge and include values, beliefs, attitudes and explanations.
2. The content and structure of social representations are important.
3. Social representations help to define and organize reality.
4. Social representations allow for communication and interaction.
5. Social representations make the unfamiliar familiar.
6. Through the use of metaphors, analogies and comparisons with prototypes social representations fit new and abstract concepts/events into existing frameworks.
7. Images are central components of social representations.
8. Abstract concepts are both simplified (through the use of images and analogies) and elaborated (through connections to existing knowledge).
9. Social representations have an independent existence once created and so can be found in social or cultural artefacts.
10. Social representations are critical components of group and individual identity.
11. Social representations are important features of group interaction and so social representations theory explicitly recognizes social conflict and the importance of power in social dynamics.
12. Social representations are prescriptive. They can direct both action and thought (especially perception).
13. Social representations are not deterministic or static. They vary along many dimensions including the level of consensus about them, their level of detail and how they are communicated. Individuals can and do influence, create and change social representations. They can be changed through individual influence, direct experience, persuasive communication, and/or group interaction.
14. Social representations connect individuals to their social/cultural worlds.
15. Social representations are both influenced by and influence science.

community marketing. Moscovici and others have used their view of social representations to describe the 'mini theories' or branches of knowledge people have about such topics as sex, health and madness. Some authors have applied the approach to tourism (Crick, 1989; Pearce *et al.*, 1996) and it is equally applicable to a broad concept like communities.

How does a social representations theory approach to 'communities' serve to enhance our understanding of these case studies and related literature? It directs attention to the following points. Tourism marketers must consider that groups receiving their communication efforts already have complex systems for understanding information about host communities and cultures. Some of this may be stereotypical, some of the linking parts of the knowledge system may be driven by cynicism, and new knowledge will be checked against the view arising from the information sources. The social representation approach also prompts people to consider how the recipients of the communication might filter the information according to their identity and the social group to which they belong. For example, a predisposition to believe that certain elements of Scottish heritage are immutable might be connected to membership in Robbie Burns' societies, thus favouring selective input of marketing messages.

The emphasis on social representations also highlights the existence and persistence of these mini-theories beyond any one individual. For example, in his attempt to understand what is Cornishness, Ireland (1997) found a high level of agreement with terms such as proud, reserved, independent and superstitious, but he also found that history, tradition, handicrafts and working life featured in the overall body of knowledge. A negative reaction to tourism development, Ireland points out, is inherent in Cornishness as the features represented in tourism promotional efforts are in conflict with the system of knowledge that defines Cornish meaning and identity.

In brief, a social representations approach alerts researchers and analysts of tourism's social force to several key items. It suggests that marketing and development efforts in tourism need to be understood in relation to existing knowledge systems, that the identity and power of the groups receiving or transmitting the communication need consideration and, further, that while social representations can change over time, an expectation that a few promotional images will be enough to do this is likely to be misplaced.

Enhancing Host Community Marketing

The complexity of the issues already reviewed concerning the tourism marketing of host communities restricts any simple recipe-like set of solutions for better outcomes. Nevertheless one potential pathway to shape future practice lies in following the perspective outlined by Freeman (2000) in his comments on the Tjapukai case. He suggests that a better result for cultural goals and community outcomes lies not by putting these issues to the fore but by focusing on business practices. In this spirit the final section of this chapter reviews some of the leading trends and recommended future practices in contemporary marketing.

One prominent concept now appearing regularly in tourism textbooks that is particularly relevant to the community tourism issues is societal marketing (Morrison, 1996; Lewis and Chambers, 2000). Essentially, societal marketing includes as a part of the planning of marketing activities some review process or reflection on the social acceptability of the product and its promotion. A societal marketing approach may take several forms, but some kind of screening or auditing by affected stakeholders or community representatives is implied. It is more than focus group testing of the success of the planned marketing exercise since some marketing efforts may appeal to target markets but be distasteful to hosts. A failure to adopt this approach is illustrated in a Sri Lankan example. Senadhira (1998) reports that an American marketing company had violated a contract to promote Sri Lanka's image. The company was hired by the Ceylon Tourist Board to handle the overall image of Sri Lanka. A promotional film was produced entitled *Ina's Journey Through Sri Lanka*. In the televised version shown on German television additional scenes to add interest were included. The result was the depiction of Sri Lanka in a semi-pornographic style. The Ceylon Tourist Board now view the incident as a debacle and remain concerned that the image of Sri Lanka as a sex paradise is likely to persist. With the auditing or checking procedure implicit in societal marketing it is most unlikely that this money would have been misspent.

A second major trend in contemporary tourism marketing practice is variously known as destination marketing alliances or partnership and collaborative practices (Palmer and Bijou, 1995; Middleton, 1998). Essentially this recommendation involves bringing organizational interests together to cooperate in tourism planning and promotion. Jamal and Getz (1995) identify three phases in this process: problem setting, direction setting and implementation. It should be noted that the collaborative practices approach can be formally distinguished from community or resident responsive tourism. The latter, often linked to the textbook written by Murphy (1985), *Tourism: a Community Approach*, essentially advocates community-based leadership of the planning and marketing process. Middleton (1998) highlights a difference between the newer terms, collaborative marketing and partnership approach and that of community or resident-responsive tourism. He suggests that collaborative or partnership planning and marketing efforts can be led by the private sector, particularly as this leadership harnesses the commercial sector energy and resources.

While this distinction clearly identifies a different leadership style in these kinds of alliances, the two trends share some very common difficulties. A fundamental problem is to assume that a power group in the community will be willing to give up some control and probably personal gain for a longer range and uncertain community goal. It is perhaps not surprising that there are few examples of this process. This is not to deny that there are numerous, in fact quite ubiquitous, tourism marketing partnerships. Often, though, these are business to business liaisons with some significant government advisors. The 'other people', the passive community, is not well represented in this approach. Ritchie (1993) also notes the pragmatic issue of sustaining the enthusiasm of participants in these partnership exercises. In an article on Calgary, Canada, Ritchie reports that the enthusiasm of the diverse group which crafted a destination vision for the future of that community started to decline as operational issues surfaced. Members started to miss meetings and the team approach devolved to the committed organizers.

Despite these difficulties some contemporary tourism commentators remain optimistic that the public voices can be heard through these partnership approaches to marketing. Middleton, for example, enthuses that:

> If it is undertaken collaboratively, negotiated and implemented jointly between the public and private sector, marketing provides the most fertile route for harnessing the professionalism and energy of modern management thinking to the achievement of sustainable goals.
>
> (Middleton, 1998: 130)

A third noteworthy trend in contemporary marketing is the expansion of distribution channels and opportunities for reaching target markets through the Internet. This facility enables individuals and small relatively poor community interest groups to establish web sites as a way of communicating to would-be travellers. Sometimes this web site activity acts as a kind of local and less official guide for visitors. It may be perceived as more trustworthy than the sites sponsored by large tourist organizations or commercial concerns. In turn travellers who become sensitized to local community and sustainability concerns may be influenced in their destination choice by this kind of informal information channel. The Sami people of the Scandinavian Arctic Circle region described at the start of this chapter as displaying placards to arriving visitors could foreseeably short circuit this form of protest by conveying similar messages to would-be travellers electronically.

One further macro trend in modern marketing deserves attention. The term relationship marketing is used to summarize marketing efforts based on the known characteristics of customers, usually those who have visited the location previously and about whom some core characteristics have been established (Powers, 1997). Analysis of guest history information in databases can be used to build customers in different seasons, to facilitate repeat visits and to manage facilities to enhance satisfaction. The use of detailed tracking and monitoring studies of previous visitors, such as exists in some businesses for relationship marketing, may provide some of the necessary evidence for encouraging sustainable practices on behalf of the industry. It is consistent with the theme of this section that sustainable tourism operating for and on behalf of host communities is likely to be driven by businesses sensitized to their own future well-being. Databases such as those outlined in the hotel and restaurant sector may be prototypes of more generic monitoring and appraisal systems to influence host community-sensitive business decisions.

Acknowledgement

Funding and resources, which facilitated the writing of this chapter were provided by Rainforest Cooperative Research Centre, Cairns, Queensland, Australia.

References

Becher, T. (1989) *Academic Tribes and Territories.* The Society for Research into Higher Education and the Open University Press, Milton Keynes.

Boum, A. (1998) Cultural commoditization, commercialization or cultural authenticity. *Contours* 8, 18–20.

Burr, S.W. (1991) Review and evaluation of the theoretical approaches to community as employed in travel and tourism impact research on rural community organisation and change. In: Veal, A.J., Johnson, P. and Cushman, G. (eds) *Leisure and Tourism: Social and Environmental Changes.* World Leisure and Recreation Association Congress, Sydney, pp. 540–553.

Butler, R. (1998) Tartan mythology: the traditional tourist image of Scotland. In: Ringer, G. (ed.) *Destinations: Cultural Landscapes of Tourism.* Routledge, London, pp. 121–139.

Carling, J. (1998) Tourism impacts on the indigenous peoples of Cordillera. *Contours* 8, 5–7.

Crick, M. (1989) Representations of international tourism in the social sciences: sun, sex, sights, savings, and servility. *Annual Review of Anthropology* 18, 307–344.

Dann, G. (1996) *The Language of Tourism: a Sociolinguistic Perspective.* CAB International, Wallingford.

Downie, R. (1996) Edinburgh's Old Town, UK. In: Middleton, V. (ed.) *Sustainable Tourism: a Marketing Perspective.* Butterworth Heinemann, Oxford, pp. 213–217.

ESD Working Group (1991) *Tourism: Final report.* Australian Government Publishing Service, Canberra.

Freeman, D. (2000) *The Tjapukai Case Study: Best Practice in Interpretation.* Tourism Queensland, Brisbane.

Graburn, N. (1997) Tourism and cultural development in East Asia and Oceania. In: Yamashita, S., Din, K. and Eades, J.S. (eds) *Tourism and Cultural Development in Asia and Oceania.* Universiti Kebangsaan Malaysia, Penerbit, pp. 194–212.

Handajani, S. (1995) Customs and traditional foods of central Java. In: Sofield, T. and Tarjana, M. (eds) *A Profile of Javanese culture.* James Cook University, Townsville, pp. 21–26.

Harrison, D. (ed.) (1992) *Tourism and the Less Developed Countries.* Belhaven, London.

Hollinshead, K. (1999) Myth and the discourse of Texas: heritage tourism and the suppression of instinctual life. In: Robinson, M. and Boniface, P. (eds) *Tourism and Cultural Conflicts.* CAB International, Wallingford, pp. 47–94.

Irawan, B. (1995) To idealise Surakarta as a tourism city: supply side views. In: Sofield, T. and Tarjana, M. (eds) *A Profile of Javanese Culture.* James Cook University, Townsville, pp. 37–41.

Ireland, M. (1997) Cornishness, conflict and tourism development. In: Robinson, M. and Boniface, P. (eds) *Tourism and Cultural Conflicts.* CAB International, Wallingford, pp. 129–160.

Jafari, J. (1990) Research and scholarship: the basis of tourism education. *Journal of Tourism Studies* 1(1), 33–41.

Jamal, T. and Getz, D. (1995) Collaboration theory and community tourism planning. *Annals of Tourism Research* 22, 186–204.

Judd, D.R. (1995) Promoting tourism in U.S. cities. *Tourism Management* 11, 175–187.

Kagami, H. (1997) Tourism and national culture: Indonesian policies on cultural heritage and its utilisation in tourism. In: Yamashita, S., Din, K. and Eades, J.S. (eds) *Tourism and Cultural Development in Asia and Oceania.* Universiti Kebangsaan Malaysia, Penerbit, pp. 61–82.

Lane, B. (1991) Sustainable tourism: a new concept for the interpreter. *Interpretation Journal* 49, 1–4.

Law, C. (ed.) (1996) *Tourism in Major Cities.* International Thomson Business Press, London.

Lewis, R.C. and Chambers, R.E. (2000) *Marketing Leadership in Hospitality,* 3rd edn. John Wiley & Sons, New York.

Mead, G.H. (1934) *Mind, Self and Society: From the Standpoint of a Social Behaviorist.* University of Chicago Press, Chicago.

Middleton, V. (1998) *Sustainable Tourism: a Marketing Perspective.* Butterworth Heinemann, Oxford.

Morrison, A.M. (1996) *Hospitality and Travel Marketing,* 2nd edn. Delmar, New York.

Moscardo, G. and Pearce, P.L. (1999) Understanding ethnic tourists. *Annals of Tourism Research* 26, 416–434.

Moscovici, S. (1973) Foreword. In: Herzlich, C. (ed.) *Health and Illness.* Academic Press, London, pp. ix–xiv.

Moscovici, S. (1984) The phenomenon of social representations. In: Farr, R.M. and Moscovici, S. (eds) *Social Representations.* Cambridge University Press, Cambridge, pp. 3–70.

Moscovici, S. (1988) Notes towards a description of social representations. *European Journal of Social Psychology* 18, 211–250.

Murphy, P.E. (1985) *Tourism: a Community Approach.* Methuen, New York.

Palmer, A. and Bijou, D. (1995) Tourism destination marketing alliances. *Annals of Tourism Research* 22, 616–629.

Pearce, P.L. (1995) From culture shock and cultural arrogance to cultural exchange: ideas towards sustainable socio-cultural tourism. *Journal of Sustainable Tourism* 3(3), 143–154.

Pearce, P.L., Moscardo, G. and Ross, G.F. (1996) *Tourism Community Relationships.* Elsevier, Oxford.

Pigram, J.J. (1990) Sustainable tourism: policy considerations. *Journal of Tourism Studies* 1(2), 2–9.

Powers, T. (1997) *Marketing Hospitality*, 2nd edn. John Wiley & Sons, New York.

Ritchie, J.R.B. (1993) Crafting a destination image: putting the concept of resident responsive tourism into practice. *Tourism Management* 14, 379–389.

Robinson, M. (1997) Tourism in de-industrializing centres in the UK. In: Robinson, M. and Boniface, P. (eds) *Tourism and Cultural Conflicts.* CAB International, Wallingford, pp. 129–159.

Robinson, M. and Boniface, P. (eds) (1997) *Tourism and Cultural Conflicts.* CAB International, Wallingford.

Ryan, C. and Page, S. (eds) (2000) *Tourism Management Towards the New Millennium.* Elsevier, Oxford.

Saarinen, J. (1998) The social construction of tourist destinations: the process of transformation of the Saariselka tourism region in Finnish Lapland. In: Ringer, G. (ed.) *Destinations: Cultural Landscapes of Tourism.* Routledge, London, pp. 154–173.

Seaton, A.V. and Bennett, M.M. (1996) *The Marketing of Tourism Products: Concepts Issues and Cases.* International Thomson Business Press, London.

Senadhira, S. (1998) Sri Lanka to sue U.S. firm for depicting it as a sex paradise. *Contours* 8(3/4), 13.

Setyaningsih, W. (1995) Architectural heritage and tourism: ancient and historic buildings in Surakarta, Central Java. In: Sofield, T. and Tarjana, M. (eds) *A Profile of Javanese Culture.* James Cook University, Townsville, pp. 27–32.

Smith, V.L. (ed.) (1978) *Hosts and Guests: the Anthropology of Tourism.* Blackwell, Oxford.

Soemanto, R. (1995) Low cost transportation and tourism. In: Sofield, T. and Tarjana, M. (eds) *A Profile of Javanese Culture.* James Cook University, Townsville, pp. 33–36.

Sofield, T. and Tarjana, M. (eds) (1995) *A Profile of Javanese Culture.* James Cook University, Townsville.

Swarbrooke, J. (1999) *Sustainable Tourism.* CAB International, Wallingford.

van den Berghe, P. (1994) *The Quest for the Other.* University of Washington Press, Seattle.

Warto, M. (1995) Inventory of traditional culture for tourism development in Surakarta, Central Java. In: Sofield, T. and Tarjana, M. (eds) *A Profile of Javanese Culture.* James Cook University, Townsville, pp. 16–20.

Yamashita, S., Din, K. and Eades, J.S. (eds) (1997) *Tourism and Cultural Development in Asia and Oceania.* Universiti Kebangsaan Malaysia, Penerbit.

Zeppel, H. (1997) Meeting 'wild people': Iban culture and longhouse tourism in Sarawak. In: Yamashita, S., Din, K. and Eades, J.S. (eds) *Tourism and Cultural Development in Asia and Oceania.* Universiti Kebangsaan Malaysia, Penerbit, pp. 119–140

Understanding Tourism and Destination Communities

14

DALLEN J. TIMOTHY,[1] SHALINI SINGH[2] AND
ROSS K. DOWLING[3]

[1]Department of Recreation Management and Tourism, Arizona
State University, Tempe, USA; [2]Department of Recreation and
Leisure Studies, Brock University, Canada, and Centre for Tourism
Research and Development, Lucknow, India; [3]School of Marketing,
Tourism and Leisure, Edith Cowan University, Joondalup, Australia

Introduction

Tourism has become so widespread throughout the world that few places today remain untouched by its direct or indirect influences. Tourism clearly has the ability to benefit destination communities economically, socially and ecologically, but at the same time it has the capacity to harm economies, societies and ecosystems. Knowledge of the former has led many communities, however these are defined, to become reliant, some entirely, some only marginally, on tourism. The terrorist events of 11 September 2001 elucidated exactly how dependent some communities are on the tourist economy. Many states, cities and rural areas of the USA, for example, suffered considerable losses in regional income, and tens of thousands of tourism industry workers lost their jobs. These effects were felt not only in the USA, but throughout the entire world as well.

It is at the destination, in the community being visited, that the core tourist experience is created. The example of 11 September is illustrative of just how intertwined the notion of place and the tourist experience are. The terrorist events also highlight many of the community elements underscored in this book: heritage and identity, economics, politics, society and culture, ethics and human rights, ecology, development, planning, management, and marketing.

One of the most notable common threads touched on by nearly every contributor to this text is power and the empowerment of destination community residents. Several chapters deal with this directly, while it is more implicit in others. Community members and all stakeholders participating in tourism can be seen on a spectrum which has a considerable range of hues, in terms of depth and variety. The spectrum lies between two extremities, from no involvement whatsoever to complete involvement. At one extreme, tourism is controlled and managed entirely by government officials and social elites. Somewhere towards the middle of this continuum is the token measure sometimes taken by governments to engage residents in decision-making. Painter (1992) terms this 'pseudo' participation, because citizens really have little say in planning and policy making, and they are often deprived of opportunities to hold a stake in community tourism programmes. At the other extreme, tenacious participation involves the growth and development of tourism being initiated and driven entirely by community members and private interests. Willingness and ability to participate will necessarily vary with the characteristics of individual communities. Traditional, less-developed and indigenous societies usually have more limitations on complete empowerment than has the Westernized, developed world. Some identifiable differences include access to information, ability to express interest, policy restrictions, ethnicity, gender, class and level of understanding of the tourism system.

Grass-roots empowerment is the foundation of sustainability in tourism. As people become more empowered in decision-making processes, and as they become more involved in the entrepreneurial side of development, their level of stewardship increases – stewardship of the environment, tourism, tourists, local cultures and the destination community in general. This places the responsibility of upholding the principles of sustainability (i.e. equity, accountability, efficiency, ecological and cultural integrity, etc.) squarely in the hands of destination residents and other local stakeholders.

Because the goals and objectives for community tourism development should be defined in accordance with the ethos and aspirations of the resident population, each situation must be tailor-made for every locale on an individual basis. Williams and Gill (1998) provide indicators for appropriate community management and monitoring programmes. They argue that community tourism programmes need to be driven by the objectives of population stabilization, increased employment and income capacities, community viability enhancement, amenity and cultural enhancement, and welfare and conservation improvement. In other words, community tourism projects should clearly reflect what destination communities choose to do, or not to do, with respect to their resources and their desires for visitor management.

Another prominent theme in this book is that of collaboration and cooperation between stakeholders in tourism, which has also recently begun to receive considerable attention in the tourism research literature (e.g. Bramwell and Lane, 2000). Collaboration, or partnership, when done correctly, has the potential to break down barriers of communication between various interest groups and stakeholders. Better communications channels and cooperative efforts can eliminate many of the administrative barriers that have long existed in most parts of the world, and more agencies, citizens and other stakeholders working together will almost always have a better chance of solving problems than any of them acting alone. More effective destination management and marketing can be achieved as resources are pooled and collective knowledge shared for the common good through formal and informal networks. Cooperation is also useful in dealing with heritage and nature conservation. Public–private sector planning and financial initiatives and volunteer work by community residents might also assist in creating meaningful interpretive programmes and conservation plans.

While this book has covered a vast array of issues that destination residents, public officials, environments and business people must face in the wake of tourism, several additional issues of recent coverage should also be noted in relation to destination communities. Volunteer tourism, or volunteer holidays, are on the rise as people are beginning to realize they can have an enjoyable holiday experience while doing something good for the environment or the society they visit (Singh and Singh, 2001; Wearing, 2001). Volunteer tourists usually engage in activities such as teaching in school, harvesting crops, planting trees and offering health-related services. Such activities are generally done in a spirit of altruism by travellers who desire to make a contribution to the destination community. Additional studies of this type of host–guest interaction would be warranted as we seek to understand better the perceptions of visitors among residents and residents among visitors.

Although it has existed throughout the ages, travel for sexual encounters has recently begun to receive more widespread scholarly attention (e.g. Oppermann, 1998; Clift and Carter, 2000; Ryan and Hall, 2001). Sex tourism exists in most destinations, and researchers are just now beginning to understand its magnitude and meaning. This clearly has significant implications for communities, particularly for resident attitudes towards tourists as local values, faiths and social mores are challenged. There is also an element of health risk associated with sex tourism that can have long-lasting repercussions in destination communities.

New forms of heritage tourism have recently been identified, such as 'dark' tourism, surrounding various forms of atrocity. Likewise, personal heritage, which has not received scholarly attention commensurate with its importance, is beginning to burgeon as society begins to age and wax nostalgic for the simpler world of the past. This is currently manifested in people travelling to the lands of their ancestors to seek out their roots, to discover who they are and where they came from. Personal heritage travel is one of the fastest growing areas of heritage tourism. Many communities find themselves a target for masses of people travelling to conduct family history or simply to see their ancestral homelands. This is particularly the case in Europe and West Africa as children of the Diasporas travel annually by the millions (Timothy and Boyd, 2003).

These are only a few of the many issues that merit additional research from the perspective of destination communities. It is critical for researchers to continue to view destination communities as a key part of the entire tourist experience in an enormous multidimensional tourism system that have their own problems, concerns and advantages. This volume attempts to do just that, but the complexities of destination communities make the subject a rich area for additional research.

References

Bramwell, B. and Lane, B. (eds) (2000) *Tourism Collaboration and Partnerships: Politics, Practice and Sustainability.* Channel View, Clevedon.

Clift, S. and Carter, S. (eds) (2000) *Tourism and Sex: Culture, Commerce and Coercion.* Pinter, London.

Oppermann, M. (ed.) (1998) *Sex Tourism and Prostitution: Aspects of Leisure, Recreation, and Work.* Cognizant, New York.

Painter, M. (1992) Participation in power. In: Munro-Clark, M. (ed.) *Participation in Government.* Hale and Iremonger, Sydney, pp. 21–36.

Ryan, C. and Hall, C.M. (2001) *Sex Tourism: Marginal People and Liminalities.* Routledge, London.

Singh, T.V. and Singh, S. (1999) *Tourism Development in Critical Environments.* Cognizant, New York.

Singh, T.V. and Singh, S. (2001) The emergence of voluntary tourism in the Himalayas: a case of Kanda community. Paper presented at the International Academy for the Study of Tourism (IAST) Conference, Macau, 10–14 July.

Timothy, D.J. and Boyd, S.W. (2003) *Heritage Tourism.* Prentice Hall, Harlow.

Wearing, S. (2001) *Volunteer Tourism: Experiences that Make a Difference.* CAB International, Wallingford.

Williams, P.W. and Gill, A. (1998) Tourism carrying capacity management issues. In: Theobald, W.F. (ed.) *Global Tourism,* 2nd edn. Butterworth Heinemann, Oxford, pp. 231–246.

Index